Bach
in
Köthen

Bach
in
Köthen

Friedrich Smend

Translated by John Page

Edited and revised with annotations
by Stephen Daw

Publishing House
St. Louis

Library of Congress Cataloging in Publication Data

Smend, Friedrich, 1893–1980.
    Bach in Köthen.

    1. Bach, Johann Sebastian, 1685–1750. I. Daw, Stephen. II. Title.
ML410.B1S53813   1985   780'.92'4   85-7695
ISBN 0-570-01325-9

1 2 3 4 5 6 7 8 9 10 PP 94 93 92 91 89 88 87 86

Contents

The traditional image of Bach's years at Köthen. The incompleteness of the records. Factual information concerning Bach's connections with the Köthen court. History of research into that period. Aims and objectives of this study.

Archive sources—accounts and records of the royal household. The evaluation of these: (1) material items of expenditure—instruments, scores, printed texts; (2) items of expenditure relating to persons—permanently engaged singers, visiting and guest vocalists and instrumentalists. Bach's visits to Köthen after 1723. The choir at the Lutheran school in Köthen. The instrumentalists in the court orchestra. The composition of the court orchestra. Bach's conducting from the viola stand.

Orchestration of Bach's instrumental works composed at Köthen. The Sixth Brandenburg Concerto (BWV 1051). The Fifth Brandenburg Concerto (BWV 1050). The remaining instrumental concertos and the ensemble suites.

Hunold's verse. *Figuralmusik* used in the divine service at Köthen. Parodies: *Durchlauchtster Leopold* (BWV 173a)—*Erhöhtes Fleisch und Blut* (BWV 173). *Die Zeit, die Tag und Jahre*

John Passion and the cantata *Du wahrer Gott und Davids Sohn* (BWV 23).

Illustrations

Frontispiece

The interior of the Spiegelsaal of the Köthen Schloss, in its restored condition. Editor's photograph, July 1983.

Enclosed Map

Detail from Zollmann's 1731 map of Saxony, showing the principalities of Anhalt and neighboring areas. From the King George V Collection, Birmingham (England) Central Library.

OTHER ILLUSTRATIONS

Author's Preface

The present study owes its origin to the discovery of the librettos of cantatas written by Christian Friedrich Hunold that Bach set to music during his years at Köthen. The find made it necessary to reexamine this chapter of Johann Sebastian's life and to pursue research into the relevant papers in the regional archive of Sachsen-Anhalt. This undertaking could not be embarked on until the documents had been returned after World War II from their place of safekeeping and relocated at Schloss Oranienbaum, near Dessau. Perusal of these archives since early in 1950 brought to light a considerable amount of hitherto unpublished material, as a result of which the picture we have of Bach's activity at the court of Köthen underwent such a fundamental transformation that it had to be redrawn. I initially gave a résumé of my work in this connection at the meeting arranged by the staff of the Theological College of Berlin to mark the occasion of the bicentennial of Bach's death. This study, which has grown out of the summary that I gave at that time, emphasizes the new information while fitting in with what was previously known. In particular, the problem of the relationship between Bach's "secular" and "spiritual and ecclesiastical" music necessitated a fuller discussion.

I am grateful to the library of the University of Halle and to the Oranienbaum Department of the regional archive of Sachsen-Anhalt for the valuable assistance they have given me. I am likewise indebted to my brother-in-law, Dr. Franz Vorländer, who twice accompanied me to Oranienbaum and helped me to make extracts from the archives and to estimate the value of their content.

Berlin
Oct. 7, 1951.

D. Friedrich Smend,
Professor, the Berlin
Theological College

Editor's Preface

Friedrich Smend was born Aug. 26, 1893; he died Feb. 10, 1980. In preparing his text for a wider market in 1985, we have tried to present his scholarship to both his and the public's best advantage. It is over 33 years since he prepared his preface, and so much has happened in the world of Bach scholarship during the third of a century that has elapsed in the meantime that it has been necessary—more than usually so—for adaptations and qualifications to be made to some of his statements; this is true particularly since the original book was clearly intended to be, in t1e best sense of these words, both stimulating and controversial. Rather than tampering more than was felt to be absolutely necessary with the main text (there are very few such editorial adjustments here), we have tried to add clearly distinguishable corrective annotations.

The first revision technique is the insertion of essential editorial notes. These are coded E throughout the book, and, like Smend's own notes, should be treated as obligatory, at least on the first encounter with the text; they should always be consulted by those who have a special interest in any part of the text of this book.

The second addition is the addition of chapter 18, printed in a clearly distinctive typeface and placed after Smend's (final) chapter 17. The main purpose of this chapter is not so much to correct as to enhance the main text; there are further details here regarding the court of Köthen, the musicians employed there (not all of whom are properly covered by Smend), the palace itself (which the editor has twice visited, once especially in connection with studies for this book), and the music that Bach is known to have prepared for performance at Köthen. Associated with this chapter— which cannot be more than introductory to its subject matter—are the illustrations and the drawings included in this book and the list of music (Appendix C). Friedrich Smend was not able (probably as a result of postwar German economies) to include an index; we have supplied two.

The third addition, a quick summary of the main achievements of post-1951 Bach scholarship insofar as it concerns Bach and his music at Köthen, most appropriately belongs in this editorial introduction. This is only a general account of an elaborate, and, if fascinating, bewilderingly international subject of concern. Therefore, in considering the many changes in our attitudes to Bach and his music that have taken place since Friedrich

17

Smend wrote *Bach in Köthen* in 1950–51, we should not forget that he, too, was partly responsible for modern approaches and attitudes towards Bach. The aforementioned summary occupies the following three paragraphs.

The most important development regarding our understanding of Bach as a creative artist has been the establishment, beginning in 1951, of the new chronology of Bach's compositions. This has completely altered our view of the significance of source materials, the value of reprographic research aids, and the relationship between preserved fact and critical speculation; more immediately, it has enabled most of Bach's choral music to be dated, through its sources, with a very limited degree of possible error. The first important published studies (which concentrated on the choral music) were issued by Alfred Dürr (in 1951, 1957) and Georg von Dadelsen (1957, 1958), but both incorporated previously assembled work on the paper of the sources compiled by the Erfurt musicologist Wisso Weiss; Weiss's work on the watermarks will be published soon as Series IX, vol. 1, of the New Bach Edition (NBA). The identification—even anonymously, but in important cases by name individually—of J. S. Bach's copyist assistants has enabled much further work on the dating of Bach's nonchoral music to be done; this subsequent work has developed gradually and has often resulted in less exact conclusions than those possible for the seasonal choral music; a Passion setting is suitable only for Good Friday in any year, but a concerto or the movement of a violin sonata may be prepared for performance on any date. The more recent work on the dating of Bach's music is partly announced in individual articles and programs all over the world and partly summarized in the Commentary volumes (*Kritischer Bericht*) designed to accompany each volume of the New Bach Edition; obviously, the earliest Commentary volumes, issued before Alfred Dürr's and Georg von Dadelsen's major studies, antedate the new chronology altogether, and later volumes have often become out-of-date regarding chronology in the light of continuing research. On detail there are disagreements between specialists, and each international scholar's impression of the new chronology will differ from that of some of his colleagues in detailed respects. But as far as dates given here in editorial notes and further commentary are concerned, reference to the new chronology denotes material regarding which there is general agreement today.

The New Bach Edition has, of course, presented us with new texts for much of Bach's music since 1954. It is to the very considerable credit of the staff respectively of the Bach-Institut in Göttingen and the Bach-Archiv in Leipzig that this edition has generally resulted in such dependable consistency; it is probably one of the most thoroughly dependable collected editions ever produced—and not simply in music. The results have established new standards in many respects and have led to the questioning of some traditional ones (such as whether or not a composer's last version of a particular composition should usually be taken to represent his ideal version of it for posterity). It should be mentioned, however, that there are some inconsistencies in this collected edition and that one of the most significant criticisms yet leveled at it was directed against the only volume that Friedrich Smend himself edited. This was the first large-scale choral work to be published in the NBA, the *Mass in B Minor* (BWV 232; NBA II/1 [Kassel and Leipzig, 1954] and its Commentary (Kassel and Leipzig, 1956). This drew from Georg von Dadelsen an extremely critical review in *Die Musikforschung* 12 (1959), entitled "Friedrich Smends Ausgabe der h-moll-Messe von J. S. Bach"; Dadelsen was writing some years after he himself had done important pioneering work on Bach's source materials, and much of his criticism springs from a comparison of Smend's discussion with his own, published the preceding year as the last chapter of *Tübinger Bach-Studien* 4/5, "Beiträge zur Chronologie der Werke Johann Sebastian Bachs" (Trossingen, 1958); this concluding chapter, "Exkurs über die h-moll-Messe," is outstanding even among von Dadelsen's distinguished contributions to Bach scholarship. Von Dadelsen also severely criticized the text of Smend's edition, claiming that in many respects that of the old Bach-Gesellschaft Collected Edition was still superior to it. In all of this, it must be admitted that von Dadelsen was as correct in his judgment as he was rigorous in his examination. From the point of view of *Bach in Köthen*, it must be said that the New Bach Edition has established standards closer to those advocated by von Dadelsen with regard to the examination and treatment of historical sources than Friedrich Smend either knew or, in his one volume, applied. This has resulted in a much more critical attitude towards speculation, as well as more demanding standards in editing, and a number of the relationships between Leipzig music and supposed Köthen originals that are suggested in the present study have not been supported by the editorial investigations of the editors working for the New Bach Edition. Where this is the case, editorial notes indicate the fact. But some of Friedrich Smend's work has been happily incorporated into the New Bach Edition (especially regarding cantatas BWV 66a and 134a, besides discussion of the Funeral Music [BWV 244a] and a number of other surviving and lost compositions), and his publication of Hunold's homage texts to Leopold of Anhalt-Köthen signaled an important discovery. It is interesting that of the three categories of postwar Bach scholarship outlined here, the first two have placed especially strong emphasis on detailed and systematically coordinated study not of Bach's music itself, but of the way in which it has been recorded for posterity; furthermore, it is clear that the New Bach Edition and the new chronology have, from before 1960, been closely associated.

The third area in which scholarship has produced new approaches to Bach is very much concerned with interpretation. But here that word should be understood in the sense of the German plural, *Interpretationen*, which in music may be undertaken at least as much by the listener as by the performer, so that, e.g., it may include biography, analysis, and criticism that arise from the music, as well as performance practice. In all of these areas of study, such factual evidence as we may possess requires careful attention, and any conclusions drawn from it may be debated, simply because the limits of our certainty are only occasionally tight enough for us to be able to state even that some particular opinion is wrong; it is usually impossible to be sure that one is "certainly right" in an interpretative assumption. One important new area of interpretation is, however, in the field of musical performance; it is the gradual establishment of the idea that music from any period may be understood more readily, and more of its problems may be solved, when it is performed on period historical instruments or copies of them. From work in this area it has been established that Bach does not really write inappropriately for voices and/or instruments, that he did have a fine ear for balance and beauty of timbre, and that he wrote music that was quite demanding—sometimes very difficult—but also realistic. In his own way, Friedrich Smend influenced this movement by suggesting that the Brandenburg Concertos were composed with an obviously small-size Köthen ensemble in mind. Bach's Köthen music is acquiring new grace and character as a result of performances that very probably do sometimes somewhat resemble his own conceptions of his music, and there is much to be learned from that. Biographically, the dispute regarding Bach's attitude to religion (and, more specifically, his involvement or otherwise in the sentiments expressed in texts that he set so admirably and illuminated so expressively in chorale preludes for organ) was already raging in 1951; we encounter it here in chapters 1 and 17—especially in the author's note 5—and elsewhere. This dispute has enlarged itself to embrace the whole of Bach's motivation, and comments on it tend to be extreme and—from either side—ill-considered, since evidence concerning motivation and belief may be expressed in the least obviously expected ways; however, in the interpreted judgment of the present editor, Bach was probably a fairly conventional, semi-intellectual, and devout Lutheran, whose Protestantism led him to take his work seriously and to feel required to serve God through his neighbor in society. This much seems to be supported by the evidence that we have; it accords very happily with the cautiously developed theses of Friedrich Smend, who was, in the area where Bach scholarship and Lutheran philosophy overlap, one of the best-equipped experts that the world has known to pronounce on this subject. In analysis and criticism, the most obvious new development has been the attempt better to understand contemporary approaches to musical expression and structure. A new emphasis has been put on our search for extramusical influences on Bach: Did he plan musical structures consciously according to the standard content of the contemporary Lutheran sermon? Did he deliberately cultivate number symbolism? Was he influenced by literature or architecture that we might suppose he admired? Then there are possible musical influences: How did he tune keyboard instruments? Was he influenced at all by theorists such as Mattheson or Mizler? What music by Couperin or Vivaldi did he know, and how familiar was he with the national performing styles? Did he model his music deliberately on that of other known composers? Why did he collect so much music in the strict polyphonic style towards the end of his life? These questions may be of increasing concern as the performing possibilities of period instruments are further explored and new styles are developed—also as the repertoire of easily obtainable early-18th-century music becomes larger in print, on microfilm, and in recorded form. After 1960, Friedrich Smend occupied himself less with Bach than he had formerly, or if this was not so, he let it be known less in print; but he did retain a considerable interest in the interpretative side of Bach scholarship, and if his work was now less immediately concerned with the Köthen period of the composer's life, that is not to be taken to indicate that he felt that the last word had been said on this subject. Indeed, it is one of the more remarkable aspects of later scholarship that, despite this author's clear invitations to others to follow up his own study with their own, there has been no serious attempt since 1951 in any country to reexamine this most interesting (and most promising) section of the composer's life. It is one of the hopes of the present editor that individuals may come forward and that avenues may be cleared, so as to facilitate the further examination of Bach's work at Köthen.

Birmingham, England
August 1984

Stephen Daw

Editor's Acknowledgments

In preparing the present book, much assistance has been afforded by individuals in detailed respects, and these are listed below; but there is not enough room here to acknowledge all of the scholars whose joint work has resulted in the substantial reappraisal since 1951 of our complete impression of Bach's life and work; not only is the new Bach literature extremely abundant, it is also mostly coordinated and coherent. This last fact is in no small respect due to three organizations: the Neue Bach-Gesellschaft, the Johann-Sebastian-Bach-Institut in Göttingen, and the Bach-Archiv in Leipzig (now under the patronage of the Nationale Forschungs- und Gedenkstätten Johann Sebastian Bach der DDR). Without all of their direct help and much incidental support (e.g., through publications), this revised version of Friedrich Smend's *Bach in Köthen* could hardly have done its author good service.

The following have given particular personal support and information: Dr. Hans-Joachim Schulze, Dr. Hans Grüss, and Dr. Winfried Hoffmann (Leipzig); Dr. Alfred Dürr, Dr. Klaus Hofmann, and Dr. Yoshitake Kobayashi (Göttingen); Professor Peter Williams (Edinburgh); Peter Dodd (London); and Professor Christoph Wolff (Cambridge, Mass.). In seeking for detailed information regarding the Köthen palace and its princely inhabitants, we were afforded useful assistance by the Staatsarchiv in Magdeburg and were given generous advice by Dr. Reinhard Plewe (Ückermünde) regarding architectural sources. In response to genealogical and historical inquiries, much assistance was afforded by the Parry Library of the Royal College of Music, London (which holds C. S. Terry's Bach papers); the German Historical Institute, London; and Birmingham University Library (England). Contemporary maps of Saxony and Anhalt were made available by the City of Birmingham Central Library, the British Library Reference Division, and the Bodleian Library, Oxford. The libraries of the City of Birmingham, Birmingham University, and the Birmingham School of Music are of continuing assistance and support to the editor, and he would like to place on record here his particular gratitude to their staff with regard to that help. In assisting with the preparation of illustrations, Lorraine

Toney (Birmingham) deserves special credit. Finally, the editor wishes to place on record his appreciation to his immediate colleague with respect to this book, Dr. John Page (Birmingham); working with him has been both easy and pleasurable.

S. F. D.

Translator's Note

Our aim has been to express clearly to readers of English the meaning of Friedrich Smend's German text. Therefore some changes in sentence structure and exact sentence content have been considered to be not only justifiable but also desirable. Having decided to opt for the German *K*, more usual today (as in *Köthen, Kammermusik*), in preference to the Latin *C* (*Cöthen, Cammermusic*), we have generally adopted this spelling except where quotation renders it unjustifiable.

Birmingham, England
1984

John Page

Abbreviations

BG	as edited for the Gesamtausgabe of the Bach-Gesellschaft (1850–1900); the volume may also be indicated.
BJ	*Bach-Jahrbuch*, hence *BJ*, 1957 refers to the 1957 yearbook of the Neue Bach-Gesellschaft.
BWV	as cataloged by Wolfgang Schmieder in his *Thematisch-systematisches Verzeichnis der Werke Johann Sebastian Bachs* [Bach-Werke-Verzeichnis] (Leipzig, 1950).
Dok I, II, III	*Bach-Dokumente*, ed. Werner Neumann and Hans-Joachim Schulze for the Bach-Archiv, Leipzig, issued as an Appendix Series to the Neue Bach-Ausgabe (1963–72). There is a fourth (pictorial) volume, issued in 1979.
E	Note numbers coded E in the text refer to editor's notes placed after author's notes in the back of the book.
KB	*Kritischer Bericht*, the editorial commentaries that are issued in the Neue Bach-Ausgabe in support of each volume of the musical text; often referred to as Critical Commentaries—but the simple "Commentary" seems no less appropriate in English.
NBA	*Johann Sebastian Bach: Neue Ausgabe sämtlicher Werke* (Neue Bach-Ausgabe); hence NBA V/8 denotes the eighth volume of the fifth series of the New Bach Edition. The edition is being published (since 1954) under the joint editorial supervision of the West German Johann-Sebastian-Bach-Institut, Göttingen, and the East German Bach-Archiv, Leipzig; it is published simultaneously in Kassel, New York, etc., and in Leipzig.

Chapter 1

The brief period from December 1717 to April 1723, happy years during which Johann Sebastian Bach was Prince Leopold's Kapellmeister and director of chamber music at Köthen, holds a special place for us in the life of the master. Here, in contrast to his previous activities in Weimar and those that followed in Leipzig, Johann Sebastian was not in the employ of the church. He was Kapellmeister at a royal court.[1] Both the principality and the court had adopted the Reformed Calvinistic faith; in consequence, the liturgy did not offer the same scope for figural music as did the Lutheran churches of Weimar and Leipzig. Thus, as distinct from both the other places, Köthen lacked a well-trained four-part choir for which Bach might regularly have composed demanding vocal music. All this clearly had a decisive influence on Bach's activities at Köthen and left its mark on those of his compositions that are now our chief concern.

To a hitherto unprecedented extent, and with an intensity unmatched in his later years, Bach devoted himself at this stage to instrumental music, more precisely to secular instrumental composition. During these years his output of works for instruments of the most varied nature, both solo pieces and compositions for combinations of instruments, is indeed considerable.[2] As examples of keyboard compositions we need mention only the English and French Suites [BWV 806–17] or the Well-Tempered Clavier [BWV 846–69];[3] as pieces for string instruments, the sonatas and suites for solo violin, for violoncello, and for viola da gamba and the sonatas for string instruments and harpsichord; of the more elaborately arranged concertos for solo instruments with string accompaniment, the ensemble suites [BWV 1066–69] and the Brandenburg Concertos [BWV 1046–51]. From these we gain an impression of the abundant wealth and variety of Bach's creative output between the years 1717 and 1723.[E1] On the other hand, these works differed extensively from those of the Weimar period; in Weimar, Bach was at first employed to compose for the organ alone,[4] though later, as a result of the commission to produce religious vocal works on a regular basis, he wrote his first series of cantatas for use in the divine service. Later in Leipzig, he was to bring this form of creative activity to perfection. In consequence, Bach's biographers are inclined more often than not to regard the period at Köthen as something of an *entr'acte*, as a lull in the composer's output of major works.

According to this version of events, Johann Sebastian strayed during these years into a backwater, admittedly one blessed with a wealth of creative activity, from which, nevertheless, the composer's move to Leipzig resembled a return to the mainstream of his life. It was further held that the years at Köthen were essentially different in that, in contrast to those of the preceding and following periods, Bach was not tied to the fulfillment of specified regular duties. Instead, he was in a position to allow free rein in his work to his own artistic imagination. In particular, attention has been drawn to the six Brandenburg Concertos, which, in their diversity and the boldness of their varied instrumentation, were proof that here Bach's creativity was completely untrammeled.[E2]

In fact, it ought to have been recognized long ago that this view of Bach's Köthen period was in need of revision.[5] With his Leipzig cantatas the master of course resumed the composition of splendidly elaborated religious vocal works. Seen from the viewpoint of their artistry, however, the first Leipzig cantatas cannot be regarded as a continuation of the Weimar vocal compositions. Thus, between Weimar and Leipzig lies a path that we ought not to regard as a detour, but rather as an integral part of Bach's development as a whole, even if, according to the present state of our knowledge, this cannot be proven in every detail.

The incompleteness of our understanding of Bach's creative activity at Köthen was demonstrated with especial clarity two years ago with the discovery of the Hunold texts that accompanied the music of Bach's cantatas of the Köthen era.[6] It then became apparent that the period 1717–23 was by no means almost entirely devoted to the composition of instrumental works. Instead, these were interspersed with a not inconsiderable amount of composition for the voice. Nor was it a question here of secular compositions alone, for alongside the latter there were figural vocal works for the purpose of divine service, in other words, church cantatas. As a result, it became necessary to undertake the task of researching afresh into these particular years in the life of Bach, in order to fill in this now quite obvious gap in our knowledge, and I should now like to set down the results of my endeavors in this field. I begin by stringing together the salient facts that relate to Bach's connections with the Köthen court:

1717   *Jan. 24.* Eleonore Wilhelmine, born Princess of Anhalt-Köthen, in her first marriage wife of Duke Friedrich Erdmann of Sachsen-Merseburg (died June 2, 1714), the elder of Prince Leopold's two sisters, married Ernst August of Saxe-Weimar, nephew of the reigning Duke Wilhelm Ernst, at Schloss Nienburg. Terry conjectures that the first face-to-face meeting between Prince Leopold and Bach, who in his capacity as *Konzertmeister* was a member of the Weimar retinue, may be traced back to this occasion.[7] There is no documentary evidence to support this. What one perhaps could draw attention to, on the other hand, which Terry omits to do, is the closeness of Bach's relationship with Duke Ernst August himself, which may in turn have been part of the reason why the duchess acted as godmother to the little Leopold Augustus Bach, the only son of Johann Sebastian born at Köthen.

Aug. 5. The signing of the deed of appointment of Bach to the post of Kapellmeister at the court of Köthen. Maria Barbara Bach immediately moved with her children to Köthen.

Dec. 2. Having surmounted the obstacles in the way of his leaving Weimar and having been released from detainment, Bach followed his family to Köthen. He had already been drawing his salary there since August.[8] The payment of certain sums over and above his salary, e.g., for the use of his premises for rehearsals on a day-to-day basis, began immediately. Payments were made on an annual basis for the first time from Dec. 10, 1717, onwards. In other words, Bach was already at Köthen on Dec. 10.

1723   *April 13.* Bach's release from active service as court Kapellmeister. But he remained "Honorary Kapellmeister."[9]

1728   *Nov. 19.* Death of Prince Leopold.

1729   *March 23–24.* Memorial service for Prince Leopold and the "Commemorative Sermon." Bach's last active music making at Köthen. He retained, however, the title of Illustrious Kapellmeister at the court of Anhalt-Köthen to his death.[10]

Before we try to add flesh to the bare bones of this chronological outline, we should briefly survey the history of research into Bach's Köthen period, which has stretched over many decades. Inevitably the monumental work of Philipp Spitta ranks high here. Describing this chapter of Bach's life, he wrote:

> Of Johann Sebastian, however, Kapellmeister and Director of the Royal Chamber Music, as he described himself in his own hand, and of the body of musicians whom he conducted, we find in none of the places where it is customary to seek signs of the existence and activity of men of substance the slightest mention, apart from one or two references in the parish register.[11]

Thus this great researcher failed to locate any documentary evidence in relation to Bach's life and work at Köthen other than church records in connection with events within the family circle (baptism of Bach's son Leopold; burial of his wife, Maria Barbara; Bach's marriage to Anna Magdalena Wülcken). Nevertheless, Spitta was able from literary sources, the obituary notice, and the Forkel biography, among other things, as well as from the actual works of Johann Sebastian that emerged during the Köthen period, to piece together a version of his life there that, though admittedly in need of revision, is substantially correct and offers us much that is immensely valuable.

Credit for the discovery of a considerable number of source documents and for being the first to make use of them must go to Rudolf Bunge.[12] He succeeded in producing details of the constitution of the court orchestra and evidence concerning the stock of instruments that have considerably enriched our understanding of the period. Of course, Bunge's interpretation of the events is not free from errors and misunderstandings. Wäschke successfully took Bunge's research a stage further, drawing on additional, previously overlooked material, and, in the process, increasing our knowledge considerably.[13] After Bethge and Götze had produced a summarized, in some circles definitive, version of all these findings,[14] the Scot, Charles Sandford Terry, returned to the theme, profiting from the groundwork of others before him in his further evaluation of the documents in the Anhalt state archive.[15] The results of his researches are, however, by no means dependable; they require detailed emendation, especially since his biography of Bach is among the most widely read at the present time.

Because the issue is one of such importance, supporting evidence must be produced here. Bunge informed us that, during the period after Bach left Köthen, the direction of the court music had lain in the hands of *Konzertmeister* Krüger, who died in the early 1780s. From among his personal effects the prince at the time inherited a not inconsiderable quantity of manuscript music for his royal collection. A brief inventory of this collection, which entered the sovereign's possession on March 22, 1785, has come down to us.[16] Terry considers this inventory to have been the subsequently extended and completed catalog of the stock of manuscript music that lay at Bach's disposal during his period of office at Köthen. He is of the opinion that both negative and positive conclusions may be drawn from the document. The absence here of any earlier music, e.g., of Vivaldi or Corelli, among others, is to him proof that these composers were unheeded in 1717–23. Coming across, on the other hand, the name of Bach among the "Sinfonien," in the company of Hiller, Stamitz, and Dittersdorf, Terry automatically assumes a reference to compositions by Johann Sebastian during the Köthen period. The dating of works by J. S. Bach known to have been composed in Köthen, insofar as this rests on Terry's inferences, is without foundation; this was already the case when Terry wrote of his discoveries and has been confirmed by more recent research.[17]

It is evident that there is a need here for very thorough clarification. At the same time, however, the research must go on under two headings:

1. It has been shown that, despite the commendable work especially by Bunge and Wäschke, our knowledge of this period remains very incomplete, and it cannot be said that the potential of the Köthen archives has been in any way exhausted. Therefore a fresh start must be made.[E3]

2. The attempt must also be made—following a method as yet untried—to go beyond the factual details so as to bring together the available information to form a coherent picture. In this way we may arrive at an understanding of this chapter of Bach's working life that may for the first time put it in its real perspective when set against his total achievement.

Chapter 2

If I now seek to make that attempt, it is obvious that to do so as things stand in this field of research is something of a hazardous undertaking. Admittedly, the archive materials have been returned from their place of safekeeping and have been reassembled to form a special section of the regional archive of Sachsen-Anhalt at Oranienbaum, near Dessau. Nevertheless, this section of the archives is still being developed, and the documentary materials have not been preserved completely enough to afford a truly comprehensive picture. We also must bear in mind the possibility that in areas hitherto left unexamined, because it was felt they would yield nothing, we may still come across important evidence that has so far escaped our notice.

At the outset, mention should be made of two sets of documents that I have used as my sources: (1) The accounts of the royal household of Anhalt-Köthen. (2) The records that relate to the salaries of the royal orchestra and the trumpeters.[18] I begin with the household accounts that take the form of annual statements (presented from one Midsummer Day to the next) of income and expenditure as part of the royal budget. For each of the years that are of interest to us, from 1717/18 to 1728/29, there exists a vellum bound volume that begins with income received. The items of expenditure relevant to us are set out in a straightforward way. At the head we find entries relating to Leopold himself, including the outlay for the orchestra. Dates and amounts of each monthly salary are recorded for all members, from the Kapellmeister down to the lowliest musician, the drummer. These are followed by individual items, arranged according to persons. Sadly, this pattern is not adhered to in all the volumes. In some years, the specific sums for the upkeep of the orchestra are scattered among those that relate to all manner of expenses.

Distinct from these household accounts, the records of the salaries paid to members of the royal orchestra and the trumpeters take the form of collections of receipts, set out on a day-to-day basis. So far only those for 1717/18 (beginning Midsummer Day) have come to light. Here again the incompleteness of the material becomes apparent, because this year already reveals discrepancies when compared with the household accounts, which in turn are shown to contain gaps when it comes to the recording of individual items of expenditure. Not separately entered here, these items are no doubt included under certain overall headings elsewhere, i.e., they are no longer individually identifiable. This peculiarity of the records is also undoubtedly the reason why in the household accounts, between the end of March 1726 and the end of 1727 (i.e., for 21 months), apart from the salaries of the permanently engaged members of the Kapelle, there are no further references to expenses arising from the provision of music. All this must be borne in mind before we reach any conclusions based on the entries in these documents. Inferences are, of course, entirely possible. We shall begin by considering Johann Sebastian Bach's period of office as Kapellmeister at Köthen, from December 1717 to April 1723, though for purposes of comparison we shall on each occasion consult the later years. We shall divide the items of expenditure into two categories, material and personal. Conspicuous among the material items of expenditure, insofar as they relate to Bach's period of office, are the purchases of musical instruments. An example from the household accounts:

> On March 1, 1719, Bach receives "for the clavier constructed in Berlin and the expense of the journey".........................130 Thalers.

> Simultaneously *Kammermusiker* Spiess "for 2 Innsbruck violins" receives
> ....40 Thalers.

> March 14. Payment made to the manservant Gottschalk for the carriage of the Berlin clavier......................................8 Thalers.

What is of interest at the outset in this information is that we learn for the first time of a visit by Bach to Berlin. If we estimate the cost of the journey that Bach undertook in order to take delivery of the instrument to have been 30 Thalers, i.e., a very large sum, that leaves a purchase price of 100 Thalers for the clavier, after the deduction of traveling costs. This again was a very large amount of money when one considers that Bach's harpsichord, which was held to be common family property and therefore omitted from the division of the composer's estate at his death, received a valuation price of 80 Thalers. Higher still in comparative terms is the 40 Thalers paid for the two Innsbruck—therefore probably made by Steiner—violins; the same distinguished maker's violin that formed part of Bach's final estate was valued at 8 Thalers.[19] Thus Prince Leopold was not averse to spending freely in order to augment his collection of instruments. We cannot assume that in the process he paid unduly high prices. As we know from the household accounts, Bach himself was in charge of the care and maintenance of instruments[20] in the prince's possession and would not have advised his master to make purchases if he felt that the price was unreasonably high. One should add immediately, however, that once Bach had left Köthen, no mention is made of payments for the purchase of instruments during Prince Leopold's remaining years.

Alongside the collection of instruments, the library of manuscript music—the "Musical. Cammer"—figures prominently in the accounts. Admittedly, we read nothing here that relates to the actual purchase of manuscript music during the years 1717–23, but we do learn of bookbinding costs. These occur throughout the period and not infrequently involve considerable sums of money; e.g., for the year 1719/20 costs amounted to around 30 Thalers.[21] Here we are led to question the actual format of the music forwarded for binding. I believe that we may cautiously assume that this consisted of parts that the copyist who was permanently attached to the court orchestra was required to prepare in the form of handwritten volumes. Among this material—and we can also say this with certainty—Bach's own work must have predominated. The entries relating to items of expenditure are very detailed and accurate on precisely this point. For this reason we can easily calculate, e.g., that the binding of one part cost 2 Groschen. By this reckoning there must have been at least 50 ensemble works in the above-mentioned year 1719/20.[22] With a court conductor of the stature of J. S. Bach at his service, there was in fact no need for the prince to buy printed scores. The situation is seen to change after April 1723, when purchases of printed music were made, among which, on Jan. 5, 1725, e.g., 12 Thalers were paid for a "new Julij Caesaris opera."

A third item relates to the printing of "Carmina." These purchases generally occur in close proximity to the prince's birthday, celebrated on Dec. 10,[23] or to New Year's Day. The cost is almost without exception 2 Thalers. This sum is of interest insofar as, according to our reckoning, the printing of a cantata or serenade text cost on average 1 Thaler. Reference is often made both to Leopold's birthday and to New Year's Day. On one occasion the term "Cantate" is expressly used, in place of "Carmen." From time to time, mention is made of "Carmina for the royal orchestra." In several instances the Kapellmeister received sums of money to forward to the printer.[24] In this way, evidence of the cultivation of vocal music comes to light; cantatas are performed, and regularly so, with two on each of the dates, Dec. 10 and Jan. 1. It is hard to avoid the conclusion here, as I intend to show later, that each date involved one piece of church vocal music and one secular. We may take it for granted that the works composed for both festive occasions during the period from December 1717 to April 1723 were always by Bach, for the simple reason that the court Kapellmeister was expected, by virtue of his office, to produce *Figuralmusik* of this kind. Thus, with these two festive occasions alone in mind, we should place 24 cantatas in the period when Bach held office at Köthen, half of them church compositions, half secular. His output of works for the voice will not, however, have stopped there.

This is clear when we turn to the items of expenditure in respect of payments to individuals that occur in both the household accounts and the records of the royal orchestra. Until now, Bach's Köthen years being regarded as almost exclusively a period of instrumental composition, interest has centered on the musicians who were permanently employed at the court. Alongside these, however, there were also vocalists who received fixed salaries. Once again, the entries in the archive documents obviously contain gaps, as the following shows. In common with the wife of Bach's predecessor as Kapellmeister, Anna Magdalena Bach was engaged as one of the salaried vocalists at court. She received 16 Thalers and 16 Groschen a month, remuneration on a par with that of *Premier Cammermusicus* Spiess.[25] (Her husband received twice that amount.) The entries that relate to the payment of her salary begin in May 1722, five months after her marriage. On Sept. 29, 1721, however, i.e., fully two months before she became Bach's wife, we come across her name in the Köthen baptismal register, where, as godmother, she is referred to as "singer at court here."[26]

In addition to Anna Magdalena Bach, there were two other permanently salaried female vocalists, the daughters of Monjou, Master of the Pages, who were occasionally somewhat casually referred to as the "Singe-Jungfern" (literally "singing maids"). It can be shown that they drew their salaries from October 1720 to November 1722 but were not paid on a full-time basis before 1720. On the other hand, in September of that year they received "occasional" payments for "demonstrating their talents," by way of introduction or at audition. On Sept. 16, for example, they were paid a nonrecurrent fee of 20 Thalers.[27]

In addition to the above, there is further evidence of the patronage of vocal music at Köthen, with the prince himself taking part, as usual, in the orchestral performances. This derives from the visits of nonresident musicians, whose estimates of expenses have been preserved. Among the instrumentalists, the wind players, horn players (always in pairs), and oboists predominate.[28] The number of singers visiting Köthen to perform at court, however, can match that of the instrumentalists.[29] It is significant that, apart from the falsettists and castrati who gave guest performances— the latter being in vogue at the time—these were exclusively tenor or bass singers, since the court was in any case already furnished with soprano and alto voices. We may take it for granted that these nonresident vocalists, whose periods of stay, to judge from the expenses for board and lodgings (with the individuals concerned sometimes named in person), were protracted, must have participated in vocal works composed by the Kapellmeister. This indicates that Bach's vocal compositions were heard at Köthen on occasions other than Leopold's birthday and New Year's Day.

Visits from outsiders increased considerably after Bach's departure.[30] That too is only to be expected. That these performances also involved unusual instruments at times is indicated by the entry for Aug. 25, 1725, according to which a "musico" who had played "upon the glasses in a manner resembling chimes" was given 6 Thalers. A week earlier, court society at Köthen had been entertained by a guest, evidently appearing as a curiosity—the horn player Beda, who "blows two French horns at the same time," for which he likewise received 6 Thalers.

Of the greatest significance in this context are the visits Bach made to Köthen from Leipzig, the last of which, that of March 1729, was on the occasion of Leopold's funeral. This will be discussed below. According to the household accounts, the Thomas Kantor appeared at Köthen on three occasions between April 1723 and March 1729.[31] In view of the importance of these visits, I quote the account entries verbatim:

1724   *July 18.* To the *Director Musicus* Bach and his wife, who gave performances, in settlement . . . . 60 Thalers.

1725   *Dec. 15.* To the Leipzig Cantor Bach and his wife, who gave a number of performances here . . . . 30 Thalers.

1728   *Jan. 5.* To the Leipzig Cantor Bach, in settlement . . . . 24 Thalers.

The exact nature of the festive occasion—for it must have been one—that brought Bach to Köthen in July 1724 is not known. None of the special events in the royal household that occurred during those years, e.g., baptisms and marriages, nor any of the birthdays of individuals within Leopold's family circle, are linked to that particular July visit. On the other hand, the December 1725 date is quite clearly Leopold's own birthday, and the January 1728 visit is associated with New Year's Day, both occasions necessitating the presence of the "honorary Kapellmeister." The difference in the fee—60 Thalers for July 1724, 30 Thalers for December 1725—can be explained by the fact that their landlord Gänseler was paid 24 Thalers for the December visit of Bach and his wife,[32] whereas in July 1724, the Leipzig guests had to meet their expenses for board and lodgings out of their own pockets, as similarly in January 1728, when Bach alone put in an appearance at Köthen. The substantial sums of money involved here are an indication of the high esteem in which the Kapellmeister was held. They further imply that the stays were not particularly brief.

As a corollary to the above, it must be stressed at this point that the entries in the accounts, for the years 1726 and 1727 in particular, are known to be incomplete. On Nov. 30, 1726, we must assume a visit by Bach for which no documentary evidence exists, the reason being that for that date, the birthday of Princess Friederike Wilhelmine, he composed the cantata *Steigt freudig in die Luft* [BWV 36a].[33] From all this it is clear that we should be thinking in terms of more frequent appearances by Bach at

Köthen, chiefly on the annual occasion of Leopold's birthday. These were festivities in which the Thomas Kantor would have had no difficulty in participating, since they coincided with the part of Advent during which there was a *tempus clausum* in the Leipzig churches, i.e., a period when elaborate music was proscribed in that city.

The entries in the Köthen household accounts, incomplete though they are, are revealing in yet another manner. In July 1724 Bach was accompanied by his wife who, as we know, had formerly sung at court. Alongside the Leipzig couple, however, there is mention of "the tenor Vetter." In December 1725 Bach and his wife were joined by a "bass singer from Gotha."[34] Here then is the evidence that the musical performances included works for the voice, as had been the case when Bach was actively engaged at the court. Of particular interest in this context is Bach's January 1728 visit, even though on that occasion the soprano singer Anna Magdalena was absent. No vocal soloist is mentioned at the time of Bach's stay. We do read, on the other hand, that six Thalers were paid to the choir of the Lutheran school for taking part in the singing on New Year's Day.[35] In other words, vocal music was also involved in Bach's visit on that occasion. We further learn from the record for the first time that singers from the Lutheran school took part, though there is no need to assume that this January 1728 appearance was the choir's maiden performance at court. Nevertheless, we deduce from this reference that Köthen did actually have such a trained Lutheran choir and that it was called on to perform in the prince's presence.

Before we come to the most important theme of this study, that of Bach's creative work at Köthen and the compositions themselves, we should discuss further instrumentalists in the court orchestra. Closer scrutiny of the entries in the Anhalt archives yields a more concrete and graphic picture of this band of musicians and their activities. Between the years 1707 and 1710, Leopold had attended the Berlin Academy for the Sons of Noblemen and had come into contact with musical circles there. His acquaintance with Augustinus Reinhard Stricker, who in 1714, i.e., before Leopold's accession to the throne, was to become Kapellmeister at Köthen, in other words Bach's predecessor, dates from this time. The enlargement of the court orchestra to 17 players took place in 1716, a year after Leopold began his reign.[36] Once again he turned to Berlin, where the thrifty Frederick William I, who, it must be conceded, had a different historical task to fulfill than that of a patron of the arts, had disbanded his court orchestra in 1713.[E4] Several of his most competent musicians emigrated to Köthen, namely,

Premier Cammer Musicus Josephus Spiess (violin)
Cammer Musicus Johann Ludwig Rose (oboe)
Cammer Musicus Johann Christoph Torlée (bassoon)

Cammer Musicus Christian Bernhard Linigke (violoncello)
Cammer Musicus Martin Friedrich Marcus (violin)

These must have been outstanding musicians, as the name *Cammer Musicus*, a title that had been conferred on no previous member of the orchestra, implies. Nevertheless, the Berlin artists discovered excellent performers among their newfound colleagues, e.g., Christian Ferdinand Abel (viola da gamba).[37] The move from the capital city of Berlin, which already had 56,000 inhabitants, to the remote and sleepy town of Köthen may initially have seemed strange to musicians who had formerly performed at the court of the King of Prussia. But they were entering the service of a man with a passionate love of music and one who, being an excellent harpsichord and viola da gamba player himself, took an active part in the music making of his orchestra. Added to that, after only a year and a half in the prince's service, they were blessed by the appointment of a Kapellmeister whose arrival was truly providential. In consequence, these performers remained loyal to their royal master until his death. Spiess became director of music after Bach's departure from Köthen, except on those occasions when the "honorary Kapellmeister" himself made his guest appearances.

We are now in a position to reconstruct an accurate picture of the court orchestra. In keeping with the baroque style of music, it was divided into soloists and ripienists. The difference was accentuated by their titles—only the soloists being described as "Kammermusiker," the ripienists being called simply "Musiker"—and by their salaries. Among the soloists we meet two violinists (Spiess and Marcus), one violoncellist (Linigke), and a viola da gamba player (Abel). These were joined by wind players, initially by an oboist (Rose) and a bassoonist (Torlée). If we at this point examine the instrumental and vocal works known to have been written by Bach in the Köthen period, we repeatedly come across two solo flutes, together with an oboe and a bassoon. This ties up with the fact that there were two other members of the Köthen orchestra in addition to those already mentioned:

Cammer Musicus Johann Heinrich Freytag
Cammer Musicus Johann Gottlieb Würdig (who was at the same time a
    member of the town band).[38]

Although we have no documentary evidence that would allow us to prove the point, we can say with certainty that these two were the flutists in the court orchestra. One place, however, was not filled by a *Cammer Musicus*, that of the viola. This was taken by Bach himself. C. P. E. Bach reports that his father, violin in hand, kept the orchestra in better order from that position than he could have from the clavier. Immediately before this, we read in the same letter from Emanuel Bach to Forkel:

> Even with the orchestra at full strength, he was able to hear the slightest musical detail. As the greatest expert and judge in matters of harmony, he best liked playing the viola in order to achieve a satisfactory balance of ensemble.[39]

In addition to the above-mentioned soloists, the orchestra also included four "musici," i.e., *tutti* players, ripienists, in the string section. More often than not, as the scoring indicates, only one of the two trumpeters, Schreiber and Krahl, was called on. Least frequently required were the services of the drummer Unger. He was, after all, an innkeeper, which enabled him to make his contribution to music by other means, since nonresident performers were regularly accommodated on his premises.

Chapter 3

Because we have these names and know something about those who bore them, we are now able to reconstruct what they actually did.[E5] Whenever His Serene Highness with his favorite instrument, the viola da gamba, joined in the music making, Herr Abel would of course move over to the second seat in the orchestra in order to vacate the first gamba position to the prince. If the sovereign took part as a soloist, however, it was a matter of honor for the Kapellmeister Bach to do likewise on his preferred instrument, the viola; in that case, Herr Spiess, normally the first violinist, would assume the accompaniment of the second viola. The chamber musician Linigke played the solo violoncello. Bach well knew how to construct a piece in such a way that no excessively demanding passages were assigned to the prince, who was thus not placed in the embarrassing position of exposing his technical limitations before his *Kammermusiker*. Thus, not only do we now have a clear picture of the instrumentation of the sixth of the Brandenburg Concertos [BWV 1051], but we also know the structure of its composition; the two violas and the violoncello shared the main burden of the solo material, whereas the violas da gamba, without exactly playing a subordinate role, were given less demanding tasks. If we pursue this line of thought a stage further, it turns out that the six concertos [BWV 1046–51] all matched exactly the possibilities of instrumentation available at Köthen, i.e., they were composed to be performed by Leopold's court orchestra. There is no doubt that in the fifth concerto [BWV 1050] Bach played the solo harpsichord with the great cadenza and thereby made use of that valuable instrument, which had been built in Berlin—probably not accidentally as it turns out, since the leading performers in the orchestra had of course come from that city. Herr Freytag or Herr Würdig would have played the solo flute, Herr Spiess the solo violin. The latter's part would have been supported in the *tutti* passages in unison by the first violin ripienist. Since Bach sat at the harpsichord, the viola was missing from the full instrumentation, which consisted of two violins, viola, and continuo on those occasions when Herr Marcus took the second violin. Because of its tone color, however, the viola was indispensable to the ensemble. Thus Herr Marcus doubled as second ripieno violinist or as viola player; in the latter instances the ensemble would have dispensed with the services of a second violin. The very striking scoring of this concerto is thus easily explained. Bach was merely adapting to the circumstances of performance at Köthen and the constraints imposed on him there.[E6]

The orchestra had no horn players. The prince, however, loved hunting, and the sound of French horns reminded him of the chase. He had, of course, got to know Bach in 1716 as the composer of a hunting piece. Thus the services of two French horn players from outside were occasionally called on.[40] Playing together with Herr Spiess and Herr Rose, these guests would have performed the solo passages in the first Brandenburg Concerto [BWV 1046]. Johann Ludwig Schreiber, the first trumpeter, must have been a virtuoso performer on this instrument, since Bach wrote for him the extremely difficult part in the second Brandenburg Concerto [BWV 1047]. (He also gave him demanding and important passages in the cantatas that we shall consider below.)[E7] We can now fit the Köthen soloists into the concertino of this concerto for mixed quartet. The trumpet was played by Herr Schreiber, the flute by Herr Freytag (or Herr Würdig), the oboe by Herr Rose. The violin part was in the hands of the trusty Herr Spiess. The wind players had thus exchanged the "flute traversière" for the "flute à bec."[E8] Both flutists used the latter when, together with the first violinist, they performed the solo parts in the fourth of the Brandenburg Concertos [BWV 1049]. In the third work of this series, however, as in the sixth, wind players were completely dispensed with, and only the string section was heard, divided into three parts. Herr Spiess led the violins, the Kapellmeister himself the violas, and Herr Linigke the violoncellos.[E9] One suspects that we may discern here a faintly amusing twist of history. Six instrumental concertos were composed for the orchestra at Köthen, the soloists in which had lost their positions at the very court of the King of Prussia and Elector of Brandenburg, which in turn had precipitated their move to Köthen. These six compositions, however, were to go down in the history of music as the Brandenburg Concertos, because the composer had dedicated a fair copy of the full score, completed at a later date, to the Margrave of Brandenburg, Christian Ludwig.[41] None of the works was performed at the latter's small court. Because of this, the margrave has gained a reputation for philistinism and a lack of appreciation of Bach's art. The probable reason why the six immortal concertos were not performed at the margrave's court, however, is that they arose entirely out of the conditions prevailing at that time at Köthen. They were centered on the musical life of that court, in the very same way as the other concertos of Bach that have come down to us from those years.

During that time Bach composed the magnificent Concerto in D Minor for violin and oboe, to be played by the *Kammermusiker* Spiess and Rose respectively. The question arises whether in the double concerto for two violins, likewise composed in D minor, the second solo violinist alongside

Herr Spiess was the Berlin exile Herr Marcus or not. Perhaps Bach himself joined the first violinist Spiess at the premiere of this incomparable piece. The situation is similar with the suites of the Köthen period. Only Herr Rose was permanently employed as an oboist. Consequently, during Bach's period of office at Köthen, they would have used a second oboist from outside, which, as we can show, was often the case in later years.[42] On those occasions, the visitor, together with Herr Rose and the bassoonist Torlée, would have formed the section of three instrumentalists in the Suite in C Major [BWV 1066].[E10] With all the above in mind, we are able to trace the musical performances at the court of Köthen throughout Leopold's reign. The move from Berlin to Köthen made by the former *Kammermusiker* of the King of Prussia is therefore seen to have been artistically providential.

Chapter 4

In addition to Bach's instrumental works, however, there were, as we now know, a large number of vocal compositions, including many cantatas. Until recently we could only point to two works in this field, apart from the wedding cantata *Weichet nur, betrübte Schatten* [BWV 202],[E11] the precise dating of which is not possible. We shall return to this work later.[43] The serenade *Durchlauchtster Leopold* [BWV 173a] has been preserved in its entirety, and together with this we have the cantata that has survived only as a fragment known by the title "Mit Gnaden bekröne der Himmel die Zeiten," after its former opening lines. We have successfully reconstructed it in the interim. The missing opening number, "Die Zeit, die Tag und Jahre macht" (by which title the work [BWV 134a] is to be called from now on), the hitherto undiscovered parts of the first aria, and the recitative that follows, have also been recovered. The date also—New Year, 1719—is now certain.[E12] Of primary importance as a pointer to further research, however, was the discovery of the identity of the librettist, Christian Friedrich Hunold, whose pseudonym was Menantes.[E13] In the collection of poems, *Auserlesene Gedichte* (1718–21), published by Hunold, which included a lengthy congratulatory ode consisting of 80 alexandrines that Bach presented to his sovereign on behalf of the court orchestra on the occasion of his birthday on Dec. 10, 1719, were found the following cantata texts set to music by Bach to honor Leopold:[44]

1718	*Dec. 10. Lobet den Herren, alle seine Heerscharen* (a church text) [BWV Anh. 5] and *Der Himmel dacht auf Anhalts Ruhm und Glück* [BWV 66a].
1719	*Jan. 1. Die Zeit, die Tag und Jahre macht* [BWV 134a].
1720	*Jan. 1. Dich loben die lieblichen Strahlen der Sonne* [BWV Anh. 6].
1721	*Dec. 10. Heut ist gewiß ein guter Tag* [BWV Anh. 7].[E14]

It must be admitted that the performance date of the last-named cantata, *Heut ist gewiß ein guter Tag*, is not specifically mentioned in Hunold. But the very publication of the text among the last of the items from Hunold's collection suggests that the work was performed in 1721. Moreover, the poem contains the clearest of allusions to the impending marriage of Prince

Leopold, which took place after the birthday celebrations (Dec. 11, 1721).[45] As a result, we are able with some certainty to nominate Dec. 10, 1721, as the date of the performance of this "pastoral dialog."[E15]

Thus, in clear contrast to the instrumental works, we are able to date these cantatas individually. If we consider them in conjunction with what we know of the details in the household accounts, where reference is made to the printing of the *Carmina*, we obtain the following picture. Vocal music was absent from no New Year's Day celebration and none of the sovereign's birthdays. Two cantatas were heard on each occasion, one religious and one secular. Mention should be made here of the way in which the compositions intended for divine service were used. As indicated earlier, both the town of Köthen and its courts subscribed to the beliefs of the Reformed (Calvinist) Church. Prince Leopold, however, in common with his father Emanuel Leberecht, who died early, was anything but narrow-minded in all matters pertaining to religion. The prince's father had given permission for a Lutheran church to be erected, alongside which arose a Lutheran school. The devout Lutheran Bach sent his children to this school at a later date. Immediately after his accession to the throne, Leopold himself had issued a decree relating to religious tolerance. A consequence of all this was that *Figuralmusik* made its way into the Reformed Church at Köthen during Leopold's reign. This happened on certain festive occasions, however; i.e., it was not a regular exercise, nor was the music tied to any strictly Lutheran religious practices. If this had been the case, the performance of music as art, particularly on Dec. 10, the prince's birthday, which always fell in the period between the first day of Advent and Christmas, i.e., during the liturgical *tempus clausum*, would have been prohibited. It is likely, however, as the choice of Hunold's text "Lobet den Herren, alle seine Heerscharen" implies, that appropriate notice was taken in the religious music composed for these occasions of both the event in the royal household and that in the church calendar. According to strict Lutheran precept, female solo singing, which we encounter at Köthen as part of the divine service, would also have been forbidden. Nevertheless, the fact that Bach's wife, the former Royal Singer, is expressly mentioned in the accounts of the royal households as part of the entry of March 25, 1729 (which we shall discuss in some detail later), is evidence that she, together with the contralto also mentioned, took part in both the funeral services ["Die Trauer Musiquen . . . machen geholfen"]. The same goes for the reimbursement of Bach and his wife in connection with their visits of July 18, 1724, and Dec. 15, 1725; once again, the available female alto and soprano singers, including Anna Magdalena, participated in both the religious and the secular vocal works presented at court, just as the two Monjou girls had been required to do in their "occasional" capacity.[46] [E16]

Turning now to the Bach texts that have come to light, we realize that in a musical sense too these cantatas ought not to be regarded as irretrievably lost. As an illustration of this we start from works with which we are already familiar and examine in the first instance the serenade *Durchlauchtster Leopold*. This work was later parodied as a sacred cantata (No. 173) for Pentecost.[47] In the process it was reduced from eight movements to six, as the following juxtaposition of the two works shows:

Serenade [173a]	*Cantata No. 173*
1. Rec. "Durchlauchtster Leopold"	1. Rec. "Erhöhtes Fleisch und Blut"
2. Aria "Güldner Sonnen frohe Stunden"	2. Aria "Ein geheiligtes Gemüte"
3. Aria "Leopolds Vortrefflichkeiten"	3. Aria "Gott will, o ihr Menschenkinder"
4. Duet "Unter seinem Purpursaum"	4. Duet "So hat Gott die Welt geliebt"
5. Rec. "Durchlauchtigster"	5. Rec. "Unendlichster"
6. Aria "So schau dies holden Tages Licht"	6. Chorus "Rühre, Höchster, unsern Geist"
7. Aria "Dein Name gleich der Sonne geht"	
8. Two-part Aria "Nimm, ach großer Fürst, uns auf "	

Entirely analogous to the above is the transformation undergone by the Köthen New Year Cantata of 1719, which reappeared in parody form as Cantata No. 134. Before we can show this, it is necessary to insert a comment on the results of the analysis of the material that has survived and the process whereby this New Year composition has been fully restored to its original form.[48] The autograph has been incompletely preserved but lacks its first sewn section. These pages contained the opening recitative, bars 1–144 of the first aria and bars 1–26a of the second recitative. As we know from a number of other manuscripts, Bach had set down here the music of the aria and the second recitative, the one below the other, using the unused space below the aria score to note down the recitative that followed.[49] This explains why not only the first movement and the beginning of the second from this work were lost, the first quire of pages having somehow become detached, but also the first great section of the recitative, which formed the third number.

Nevertheless, it has been possible to reconstruct the entire work, as the following shows. The sacred Cantata No. 134 came about as a parody of the Köthen composition. However, Bach did not at first give the religious work the shape we know today, where only the music of the aria "Auf, Gläubige, singet," the duet "Wir danken und preisen," and the final chorus "Erschallet, ihr Lieder" matches the original. Initially the entire work, including the recitative passages, had been given a new libretto, while the music remained unaltered. The individual parts in this oldest version have been preserved, and we can even show that the instrumental parts among these already belonged to the 1719 Köthen piece and had therefore already once been used at Köthen.[E17] If we insert the Hunold libretto below the vocal line of this earliest parody version, we obtain such a convincing rendering of the text that the singing parts now enable us to recognize the original arrangement of the Köthen score.

Here two small conjectures are necessary, the first of which concerns the opening recitative. The modern wording of the first line of the religious text, "Ein Herz, das seinen Jesum lebend weiß," contains two syllables more than the corresponding opening Hunold line, "Die Zeit, die Tag und Jahre macht." It can be shown, however, that the word "seinen" in the church text is a later addition on Bach's part. On the earliest cover of the score we find the title of the piece in what must have been its original form: "Ein Herz, das Jesum lebend weiß." Thus, in place of the opening phrase that has come down to us:

we should have:

Furthermore, this version is musically superior to the one first quoted above, having an underlay that combines effectively with Bach's phrasing in all the recitatives of the work, and including here (as throughout the rest of the composition) a pause sign in the musical line corresponding to a punctuation mark in the libretto. Our recitative in the Köthen version [BWV 134a] therefore looked like this:

The second of our interpolations that enables us to recreate the original form needs no elaborate justification. It concerns the third movement, more precisely the beginning of its third bar. Here, in the vocal line, we should replace the tone f′ with f. At this point the parody libretto contains the word "Hölle" (hell), as against "Himmel" (heaven) of the original. In the revised libretto Bach altered only the octave position of this note. This discovery of the early wording, however, enables us to identify the former pitch (i.e., f instead of f′) as undoubtedly that of the original version of this bar. Accordingly, the opening of the number, missing until now, would sound as follows:

48

The use of Hunold's verse as the libretto of the aria that stands between the two recitatives presents no difficulties.

Thus, by careful and prudent tailoring of the fragments that have survived, we are able completely to restore the score of the Köthen New Year's Day Cantata of 1719. The order of its movements and that of the parody composition of which it gave rise, Cantata No. 134, are juxtaposed below:

Köthen 1719 [BWV 134a]	*Cantata No. 134*
1. Rec. "Die Zeit, die Tag und Jahre macht"	1. Rec. "Ein Herz, das (seinen) Jesum lebend weiß"
2. Aria "Auf, Sterbliche, lasset"	2. Aria "Auf, Gläubige, singet"
3. Rec. "So bald, als dir die Sternen hold"	3. Rec. "Wohl dir, Gott hat an dich gedacht"
4. Duet "Es streiten, es prangen/siegen"	4. Duet "Wir danken und preisen"
5. Rec. "Bedenke dann"	
6. Aria "Der Zeiten Herr"	
7. Rec. "Hilf, Höchster, hilf daß mich die Menschen preisen"	5. Rec. "Doch wirke selbst den Dank in unserm Munde"
8. Chorus (soloists and *tutti*) "Ergetzet auf Erden"	6. Chorus "Erschallet, ihr Himmel"

One recognizes immediately that the reshaping process here closely parallels that of the serenade, *Durchlauchtster Leopold*, discussed above. There, too, a parody containing six numbers was developed from an original eight-movement composition.

Chapter 5

The preceding remarks are of the greatest importance when we come to examine the other Hunold texts, in particular that of the cantata for Dec. 18, 1718, *Der Himmel dacht auf Anhalts Ruhm und Glück.*[50] The point is that this work was reshaped for performance in church on the second day of the Easter festival at Leipzig. It has come down to us as Cantata No. 66, *Erfreut euch, ihr Herzen,* regarded until now as an original piece. We shall now demonstrate that it was a parody and shall begin by juxtaposing the numbers of the original parodied in the revised version:

Köthen 1718 [BWV 66a]	Cantata No. 66
1. Rec. "Der Himmel dacht"	2. Rec. "Es bricht das Grab"
2. Aria "Traget, ihr Lüfte"	3. Aria "Lasset dem Höchsten"
3. Rec. "Die Klugheit auf dem Thron zu sehen"	4. Rec. "Bei Jesu Leben freudig sein"
4. Duet "Ich weiche nun/nicht"	5. Duet "Ich fürchte nicht/zwar"
5. Rec. "Wie weit bist du"	
6. Aria "Beglücktes Land"	
7. Rec. "Nun, teurer Fürst"	
8. (Soloists and full chorus) "Es strahle die Sonne"	1. Chorus "Erfreut euch, ihr Herzen."

As may be seen, three movements of the original version—the recitative "Wie weit bist du," the aria "Beglücktes Land," and the recitative "Nun teurer Fürst"—were omitted from the revised version. Furthermore, a final chorale setting was added in the parody. Once again, it appears that the revised version consisting of six numbers developed out of an eight-movement original. The final number of the Köthen piece, "Es strahle die Sonne," reappeared in the Leipzig version at the start of the work as the chorus "Erfreut euch, ihr Herzen." Minor alterations were also made within the movements themselves; for example, Bach removed two lines of verse from the congratulatory recitative "Die Klugheit auf dem Thron zu sehen" to make the Easter cantata more direct in expression. The close parallels in the text, however, make it abundantly clear that all the numbers of Cantata No. 66, with the exception of the final chorale, owed their origins to the Köthen work. Movement by movement this can also be demonstrated by the parody form of the musical score as it has come down to us. A few examples will serve to show this.

The Köthen congratulatory piece began with the recitative that formed the second number of the Easter cantata. The strings accompany the bass aria, at first in sustained chords. They conclude, however, with a passage containing eighth-note movement in combination with descending chords. The text that forms the basis of the religious work, "So ist in Not und Tod den Gläubigen vollkommen wohl geraten," provides no obvious reason for this change in the mode of expression, though the latter is clearly appropriate in relation to Hunold's original text:

from BWV 66, 2 (reconstructed)

N.B. The character Anhalts Glückseligkeit was probably sung by a contralto, i.e., one octave higher than this.-Ed.

As becomes clear from the later numbers, the role of "Glückseligkeit" (Fortune) was sung by a contralto singer as was the opening recitative. The transposition to the bass register in the Leipzig version will have presented no difficulties. Here again the theme of the vocal part is only really intelligible when we set Hunold's words to the music. Bars 33–57 of the work are given as an example of this:

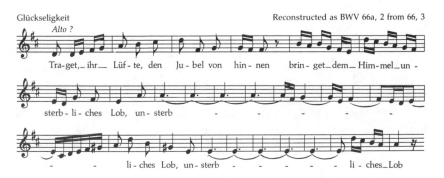

Reconstructed as BWV 66a, 2 from 66, 3

52

But not only does the way in which the words are declaimed come to light as a consequence of the discovery of the original text; we also perceive more clearly the links between the various movements, and thus the dialog structure of the work as a whole. As an illustration of this, two examples from the central section of the aria have been chosen. This section (bars 126–30a) begins with the phrase:

Transposed to A major, this is repeated at bars 148–52:

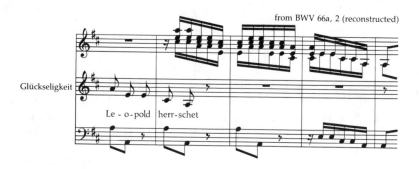

In both instances the final phrase of the opening recitative is taken up by the singer and orchestra. The accompanying words bring out the reason for the "Jubelfest" (jubilee) and its meaning: "Leopold lebet" (Leopold lives) and "Leopold herrschet" (Leopold reigns). Unmistakable here is the thematic relationship with the fourth Brandenburg Concerto, where in the opening movement the same motifs, taken a stage further, appear in the main theme of the solo violin, to be underlined and heightened by the ripienists. Bars 12–22a are quoted below in illustration:

from BWV 66, 3

In both instances, in the cantata and in the concerto, we hear celebratory music as performed at the court of Köthen. In both our serenade and Cantata No. 66 a dialog-recitative succeeds the aria quoted above. Syllable by syllable, we can set the newly discovered original text to the music of the vocal line as we have it from the Easter version. Most characteristic of this process are the rhythmically distinctive bars 22–51, the beginning of which is quoted. Here the discrepancy between the parody text that has come down to us ("mein [kein] Auge sieht den Heiland auferweckt") and the musical phrasing becomes particularly apparent, while the tone coloring of the lines matches the original text extremely well:

from BWV 66a, 3 (reconstructed)

We watch as Prince Leopold's carriage, weighed down with all his glory, rumbles over hill and dale into the far distance. In both the secular and the religious cantatas a duet follows. Here again, because of their diversity, the handling of the singing parts becomes intelligible only when we apply Hunold's lines. The entry of the voices illustrates this:

"Fortune" remains in the state of Anhalt, as it does within the score, whereas "Fame" swiftly sets off to spread the sovereign's praises far and wide. The three sections that follow in the serenade were not carried over into the parody. The original final chorus has been preserved, however, as the opening chorus of Cantata No. 66. When we add Hunold's text we obtain the most sublime expressive effect. Only now does the structure of the composition become clear, as the very first vocal entry demonstrates:

In strict obedience to the instructions of the librettist, the two vocal soloists, "Fortune" and "Fame," are the first to enter, and only then does the full chorus join in. The same thing occurs in the middle section, from which are quoted bars 157–202 of the vocal parts; in bars 165–70, the bass part was to be raised into the tenor register by placing it an octave higher:

In his parody, Bach set the word "trauern" (mourn) in the text to the chromatic lines of this part with great skill; it fits the sequence of notes just as well as the original "flehen" (beseech). Undoubtedly, the leap of a seventh, used as an opening motif, arose because of the cry "Ach Himmel" (Oh, Heaven). Its true significance was forfeited in the revised version, which has "Ihr könnet" (You can).

Lastly, attention is drawn to a short passage in the movement, where on three occasions (at bars 20ff., 70ff., and 152ff.—i.e., at the end of the orchestral ritornello) we meet the following phrase in the continuo part:

We are familiar with these from the first numbers of the piece. In the repeat of the chorus, bars 152–56 bring the entire work to an end. In this way the congratulatory serenade is rounded off musically with a return to the motifs of the opening movement. Furthermore, it provides a conceptual link between the end and the beginning with its reference to the sovereign's "jubilee." It is thus evident that Cantata No. 66, from the viewpoint of its musical structure, is comprehensible only when we combine it in conjunction with Hunold's text.

This alone represents a gain, but the discovery has a more general importance, conveying as it does an impression of the way in which parts of Hunold's verse were set to music in scores by Bach that have not survived, either in the original or parody form. The fact is, however, that we may take it for granted that Bach did compose scores for the other cantata texts by Hunold that I have listed. These are occasional verses, invariably written to be set to music and most probably commissioned for performance at a particular celebration. Bach was of course the resident Kapellmeister, and it was incumbent on him to provide music of this kind. At the same time we recognize from the texts themselves the close affinity with the type of composition we examined earlier. An instance of this is the pastoral dialog "Heut ist gewiß ein guter Tag" [BWV Anh. 7], which we find in the 27th section of Hunold's verses. In the recitative "Du redest nicht," the third number of the work, which takes the form of a dialog between the shepherdess Sylvia and the huntsman Phillis, the pair are brought together to form a vocal duet in a way that is characteristic of the Köthen cantatas:

> Doch so erfreuet unsere Brust
> Dich, aller Hirten Aug und Lust,
> Dich, holden Daphnis, in den Auen
> Gesund, vergnügt und wohl zu schauen.

Daphnis is the pastoral pseudonym assigned to Prince Leopold in the verses. He celebrates his birthday in the depth of winter. The recitative "So schenket nach dem Leiden der Himmel tausend Freuden," the seventh movement in the pastoral dialog, alludes to this and includes a thanksgiving for the recovery of the prince, whom we know to have been invariably in delicate health. Again the number takes the form of a conversation, this time between Thyrsis and Phillis. Once more their lines are interspersed with choral singing, which also brings the piece to an end:

> Thyrsis and Phillis:
> Da hört man nichts von Drangsal und Beschwerden,
> Da muß durch seine Gütigkeit,
> Durch seine Huld und freundliche Gebärden
> Die rauhe Winterszeit
> Zum schönsten Frühling werden.

We may safely assume that these two duet parts within the recitative are sung in a marked rhythmic style, since that was a feature of Bach's occasional compositions of the period. As the text clearly shows, the form of the "Aria a 3," the sixth movement, also belongs to this time:

$$\text{Auf!} \left\{ \begin{array}{l} \text{lobet} \\ \text{danket} \end{array} \right\} \text{dem} \left\{ \begin{array}{l} \text{gütigsten} \\ \text{herrlichsten} \end{array} \right\} \text{Gott,}$$

$$\text{Der unseren} \left\{ \begin{array}{l} \text{edelsten} \\ \text{teuersten} \end{array} \right\} \text{Daphnis bekrönet,}$$

$$\text{Ihn} \left\{ \begin{array}{l} \text{vergnügt} \\ \text{gesund} \end{array} \right\} \text{und wohl zu sehn,}$$

Ist des Landes Wohlergehn,

Wo alles anjetzo von { Jauchzen / Freuden } ertönet.

Auf! { lobet / danket } dem { gütigsten / herrlichsten } Gott,

Der unseren, etc.

The text of this pastoral conversation has the appearance of a two-stanza "Aria," in common with that of *Durchlauchtster Leopold.* There we even have a three-stanza structure on a similar pattern. This is the "Aria. Al Tempo di Menuetto," the three stanzas of which are assigned to the singers' voices in such a way that the first is taken by the bass, the second by the soprano, and the third by both simultaneously:

Unter seinem Purpursaum
Ist die Freude nach dem Leide.
Jedem schenkt er weiten Raum,
Gnadengaben zu genießen,
Die wie reiche Ströme fließen.

Nach landesväterlicher Art
Er ernähret—Unfall wehret,
Drum sich nun die Hoffnung paart,
Daß er werde Anhalts Lande
Setzen in beglückten Stande.

Doch wir lassen unsre Pflicht
Froher Sinnen—itzt nich rinnen,
Heute, da des Himmels Licht
Seine Knechte fröhlich machet
Und auf seinem Szepter lachet.

Structures of this kind seldom recur in Bach's later cantatas. What gives this movement its special character is the progressive key in each of the three sections; the first is in G major, the second in D major, and the third in A major. We are, of course, unable to trace anything of the music of the corresponding number in the pastoral dialog. Its textual form, however, displays the greatest similarity with the lines from *Durchlauchtster Leopold,* to such an extent that we might even have assumed from this feature alone that the piece was to be set in minuet style:

1.

Ein vergnügt und ruhig Leben
Ist das beste dieser Zeit.
In den Feldern, in den Auen
Ist nichts Schöneres zu schauen
Als des Herzens Fröhlichkeit.

2.

Unsers Herzens liebste Weide
Bleibet wohl vergnügt zu sein.
Aber von des Himmels Güte,
Daphnis edelstem Gemüte
Kommet unsre Lust allein.

As in the minuet aria in *Durchlauchtster Leopold*, changes of role and voice occur from stanza to stanza. The first of the two five-line verses above is sung by the shepherdess Sylvia, and the second by the huntsman Phillis.

Chapter 6

The foregoing examples were intended to demonstrate that the cantatas written for performance at court festivals in Köthen, which were set to music by Prince Leopold's Kapellmeister as a matter of course, shared a textual structure that linked them with the type of composition we met in the earlier three works—*Durchlauchtster Leopold; Die Zeit, die Tag und Jahre macht;* and *Der Himmel dacht auf Anhalts Ruhm und Glück.* It is also possible, however, to make *a posteriori* deductions from later source materials. In the case of certain of the vocal works whose musical structure displays the closest relationship with established Köthen vocal compositions we may infer that these were first written during that period. This is particularly so where the material that has come down to us clearly indicates that the existing religious forms of these works are adaptations from earlier originals. They are parodies of compositions that have been lost.

We shall begin with the cantata *Erwünschtes Freudenlicht* [BWV 184]. As will be shown, this composition undoubtedly derives from the period of the Köthen court music. The sequence of movements in the cantata is as follows:

1. Rec. "Erwünschtes Freudenlicht"
2. Duet "Gesegnete Christen, glückselige Herde"
3. Rec. "So freuet euch, ihr auserwählten Seelen"
4. Aria "Glück und Segen ist bereit"
5. Chorale "Herr, ich hoff je"
6. Chorus (*tutti* and soloists) "Guter Hirte, Trost der Deinen."

As the manuscripts prove, the chorale (the 5th movement) is a later substitute for a recitative that previously occurred at this point. This alone indicates that we are dealing with a revised version. If, however, we consider the original form, with its six movements, we again have before us a framework that bears a very close resemblance to the religious parodies of the known Köthen compositions. The same deep affinity can be demonstrated when we examine its individual movements. As with the serenade *Durchlauchtster Leopold*, Cantata No. 184 begins with an instrumentally accompanied recitative. We note the concurrence of the stanzaic structure of the two textual openings:

Köthen Serenade
Durchlauchtster Leopold
Es singet Anhalts Welt
Von neuem mit Vergnügen

Cantata No. 184
Erwünschtes Freudenlicht,
Das mit dem neuen Bund anbricht
Durch Jesum unsern Hirten.

The subsequent solo number in Cantata No. 184, the duet "Gesegnete Christen," displays in its main theme the same form as the Köthen duet "Es streiten, es siegen die künftigen Zeiten" from the New Year composition *Die Zeit, die Tag und Jahre macht:*

Köthen Music for New Year
Es streiten, es siegen die künftigen Zeiten
Im Segen für dieses durchlauchtigste Haus.

Cantata No. 184
Wir danken und preisen dein brünstiges Lieben
Und bringen ein Opfer der Lippen vor dich.

Musically, this duet harks back to *Durchlauchtster Leopold.* The instrumental accompaniment consists of strings and two flutes that combine with the first violin in the ensemble passages. Bach follows the same procedure in the aria "Güldner Sonnen frohe Stunden," the second number of *Durchlauchtster Leopold.* In the duet movement of the religious work the first violin joins with the flutes, playing soloistic material both in unison with them and in alternation; this corresponds exactly to the arrangement in the above-mentioned Köthen parallel. It also matches the duets "Ich weiche nicht, ich will der Erde sagen" (fourth number of *Der Himmel dacht auf Anhalts Ruhm und Glück*) and "Es streiten, es prangen die künftigen Zeiten" (the fifth movement of *Die Zeit, die Tag und Jahre macht.* The recitative "So freut euch, ihr auserwählten Seelen," the third movement of Cantata No. 184, shares with the Köthen recitative passages, with which we are now familiar, the transition from a freely declaimed performance to one of fixed rhythms (cf. bars 22ff.). The same was true of the original penultimate movement, the recitative, which is now mainly lost [BWV 184, 5]. The cello part has been preserved (cf. BG 37, p. xxiii); it runs as follows:

Continuo   fragment from BWV 184a, 3 (?)

Finally, there is a quite different feature of our cantata to which attention should be drawn—a characteristic that it shares with the serenade *Durchlauchtster Leopold*. In this serenade, Bach prefaced the fourth number, the duet "Unter deinem Purpursaum," with the heading "Al Tempo di Menuetto." This passage is in fact representative of the minuet type, i.e., of a dance form. The same is true of the tenor aria "Glück und Segen sind bereit," the fourth movement of Cantata No. 184, the instrumental ritornello of which runs as follows:

This movement is obviously in the style of a polonaise. The final chorus, however, the opening of which is shown below, is clearly a gavotte:

Thus, as in *Durchlauchtster Leopold*, we have dance forms in both instances. What this signifies as a whole will be analyzed later in some detail.[E18] Suffice it to say here that the link between Cantata No. 184 and the Köthen cantata has been demonstrated from a number of different points of view.[E19] Since we can also show that the religious cantata came about as a parody, there can be no doubt that it was based on a vocal composition by Bach, probably secular, from the years 1717–23.

I am convinced that the same is true of the cantata for the Third Day of Easter, *Auf, mein Herz, des Herren Tag* [BWV 145]. The authenticity of this piece has been, in my opinion, wrongly contested. Doubts about its genuineness could only be expressed while the work was held to be a new church cantata.[E20] Admittedly, the piece underwent a far more rigorous transformation than the two cantatas, Nos. 134 and 184, previously discussed. The two chorales, with which Cantata No. 145 begins and ends, are undoubtedly additions in the parody. (We have already encountered the later insertion of chorale movements into Köthen works parodied for church use.) We shall now look at the second number of the work, the chorus "So du mit deinem Munde bekennest Jesum, daß er der Herr sei." A section such as bars 3ᵇ to 7 is striking not only in a musical and declamatory sense, but also from the textual and grammatical aspect:

from BWV 145, 2 (by Telemann.-Ed.)

Daß er der Herr— sei, daß er der Herr— sei, Herr,   Herr,   so du   mit dei-nem

These bars not only lead us to suspect that the accompanying libretto did not originally belong to the music, i.e., that we have a parody here; they may be taken to demonstrate it conclusively. Particularly improbable is the repetition of the freestanding "Herr" (Lord). In any case, we cannot regard this piece as a complete choral movement. Even so, its form does gain significance, once we consider it as having derived from an internal movement of a secular cantata chorus dating from Bach's Köthen years. Here, once again, the music opens with two vocal parts performing solo in duet, to be joined by the chorus only at bar 40 (as the instruments that enter at this point and perform *colla parte* indicate).[51] This is a replica of the example I quoted in detail earlier from the cantata *Der Himmel dacht auf Anhalts Ruhm und Glück* [BWV 66a], where the four-part vocal section did not begin until the 42d bar of the central movement. The core section of the final chorus of the cantata *Die Zeit, die Tag und Jahre macht* [BWV 134a] has a similar structure, where once again a long solo duet passage (13 bars) precedes the entry of the choir. The orchestral accompaniment of the chorus "So du mit deinem Munde bekennest," where only a single instrument is used alongside the strings, also finds parallels among the vocal works of the Köthen period. The same is not true of the thematic materials accorded to the vocal parts, which one would have to describe as untypical of Bach, if one were to consider the piece as an autonomous work by the composer. However, the overall design of the movement accords with our impression that it originated as an inner movement of a lost Köthen cantata.

The passage that does fit as movement three of Cantata No. 145 is a vocal duet. This again brings to mind Köthen, the form of the duet clearly demonstrating its links with the vocal works performed at court there. As in those duets, we are again presented with a dialog, the text of which has the following now familiar form:

| Seele | Du lebest, mein Jesu, ⎫ | zu | ⎰meinem⎱ | Ergetzen, |
| Jesus | Ich lebe, mein Herze, ⎭ | | ⎱deinem⎰ | |

Dein ⎫ Leben erhebet ⎰mein⎱ Leben empor.
Mein ⎭ ⎱dein⎰

in ⎧ Die klagende Handschrift is völlig zerrissen,
⎨ Der Friede verschaffet ein ruhig Gewissen
unison ⎩ Und öffnet den Sündern das himmlische Tor.

In this duet, as with the related Köthen numbers, the obbligato accompaniment is entrusted to the solo violin. Its theme clearly echoes Bach's Köthen style. Schering is right when he conjectures that Bach undertook a series of alterations to this movement, a view that closely supports our assumption that we are dealing with a parody here.[52]

Of the bass aria that immediately follows, Spitta writes: "The lively bass aria 'Merke, mein Herze, beständig nur dies' has something dancelike about it; we almost fancy we are watching happy, sturdy figures dancing in the spring."[53] Schering, on the other hand, goes so far as to surmise that this number owes its origins to a secular cantata.[54] We find this view fully confirmed with the entry of the first violin, from which are quoted bars 1–28:

Vln. I   from BWV 145, 5

Less of the original work has been carried over into the parody than was the case with cantatas 173, 134, 66, and 184. Nevertheless, we may take it as certain that three numbers of Cantata No. 145 derive from a lost Köthen original. The use of the oboe d'amore is a help when we come to date this original composition, suggesting, as it does, Bach's later years at Köthen, since this particular instrument occurs in his work only after 1720/21.[E21]

Chapter 7

Our studies of cantatas 184 and 145 necessarily raise the question whether these really are the only works we have that in their modern form are associated with Leipzig, but which in fact derive from pieces originally composed during the years 1717–23. To continue the search means that in each instance we must focus our attention on three aspects of the compositions:

1. Do the individual movements belong structurally to the Köthen types identified above?
2. Do the libretto and the music of the composition suggest alternative origins?
3. Does other evidence point in this particular direction?

Let us begin by addressing all these questions to Cantata No. 190, *Singet dem Herrn ein neues Lied,* which consists of the following movements:

1. Chorus "Singet dem Herrn ein neues Lied"
2. Chorale with recitative "Herr Gott, dich loben wir"
3. Aria "Lobe, Zion, deinen Gott"
4. Rec. "Es wünsche sich die Welt"
5. Duet "Jesus soll mein Alles sein"
6. Rec. "Nun, Jesus gebe, daß in dem neuen Jahr"
7. Chorale "Laß uns das Jahr vollbringen"

The source materials at our disposal are:

A. An autograph score containing, however, only numbers 3–7.
B. Six individual parts (four vocal parts and the two violins) for the entire work, as written out by a copyist and revised by Bach.
C. The old front cover for the parts, the inscription of which, written in the hand of a copyist,[E22] informs us that apart from the vocalists, strings, and *basso continuo,* the following belonged to the full complement of the orchestra: 3 *clarini,* drums, 3 oboes, bassoon.

The fragmentary character of these source materials explains why the first two movements of this cantata have come down to us only in incomplete form. The nature of the manuscript material can nevertheless be explained quite satisfactorily from what we have learned in recent years of Bach's parody technique. In the version we have, which belongs to the early Leipzig period, the composition was intended for the New Year. Bach parodied it in 1730 to create a celebratory cantata on the occasion of the jubilee of the Augsburg Confession. Picander furnished the libretto of the parody. The music used in 1730 has been lost, though we can say with certainty that no overall score was produced, simply parts for the individual singers and instrumentalists. Even so, we can have a very clear idea of how the piece looked. Bach constructed the work in the same way he always did when a parody was intended for a specific occasion, i.e., it could only be used once. He took from the vocal score of the original whatever he needed for the revised version. In this instance, the four singing parts were of no use because they would have necessitated substantial rewriting for the insertion of the 1730 libretto. The two copies of each of the violin parts, however, were indispensable, and for this reason these four parts from the performance material of the New Year cantata were retained in the folder. The fact that the remaining instrumental parts were not replaced shows that Bach did not use the cantata again after that year. This also explains why the scoring was left incomplete.

It is important to understand at this point that Bach's works, or the movements from them that he parodied, were usually further revised on many occasions. It is rare for a piece to be reused only once.[55] This suggests that the New Year's music "Singet dem Herrn" was not an original work either and that it contained older reworked material. As was frequently the case, the latter was combined with passages that had been newly composed or with music that was derived from elsewhere. The piece matches this view, both in terms of its musical structure and of the actual score in our possession. This has two components that were quite clearly originally separate, the one an introductory chorus and chorale recitative, the other the numbers that follow in the score. The score as such is, however, incomplete. The presumed earlier version did not include the opening two movements of Cantata 190 as we have them today. Thus, numbers 3–7 refer to an earlier period, being a fragment, almost certainly the concluding movements of an earlier cantata, probably from the Köthen repertoire. The structure of the movements fully concurs with this view. Spitta himself drew attention to the "dancelike character" of the alto aria "Lobe, Zion, deinen Gott."[56] The introductory and closing ritornello, where the opening bars:

Strings and Continuo   from BWV 190, 3

are repeated *piano*, with bars 14ᵇ to 17ᵃ providing an analogous *piano* repeat, corresponds in instrumentation with Bach's compositional practice at Köthen. Towards the end, the recitative "Es wünsche sich die Welt" changes to the measured *andante* for which Bach had a special liking at that time. The inclusion of one duet had been a feature of the Köthen cantatas, and the one that follows in [BWV] 190 is structurally very closely related to those discussed above, notably in the manner of its effective deployment of canon. The penultimate movement of Cantata No. 190 is, however, noteworthy above all because of its libretto, which begins:

> Nun, Jesus gebe,
> Daß mit dem neuen Jahr auch sein Gesalbter lebe;
> Er segne beides, Stamm und Zweige,
> Auf daß ihr Glück bis an die Wolken steige.

There is no mention in any original Leipzig work for New Year's Day of a prayer for a "Gesalbter" (Anointed One), a prince, or his family ("Stamm und Zweige"). Such references would have been entirely inappropriate in those compositions. (In Cantata No. 171, *Gott, wie dein Name*, there is a reference to "Obrigkeit und Land" [the supreme authority and the state] and in Cantata No. 41, *Jesu, nun sei gepreiset*, to "Stadt und Land" [city and state]). In other words, the libretto of Cantata No. 190 points to a specifically royal environment, i.e., Köthen. This means, however, that in this instance we are dealing not with parody procedures but with movements that have come down to us with their original texts. These words derive in fact, as we know, from one of the Köthen religious cantatas that were regularly performed on New Year's Day at court.[57]

It is even possible to give a fairly accurate date to this composition, both from the libretto and the score. As in the case of Cantata No. 145, the use of the oboes d'amore precludes a dating before 1720/21.[E23] The reference to the "Stamm und Zweige" (stem and branches) of the royal household, however, inevitably points to the time after Leopold's marriage (Dec. 11, 1721), probably even to the period after the birth of the first child that ensued from the marriage, Princess Gisela Agnes (born Sept. 21, 1722). The religious New Year's composition, from which the movements of Cantata No. 190 that we discussed earlier originate, might, therefore, have been originally performed on Jan. 1, 1722, but was probably first heard a year later, on the last occasion on which Bach was to experience the turn of the year at Köthen in his capacity as the resident Kapell-meister.[E24]

Whenever he subjected a composition of this kind to revision, Bach would parody a work on more than one occasion. The fact that a piece that had been given a new libretto could only be used once contributed to these numerous revisions. Considerations of this kind led to an examination of Cantata No. 190 and the discovery of numbers taken from a Köthen religious cantata that had been preserved entirely in their original form. We can apply quite similar methods of analysis, modified slightly to take account of the special nature of the available materials, to a cantata written for the Leipzig Council election, *Ihr Tore zu Zion* [BWV 193]. As in the case of Cantata No. 190, this work has survived only fragmentarily. As source materials we have only nine of the original parts (the two violins twice, soprano, alto, viola, and the two oboes once each). Among the vocal parts we are certainly lacking those of the tenor and bass. Of the instrumental parts, the music for the three trumpets and timpani is missing. Nor do we have a score from which we might insert the parts we lack. Nevertheless, a number of very significant conclusions may be reached on the basis of these materials alone. The order of the movements is as follows:

1. Chorus "Ihr Tore zu Zion"
2. Rec. "Der Hüter Israels"
3. Aria "Gott, wir danken deiner Güte"
4. Rec. "O Leipziger Jerusalem"
5. Aria "Sende, Herr, den Segen ein"
6. Rec. (text unknown).
7. Chorus "Ihr Tore zu Zion" (repeat of first movement)

Elsewhere[58] I have been able to demonstrate that the chorus that opened and closed this work and the two arias were not original compositions but parodies. I was able to prove this by reference to the congratulatory piece composed for Augustus the Strong's name day (Aug. 3, 1727), the libretto of which was written by Picander and published in the second volume of his *Ernst-, scherzhafte und satyrische Gedichte* (Serious, frivolous, and satirical poems) of 1729 (pp. 11ff.). Examination of these verses revealed that the chorus, "Ihr Tore zu Zion," may be traced back to Picander's first movement, "Ihr Häuser des Himmels," and that the two arias, "Gott, wir danken deiner Güte" and "Sende, Herr, den Segen ein," have their origins in the fourth and seventh movements of 1727, "Herr, so groß als dein Erhöhen" and "Sachsen, komm zum Opferherd." However, even with no knowledge of these Picander verses, one could have recognized from the materials we have of "Ihr Tore zu Zion" that we are concerned here with a parody. In the alto part we find the following bars that were subsequently struck out by Bach:

O Leich-zi-ger Je - ru - sa-lem Ver-gnü-ge dich an dei-nem Fe-ste,der Fried ist noch in dei-nen Mau - ren es stehn an-noch die Stüh-le zum Gericht und

die Gerechtigkeit bewohnet die Palläste. Ach, bitte, daß dein Ruhm und Licht, also beständig möge theuren.

The question of how this passage, containing a declamation that misfires to such an extent that it produces a downright comical effect, nearly found its way into a Bach composition, is easily answered. The copyist took as his model a score from which he had to write out certain numbers only. The recitatives were not among these, since they were not required. As was the custom in copywork of this kind, the scribe first of all, for the fourth number of the cantata, which celebrated the inauguration of the new council, "O Leipziger Jerusalem," wrote the words of the text below what were at that stage empty staves, in order to be able to enter the music of the vocal parts more easily at a later date.[59] However, at this point he inadvertently took the wrong score as a model, i.e., the score from which he was required to copy out the opening chorus and the arias and nothing more. We may assume that Bach spotted the error at the time when the wretched copyist, probably a pupil, was committing his folly to paper, and that the Kantor thereupon struck out the offending contents but later inserted the passage at another place in the score, indicating the point at which the addition was to be made. In other words, the scribe's error could have supplied the proof to anyone who was unaware of Picander's text that Cantata No. 190 was the result of the parody technique.[E25] This can now be shown unequivocally from Picander's verses, even from this small fragment of a recitative, since, if we superimpose the lines taken from Picander's version, we are left with the best possible declamation.

Wie bin ich doch er - götzt, daß Sach-sens Wunsch und Pflicht nun der Er-

hör-ung wert-ge - schätzt. Das uns er-freu-te Licht er-regt im Lan-de Ju-bel - lie-der

The application of the parody process, i.e., in this instance the superimposition of a new libretto, also enables us to understand the otherwise virtually inexplicable indecision in the text of the council inauguration cantata, where we have "Ihr Pforten zu Zion" (after Gen. 27:17 and Neh. 2:8) as compared with "Ihr Tore zu Zion" (after Ps. 122:2; 147:13; Is. 60:11 and 18; 62:10; Rev. 22:14). The view that textual indecision of this kind points to a parody should be further extended to Picander's congratulatory verse of 1727 for Augustus the Strong.[60] In both the presentation copy itself and the 1729 reprint of the verses, the piece begins:

Ihr Häuser des Himmels, ihr scheinenden Lichter, Seid gebückt.

The poet addresses the stars. The designation "Häuser des Himmels" (houses of heaven) is to be taken as meaning that the heroes, who have been raised to the heavens, now reside there. The image of these "houses" being "bowed down" as their contribution to the glorification of the mighty elector—a physical impossibility—is explicable only if we try to visualize the difficulties confronting the poet in his attempt to create a text that, both rhythmically and declamatorily, could be applied to an existing piece of music. Not until later did it occur to Bach's librettist that the solution was to replace the word "Häuser" by "Häupter" (heads), thus achieving a meaningful image, since heads may easily be bowed. The parodist escaped from his predicament and the text was improved.

Thus, we should regard not only the council inauguration cantata, *Ihr Tore zu Zion* [BWV 193], but also the serenade of 1727, *Ihr Häuser des Himmels*, as parodies. In that case, the two arias, "Herr, so groß als dein Erhöhen" and "Sachsen, komm zum Opferherd" ("Gott, wir danken deiner Güte" and "Sende, Herr, den Segen ein" in the council inauguration text respectively), are of significance, since we have their musical scores virtually complete. From the first of these two I quote from the introductory ritornello the parts of the first oboe and the first violin:

Oboe I
from BWV 193, 3

Vln. I

A characteristic of both lines is that the unison playing of the two instruments is on each occasion interrupted by sections in which the oboe and violin separate, the one taking the actual melodic line, the other providing simple accompanying figures or adding rhythmic point to the melody. This method of composition is a feature of the instrumentation of Bach's Köthen vocal compositions. Above, an instance of this device is referred to in the opening ritornello from the final chorus of Cantata No. 184 (see page 62). There we had a gavotte movement into which the choral part had been inserted. In our aria "Herr, so groß als dein Erhöhen" we are likewise confronted by a dance form, a minuet that precedes the vocal section in the shape of a complete instrumental movement, thus:

> Bars 1–16: First section modulating from E minor to G major.
>
> Bars 17–32: Second section modulating back to E minor.

Both elements, the use of a dance form and its complete, purely instrumental presentation as an opening and concluding ritornello, are characteristic of the Köthen period.

The second of the two arias, "Sachsen, komm zum Opferherd," likewise belongs to the years 1717–23. The soloistically elaborate treatment of the oboe in the obbligato accompaniment is encountered in many parts of the Köthen cantatas, above all in the solo arias.

No less significant than the parts of the secular cantata of 1727 where the score is still recognizable are the sections for which we still have only Picander's libretto. The last movement, "Himmel, erhöre das betende Land," gives us the contrast of soloists and *tutti* entirely typical of the

Köthen compositions, where, as the text alone indicates, the full chorus makes its appearance in a homophonically assertive passage. Equally important is the duet between "Fama" and "Providentia," two allegorical figures whom we meet again and again in those of Bach's Köthen cantatas with which the reader is already familiar.

Duet Aria
Fama and Providentia

| F. | Ich will $\Big\}$ rühmen $\Big\{$ ich will $\Big\}$ |
| Pr. | Du sollst $\qquad$ du sollst |

| Duet | Von den angenehmen Tagen; |
| | Wie sich Reich und Land erfreut: |

| Pr. | Aber von der Seltenheit |
| | Deines Königs Herrlichkeit |

| F. | Will ich $\Big\}$ selbst die Sterne fragen |
| Pr. | Sollst du |

As in Hunold's duets between Fame and Fortune: "Ich weiche nicht, ich will der Erde sagen" (from *Der Himmel dacht auf Anhalts Ruhm und Glück* [BWV 66a]) or between Time and Divine Providence: "Es streiten, es prangen die vorigen Zeiten" (from *Die Zeit, die Tag und Jahre macht* [BWV 134a]) or in the three-part song "Auf! Lobet den gütigsten Gott" (from *Heut ist gewiß ein guter Tag* [BWV Anh. 7]), we have interchanging passages where the vocalists alternate between singing alone and simultaneously in duet. All this enables us to identify how Picander superimposed his congratulatory piece of 1727 on an existing score, and how in this case too, as so often with Bach, the same work, or at least sections from it, underwent the parody treatment on several occasions. Consistent with this view is the fact that both the lost original version and the first parody of 1727 were suitable for use on one occasion only. As we have demonstrated, however, the original version was surely composed in Köthen.

Chapter 8

Using the various preceding examples, an attempt has been made to show that behind many of the cantatas of the Leipzig period, hitherto held to be original compositions, we may with some degree of success seek lost vocal works written at the time when Bach was actively engaged as Prince Leopold's Kapellmeister. No claim is made here to have grasped all the implications of these documents or to have exhausted their research potential. We can, however, add to the material. Hitherto, a vocal work by Bach that may rightly be placed in the Köthen period has not been discussed; this is the secular wedding cantata *Weichet nur, betrübte Schatten* [BWV 202]. This is because the work calls for only one soprano. In other words, the movement structures that enable us to recognize Bach's method of vocal composition at that time with especial clarity, the duet and the chorus consisting of homophonous *tutti* sections and solo parts sung in duet, are not to be found in this particular composition. Having familiarized ourselves with Bach's Köthen style of vocal composition, however, we must now turn our attention to the wedding cantata. First and foremost, mention should be made of the dance forms that we find here. The final movement bears the inscription "Gavotta" and displays the tripartite structure that we associate with Bach's Köthen suites. In this instance, only the central section is sung, while the main musical material, which is repeated after the central section, is purely instrumental. The preceding aria, "Sich üben im Lieben," with its introductory ritornello:

has the dance character of a *passepied*.[E26] These cheerful passages, to which the second and third arias of the cantata ("Phöbus eilt mit schnellen Pferden" and "Wenn die Frühlingslüfte streichen") with their associated recitatives also belong, form a delightful, one might even say an enchanting, counterpart to the movement that introduces the whole work, "Weichet nur, betrübte Schatten":

Above the wind instruments, rising *piano* in broken chords, we hear the elegant theme of the solo oboe, to be joined by the soprano in the middle of the fifth bar. The delicately fashioned melody intertwines with the even more richly ornamented line of the oboe and is surrounded by the continuing accompaniment of the spread chords in the violins and the viola, creating an exquisitely wistful impression.[E27]

We have one religious cantata by Bach, belonging, like those discussed in previous chapters, to the early Leipzig years, which matches the above in its musical structure—Cantata No. 32, *Liebster Jesu, mein Verlangen*. Close examination of the work discloses that it too should be counted among the parody works and that the lost original belonged to the Köthen period.[E28] It consists of the following movements:

1. Aria "Liebster Jesu, mein Verlangen"
2. Rec. "Was ists, daß ihr mich gesuchet?"
3. Aria "Hier, an meines Vaters Stätte"
4. Rec. "Ach! heiliger und großer Gott"
5. Duet "Nun verschwinden alle Plagen"
6. Chorale "Mein Gott, öffne mir die Pforten."

Cantata No. 32 has the same instrumentation—oboe, strings, continuo—as *Weichet nur, betrübte Schatten* [BWV 202]. Its overall structure, six movements including two arias and a duet with a preceding dialog recitative, brings to mind cantatas [BWV] 134 and 66, which we know developed from eight-movement originals. As in the case of other parodies, the chorale that comes at the end of Cantata No. 32 is to be regarded as an addition occasioned by the new religious libretto, substituted perhaps for an original final chorus. The above assumes that we can prove that this cantata was in fact a parody.

We can show this to be the case first of all from the source materials in our possession. There are two pieces of evidence of primary importance, namely,

a. The autograph score.
b. One set of the original parts.

Of the vocal parts, those for the alto and tenor are complete and in Bach's own hand, though for the soprano and bass we have only the parts for the fourth, fifth, and sixth movements. Of the instrumental parts, however, we have only the last page in Bach's hand; for some parts this gives us only the chorale, for others we have in addition the end of the preceding duet. This is entirely in keeping with the assumed parody nature of the work. The copyist was able to transcribe the material for the oboe and strings directly from the score of the original work with which he was supplied. The composer himself wrote down only the final page, inserting the chorale, which did not appear in the original work. Because of the new libretto, however, the vocal parts presented greater difficulties and the copyist probably made little headway here. As a result, Bach chose to collaborate more closely with him at this point, writing out himself two of the parts in full and more than half of the other two.

Thus the source materials we have inherited indicate that we should be thinking of the reworking of an older cantata here, one that would have a very close affinity with the Köthen vocal compositions. The opening aria of Cantata No. 32, the beginning of the prelude of which is quoted below, sounds thus:

We need only compare the sequence of notes here with the opening of the cantata *Weichet nur, betrübte Schatten* to perceive the close relationship. As there, here too the oboe performs a widely ranging elegiac melody, to be joined later by the soprano interweaving its richly structured line with that of the wind instrument. Here again both soloists and their parts are supported by broken chords in the strings with their bittersweet harmonies. On both occasions a broadly sustained tempo is expressly called for, and on both occasions Bach stipulates *piano* for the string parts.

From the second aria we may single out the main theme of the vocal melody:

This is a perfect example of a minuet. The following recitative, accompanied by the strings, takes the form of a dialog; as such, it is very similar to the recitatives of the Köthen years. It also includes bars of true arioso in rhythmic notation. From the text of the soprano part (bars 15 and 16), "Ach Jesu! meine Brust liebt dich nun inniglich," one recognizes that this movement consists of a conversation between Jesus and the soul. Bach has retained dialogs of this kind in this piece whenever a duet with the same vocal scoring follows a recitative. Only then is the juxtaposition of dialog pairs for one voice meaningful. The reader is reminded of the following examples from the Köthen cantatas:

Der Himmel dacht auf Anhalts
Ruhm und Glück [BWV 66a]

Rec. "Die Klugheit auf dem Thron zu sehen"
Duet "Ich weiche nicht, du sollst der Erde sagen"
On both occasions: Fame and Fortune

Die Zeit, die Tag und Jahre macht [BWV 134a]

Rec. "So bald, als mir die Sterne hold"
Duet "Es streiten, es siegen"
On both occasions: Time and Divine Providence

Of the religious parodies, we should mention:

Erfreut euch, ihr Herzen (Cantata No. 66)

Rec. "Bei Jesu Leben freudig sein"
Duet "Ich fürchte zwar des Grabes Finsternissen"
On both occasions: Fear and Hope

In the later religious cantatas Bach retains this procedure:

O Ewigkeit, du Donnerwort (Cantata No. 60)

Rec. "O schwerer Gang"
Duet "Mein letztes Lager will mich schrecken"
On both occasions: Fear and Hope

In similar vein, we must regard the duet for soprano and bass, "Nun verschwinden alle Plagen," from Cantata No. 32 as a continuation of the dialog contained in the preceding recitative. The dialog, however, comes to grief because of the general style of the duet number. One after the other, the two voices intone the following in a happy, lilting rhythm:

Delightful though this movement is from a purely musical standpoint, the piece is totally out of keeping with the textual and conceptual subject matter both of the composition as a whole and of this particular passage. The joy of the redeemed soul could conceivably be expressed by means of this cheerful dance form; it is, however, not appropriate for the part of the risen Savior.[E29] This difficulty is removed at once if we regard the duet as a revision of an original Köthen work. A characteristic of Bach's method of composition at that time was his preference, particularly in the vocal duets, for allowing the first violin, as here, to stand out in its thematic material and its soloistic style from the rest of the strings. At the same time, we find the identical technique used in the parallel relationship between the wind instrument and the first violin, a feature we have encountered several times already in this study. The two instruments are used in some passages in unison; elsewhere the wind instrument merely emphasizes the salient rhythmical features of the violin melody:

All this allows us to recognize a lost Köthen original behind Cantata No. 32, *Liebster Jesu, mein Verlangen.* Our point of departure, however, was the striking resemblance between the opening movement and the first aria of the Köthen wedding cantata, *Weichet nur, betrübte Schatten*, and we must return once again to this charming piece. Spitta himself pointed out that the continuo line of the aria "Phöbus eilt mit schnellen Pferden":[61]

Continuo   from BWV 202, 3

is closely related to the main theme of the last movement of the Sonata for Violin and Harpsichord [BWV 1019, 5], which likewise originated in Köthen:[E30]

Vln.   from BWV 1019, 5

This sonata must be mentioned in this context because, particularly in connection with our present theme, it takes us a surprising step further. The point is that this work displays not only a thematic relationship with the Köthen wedding cantata, but also an overall structural resemblance. In his study "Der modulatorische Aufbau in Bachs Gesangswerken,"[62] Hans Stephan summarized the composition of the wedding cantata as follows:

Aria "Weichet nur" G major
Rec. "Die Welt wird wieder neu"
Aria "Phöbus eilt mit schnellen Pferden" C major
Rec. "Drum sucht auch Amor"
Aria "Wenn die Frühlingslüfte" E minor
Rec. "Und dieses ist das Glücke"
Aria "Sich üben im Lieben" D major
Rec. "So sei das Band der treuen Liebe"
Aria "Sehet mit Zufriedenheit" G major

Here we have a five-part structure that encloses a central section within a double framework. Three versions exist of the Sonata in G Major [BWV 1019] (the same key as that used in the cantata), the earliest of which deserves our special attention. It has the following form:

Presto . . . . G major
Largo. . . . . E minor
Cantabile, ma un poco Adagio . . . . G major

Adagio. . . . . .B minor
Presto ab initio repetatur et claudatur . . . . .G major

Here too, as distinct from all the other Bach sonatas, we have a five-part
structure. The clearly identifiable outer movements provide a firm framework. The second and penultimate movements are linked together by their
dignity of character and similarity of key. Both pairs of movements, however, enclose a central passage that in this instance is written in the key
that is basic to the piece as a whole, G major. Only the last of the three
versions of the work also shows in its key structure any close relationship
to the form of the wedding cantata. Here Bach replaced the G major movement that was originally at the center of the work by a solo clavier piece
in E minor.[E31]

We now turn our attention to the central movement, which Bach left
out of the sonata. Of this Spitta wrote:

> This is a fully developed and extended piece in a 6/8 time and in three
> sections, remarkable for a singularly bridal feeling: it is marked by a sweet
> fragrance and a breath of lovely yearning such as are seldom found in
> Bach. The lengthy superscription—which Bach was wont to disdain as a
> rule—is remarkable; and there is developed in the two upper parts a
> kind of loving intercourse, a dialog as from mouth to mouth, carried on
> above a bass that has nothing to do but to support the harmony. All these
> are quite at variance with the style of Bach's trios in other places; and
> what is just as unique is that all three parts do not conclude at the same
> time: the clavier melody ceases 12 bars before the end, while the violin
> repeats the whole of the opening phase of the melody, supported by the
> bass.[63]

Thus, according to Spitta, this movement is completely different from the
normal trio style of Bach's sonatas. Two features most clearly bring this
out, the treatment of the bass, which remains completely distinct from the
music of the upper parts, and the arrangement of the last 12 bars, where
the violin alone remains to accompany the basso continuo. However, we
may go a stage further. The two upper parts do indeed combine to create
a splendid duo, though structurally they fulfill distinctive roles. The lavishly
employed 32d-note passages in the violin part occur only sparingly in the
right-hand part for the clavier, which follows a more graceful, songlike
course. Furthermore, the range of notes employed in the two upper parts
is remarkably different. In that of the violin these extend from g to d''',
i.e., a span of two and a half octaves, whereas for the right hand of the
clavier part we have only d' to a'', a full octave less.

If we examine the movement from all these aspects, we recognize that
we are dealing with a soprano aria minus the libretto. The vocal line has

been allocated to the upper part of the clavier, Bach confining himself here to the precise vocal range of the soprano. In the same way, the treatment of the violin part, which is essentially different from that of the right hand of the clavier, becomes intelligible down to the last detail. Phrases in the violin part such as:

i.e., motivic decorations of the main theme that occur in only one of the parts, counterparts of which we may seek in vain in the other, may be explained as a technique that Bach habitually used in arias involving obbligato accompaniment. The instruction *piano*, which occurs twice in the instrumental parts, at bars 14 and 47, derives from the aria form. The vocal line enters for the first time at bar 13 after the great instrumental prelude; the solo violin withdraws *piano*. The beginning of the central section corresponds to the opening of the vocal passage in the main part of the aria. It had begun with a two-bar violin interlude (bars 43 and 44), to be played *forte*, of course. At this point the vocal line enters again, for two bars at first, accompanied only by the basso continuo. At the reentry of the violin (bar 47) we find the instruction *piano*, exactly as it has occurred at bar 14. Spitta compared this work, which is headed, probably not by chance, "Cantabile, ma un poco adagio," with certain arias from Bach's wedding cantatas, though it should be added that he had only the atmosphere of the piece in mind. The similarity, we might even go as far as to say concurrence, in terms of form, indicates that it is indeed an aria divested of its libretto. As such it sits awkwardly within a purely instrumental work, a sonata, which may be the reason why Bach omitted the movement at a later date, replacing it by another.

Later, however, we come across the piece again, significantly now as an aria, with the following text:

Heil und Segen
Soll und muß zu aller Zeit
Sich auf unsre Obrigkeit
In erwünschter Fülle legen,

Daß sich Recht und Treue müssen
Miteinander freundlich küssen." Da Capo.

(Fourth movement of Cantata [BWV] 120, *Gott, man lobet dich in der Stille*)

Thus Bach did not, as was originally supposed, fit words to an original instrumental work; he was parodying an aria that had previously been composed to a different libretto. The fact, however, that the oldest version of this movement that we have is to be found in a Köthen instrumental work shows that it must have derived from a lost vocal composition of the years 1717–23. Its conclusion, temporary though it was, in the Sonata in G Major has thus enabled us to discover a new fragment from one of these lost vocal works. Since it was Bach's custom, whenever he parodied a piece, to give his newly composed libretto the same strophic form, we may assert that the original text, in terms of its form, is preserved in the aria libretto "Heil und Segen." This could be of considerable value for further research into Bach's vocal works from the years 1717 to 1723, particularly should any more librettos come to light.

The assumption that "Heil und Segen" represents the libretto structure of the original text set to the specified music from the Sonata in G Major is corroborated by our discovery that Bach (as was so often the case) parodied this particular Köthen aria on several occasions. We meet it in the cantata *Gott, man lobet dich in der Stille*, [BWV 120b], a version of BWV 120 adapted by Bach for the jubilee celebrations of the Augsburg Confession,[E32] on this occasion with a different text. The latter, however, displays the same strophic form:

Treu im Glauben,
Unbeweglich in der Not,
Treu im Leben, treu im Tod
Müssen wahre Christen bleiben
Daß sie nach dem frohen Sterben
Jenes Lebens Krone erben." Da Capo.

At the same time, however, the fact that Bach went back to a Köthen original significantly reinforces the contention that Cantata 190, *Singet dem Herrn ein neues Lied*, which was likewise performed at the *Confessio Augustana*, made use of material from the same period.

Between the two church compositions that formed part of the celebration of the Augsburg Confession there is yet another remarkable parallel. We can show that in both works Bach derived his material from not one, but several sources. This sheds new light on the opening aria of Cantata No. 120, *Gott, man lobet dich in der Stille*. Quoted below are a few bars of the vocal part:

These figurations are not intended for a vocal part; they have an unmistakably violinlike character. It follows, however, that the two arias of Cantata No. 120 are to be interpreted in a way that is exactly opposite of that previously adopted. "Heil und Segen" did not evolve from a purely instrumental work, and *Gott, man lobet dich in der Stille* is not originally a vocal composition. If we, however, state this categorically, then our aria can only have been the central movement of a lost violin concerto that received a libretto at some later date. Let us compare this with the church Cantata No. 35, *Geist und Seele wird verwirret*, which appeared only a year after Cantata 120. It is well known that this contains the three movements of a lost clavier concerto by Bach. The opening number of the cantata gives us the first of the concerto movements, of which moreover at least nine of the original bars are preserved. The finale of the concerto forms the opening number of the second part of the cantata, which, like the opening number, is designated *Sinfonia*. The central movement has been transformed into the aria "Geist und Seele wird verwirret," which begins:

The three double-reed instruments double the strings *colla parte;* the clavier, however, adopts the part of the first violin with the right hand, that of the basso continuo with the left. Only as the movement progresses are the groups of instruments accorded individual tasks. The same holds true for the wind instruments and the strings that accompany the aria "Gott, man lobet dich in der Stille." Their main theme is very closely related to that previously quoted:

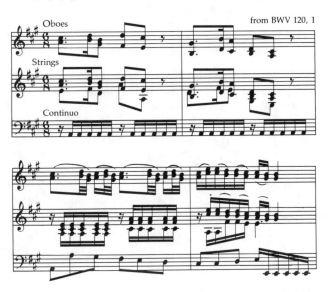

As we see immediately, this A major movement is a close relation of the A minor passage in the clavier concerto. We must place both in the Köthen period, the great period of Bach's concertos.[E33] The appearance of the two oboes d'amore in "Gott, man lobet dich" leads to the same conclusion reached with cantatas [BWV] 145 and 190, namely that the original version belongs to the later Köthen years. This then was one of the previously available instrumental ensemble works of Bach, and there were many of these, as we established in the opening chapter of this study, that would have been composed for the Köthen court orchestra and that, regrettably, have for the most part been lost. The form of the A major movement, which points throughout to the central movement of the clavier concerto that became Cantata No. 35, is clear evidence that the violin concerto from which both originate must have been a highly significant work. This is, moreover, the only violin concerto we have so far been able to ascribe to Bach in which, apart from the strings, wind instruments were also used.

Chapter 9

Our investigations into the remnants of long-lost Köthen cantatas have thus set us on the trail of an instrumental work, the original version of which is likewise missing. This piece too, as we shall see, is of great interest. Here it should be stressed again that the present study, which seeks to rediscover or verify compositions by Bach during the years 1717–23 that have gone astray, cannot lay claim to have exhausted the possibilities of the relevant research material. Further work will no doubt bring both additions and rectification. Nevertheless, we already have a wealth of verified material from which we may extract much of value. Before we examine these issues more closely, it is appropriate at this stage to survey the known Köthen vocal works by Bach, of which we have, either as fragments or in their entirety, the score or only the libretto.

Vocal works preserved in their entirety:

Durchlauchtster Leopold (undated) [BWV 173a]

Six movements of this parodied in Cantata No. 173, *Erhöhtes Fleisch und Blut*

Die Zeit, die Tag und Jahre macht (Jan. 1, 1719) [BWV 134a]

Five movements of this parodied in Cantata No. 134, *Ein Herz, das (seinen) Jesum lebend weiß*

Weichet nur, betrübte Schatten (undated) [BWV 202]

Surviving in fragmentary form:

A sacred church cantata for New Year's Day (probably 1723)

Five movements of Cantata No. 190, *Singet dem Herrn ein neues Lied,* derive from this cantata and have come down to us with the original libretto.

Surviving as a result of the parodying of certain numbers:

Der Himmel dacht auf Anhalts Ruhm und Glück (Dec. 10, 1718) [BWV 66a]

Five movements of this parodied in Cantata No. 66, *Erfreut euch, ihr Herzen.*

The original form of Cantata No. 184, *Erwünschtes Freudenlicht*

Four movements of this, together with the continuo part of a recitative, may be traced back to a lost Köthen original.

The original form of Cantata No. 145, *Auf, mein Herz, des Herren Tag*

The chorus "So du mit deinem Munde" and the following solo movements (duet, recitative, aria) derive from a Köthen original.[E34]

The original form of the cantata *Ihr Häuser des Himmels*

The libretto of the parody, several movements of which originated in Köthen, has been preserved in full. Only fragments of the score have come down to us, namely, remnants of four movements of the council inauguration cantata, *Ihr Tore zu Zion* [BWV 193].[E35]

The original form of Cantata No. 32, *Liebster Jesu, mein Verlangen*

We may regard the whole of this work, apart from the final chorale and the recitative, as a parody of a Köthen original.[E36]

The original form of a movement from Cantata No. 120, *Gott, man lobet dich*

The aria "Heil und Segen" (other parody text, "Treu im Glauben"). This movement appears as a purely instrumental piece in the Sonata for Violin and Harpsichord in G Major [BWV 1019a]. In its original form, however, it was a soprano aria.[E37]

Cantatas preserved in literary form only:

Lobet den Herrn, alle seine Heerscharen [BWV Anh. 5]

Sacred cantata for Dec. 10, 1718. Text to be found in Hunold (No. 13).

Dich loben die lieblichen Strahlen der Sonne [BWV Anh. 6]

Secular New Year's cantata, 1720. Text to be found in Hunold (No. 21).

Heut ist gewiß ein guter Tag [BWV Anh. 7]

Secular cantata to celebrate Prince Leopold's birthday, 1721. Text to be found in Hunold (No. 27).

We should begin by listing briefly the salient characteristics of Bach's "Köthen Cantatas," starting with their constituent parts, first considering the music he composed for voices.

Examination of the handling of the chorus reveals the following: It is used only occasionally within the movements as a full, four-part entity, mainly in solid chordal harmony and without any marked figurative polyphony. The main thematic material in the vocal music is borne by the soloists, who perform in duet. Likewise, in the solo numbers, the duet, which is a form rarely used afterwards by Bach, plays an outstanding part. Most of the "Köthen Cantatas" now known to us contain a solo movement for two voices. Of interest when we consider the sequence of the movements is the fact that recitative is preferred at the start of a cantata. Similarly, the overall structure of the cantatas (these were evidently generally eight-movement compositions) is strikingly uniform. A typical feature of the textual basis, and therefore also of the score, is the preference for dialog passages where the partners appear in pairs. As a result, we have the duet form as part of the musical score, not only in the elaborately structured numbers, but also in recitative. In the recitatives, freely declaimed parts alternate with others demanding metrical treatment; in these more exactly notated passages the two-part material is often treated canonically. Generally, the words slightly diverge in the two parts, which results in arrangements such as the following:

Fame: Ich ⎱ aber ⎰will ⎱ auf ⎰meinem⎱ Ehrenwagen
Fortune: Du ⎰   ⎱kannst⎰   ⎱deinem⎰

Dein ⎱ Lob zu allen Völkern tragen
Sein ⎰

(*Der Himmel dacht* [BWV 66a], 3d movement)

Allegorical figures perform the dialogs, in this instance "Die Fama" (Fame) and "Die Glückseligkeit Anhalts" (the Fortune of Anhalt), elsewhere "Die Zeit" (Time) and "Die Göttliche Vorsehung" (Divine Providence) or pastoral couples such as Phillis and Thyrsis. The latter become "Hoffnung" (Hope) and "Furcht" (Fear) in the sacred parodies, or Jesus and the Soul.

There are further important features to be observed regarding the instrumental music within these works. The great duet numbers are regularly furnished with an obbligato accompaniment, and in many instances this is performed on a solo violin. Alongside this, the single oboe and the paired flutes often feature as soloists in these works. This again is an indication, as we showed in our description of the Köthen orchestra, of the instruments available at the court, together with its limitations. In fact, evidence of this kind makes it possible to speak of Bach's "Köthen Cantatas" as a specific type. On the other hand, their very variety allows us, when we examine them individually, to establish the chronological order of their composition and perceive a clear development in their artistry. Of course, the fact that the Hunold librettos are dated is of great significance. Only one of his verses, "Heut ist gewiß ein guter Tag," bears no date. Here, however, the allusion to the impending marriage of Prince Leopold is so unmistakable that the establishment of the chronological sequence of the composition presents no difficulties.[64] It was first heard on Dec. 10, 1721, on the eve of the royal wedding.[E37]

Thus, if we study the cantatas in the order in which they were composed, or seek to establish this order in those that are undated, the first thing we notice is their instrumentation. The serenade *Durchlauchtster Leopold* [BWV 173a] is in every respect the simplest of the vocal works. It does not use a chorus and, apart from the strings, there are only two flutes and a bassoon. The tasks assigned to the flutes are not particularly difficult; the first violin, on the other hand, and the bassoon are given solos. Without question this work is the first of the Köthen cantatas. Bach arrived in Köthen in 1717, at the earliest only a week before Leopold's birthday. Maria Barbara, however, who had already moved to Köthen from Weimar in August, would have instructed her husband about the musical talent at his disposal, stressing no doubt the abilities of the first violinist of the court orchestra, Spiess, and the bassoonist, Torlée, both of whom had earlier performed at court in Berlin. Evidently, Bach knew nothing of the existence of the choir at the Lutheran school before taking up his new post. Either that or he wanted to check on the competence of the singers at first hand before using them. At any rate, he managed without them entirely in this his first Köthen vocal work. As early as New Year's Day, 1718, however, he made use of them, albeit not with any particularly demanding tasks, as the cantata *Erwünschtes Freudenlicht* [BWV 184a] shows. Admittedly, the original of this piece is lost, and therefore we cannot date it from the evidence of text or score alone. Nevertheless, we may with certainty place this lost original at New Year, 1718. As the parody demonstrates, in formal terms it was very close to the congratulatory music of December 1717, *Durchlauchtster Leopold*. There is no other preserved composition by Bach written for the first New Year's Day he spent in Köthen. In addition, the birthday music composed for December of the same year displays, as we shall see, greater complexity. Of the instrumentalists who performed on Jan. 1, 1718, the *Premier Cammer Musicus* Spiess was given a major solo role.

The royal birthday of that year brought us, as we know from Hunold, the cantata *Der Himmel dacht auf Anhalts Ruhm und Glück* [BWV 66a], the bulk of the movements of which we know through their later parody. By this stage Bach had spent a full year in Köthen and was now thoroughly acquainted with the orchestra under his charge. Among the musicians— and Maria Barbara had probably not conveyed this fact to him in her letter— there was an excellent oboist, the *Kammermusiker* Rose. Bach assigned to the latter, together with the violinist Spiess and the bassoonist Torlée, artistically rewarding tasks in all the preserved Köthen cantatas he subsequently composed. The royal household accounts for Dec. 16, 1718, include payment of fees to a bass singer Binenschneider,[E38] a descant singer Pröse, Konzertmeister Lienigke from Merseburg, and Vogler from Leipzig. Thus, as one can clearly see, the festival in the royal household was on this occasion especially richly endowed with music. The printing costs for the "Carmina" came to four Thalers. In this instance we also know from Hunold's *Auserwählte Gedichte* (Selected poems) the libretto of the "cantata" that was sung at the divine service that was held: *Lobet den Herrn, alle seine Heerscharen* ([BWV Anh. 5, referring to] Psalm 13:21). Unfortunately, research into the music composed for this libretto has yielded nothing. As I said earlier, there is a distinct affinity between the serenade *Durchlauchtster Leopold* and the original of Cantata No. 184, and consequently we should regard the chronological sequence of the two works as being very close (December 1717 and New Year, 1718). There is a parallel relationship between the birthday cantata for 1718 and that composed for New Year's Day, 1719. Even if we were not in a position to date the latter from Hunold's published text, we should still have to place it at New Year's Day, 1719.

On the occasion of the royal birthday of the same year Bach presented to his sovereign the celebratory poem mentioned earlier, which is printed in the Hunold collection and which has come down to us.[65] The poem lays great emphasis on the prince's love of music. Thus, the birthday too, as was the custom, would have been celebrated with music, more precisely with performances of vocal works. It is true that we have no record of the libretto used on this particular occasion, nor do the household accounts contain any reference to expenditure on printing costs for the cantata texts. This should not, however, be taken as evidence to the contrary, since if Bach had really composed no vocal works for Dec. 10, 1719, this birthday of Leopold would have represented a sole exception during the whole period of the composer's musical activity at Köthen. We know from the sums set aside for printing that two cantatas were performed three weeks later, on Jan. 1, 1720. Again, we know the libretto of one of them from the Hunold collection. It began: "Dich loben die lieblichen Strahlen der Sonne."

Precise dating becomes more difficult from now on. Hunold seems to have provided no "Carmen" for Leopold's birthday in 1720. Perhaps Monjou, Master of the Court Pages, was the librettist that year; a fee to that effect recorded in the accounts might lead us to such a conclusion.[66] As a result of the engagement of his two daughters as royal singers the previous autumn, Monjou had become more closely involved with music making at the court.[67] Likewise it is highly probable that Monjou translated the French dedication of the Brandenburg Concertos of the following March

24. This would at any rate most easily explain Bach's use of French, which would otherwise have been difficult to demonstrate.[68] [E39]

So far we have been unable to establish any trace of the music performed on New Year's Day, 1721. We do know, however, that, according to the household accounts for Dec. 10, 1721, one of the two vocal works, the texts of both of which were printed, was the Hunold poem "Heut ist gewiß ein guter Tag." This is the last contribution by the Halle poet that we can show was used for court festivities at Köthen. It is not known whether Bach's composition for the royal wedding on Dec. 11, 1721, was also a vocal work or whether it was an instrumental piece.[69] It is clear from the household accounts, however, that two cantatas were performed during the following year, on the occasion of the royal wedding and three weeks later on New Year's Day. In both instances Bach was paid the sum involved for forwarding to the printer.[70] Of the secular work composed for New Year's Day, 1723, the last in which Bach was to be engaged as active Kapellmeister, the title page has survived and is kept in the Bach Museum at Eisenach.[71] Unfortunately, the preserved fragment contains none of the words of the text. Nevertheless, we probably have in the numbers of Cantata No. 190, *Singet dem Herrn ein neues Lied*, discussed in detail earlier, original components of the work performed at divine service on that Jan. 1. It was likewise shown above that the vocal music recognizable behind Cantata No. 145 is to be placed during the period of Bach's final months of office. Not only the use of the oboes d'amore but also, as we are now able to add, the greater sophistication in the form of the movements point to this conclusion regarding the date. Similarly, the choir receives more demanding tasks than Bach had wanted to risk giving it earlier.[E40]

This brings us to discuss briefly the way in which the composer dealt with this body of singers. The birthday music for Dec. 10, 1717, the serenade *Durchlauchtster Leopold*, was composed without chorus. Evidently, Bach was unaware before his arrival in Köthen that the choir of the Lutheran school could undertake even the simplest of choral tasks. When we review the works known to us from this period, however, we observe that increasing use was made of these singers in his performances.[E41] It is clear that Bach, whose own children attended the school and were undoubtedly members of the choir, was able to make greater demands on these singers as time went on. It is, however, equally evident from the parts as allocated that up to the last the main burden of the vocal *Figuralmusik* was carried by the solo singers, in particular in the outstanding duet movements contained in these works.

Before we turn to the period after Bach's departure from Köthen, I should like to insert here a few remarks that, like so many others in this study, seek to correct the traditional image of the years 1717–23. On Oct.

28, 1730, Bach wrote his famous letter to his old schoolmate from Lüneburg, Georg Erdmann,[72] in which, as is well known, he described his time at Köthen and the move to Leipzig. He links his departure from his position as Köthen Kapellmeister with the fact that Prince Leopold, in Bach's words, had taken an "amusa" as his wife and that thereafter the sovereign's "musical inclination waned." From these references an image of the princess from Anhalt-Bernburg has evolved that pictures her as not only being fundamentally unmusical but even vindictively hostile to the art. The documents in the Anhalt State Archive, however, do not reveal any decline in the patronage of music at the court of Köthen during the period after the royal marriage. It in no way impairs the stature or impugns the character of Johann Sebastian Bach, however, when one reflects that the letter to Georg Erdmann was written at a time when the composer was particularly disgruntled at the stresses and difficulties imposed on him by his situation in Leipzig. Too much weight, therefore, should not be attached to the individual words of the letter, nor should their meaning be taken too literally. It was not the first time that Bach had contemplated leaving Köthen; a year before Leopold's marriage, for example, he had applied for the post of organist at the Jakobikirche in Hamburg. And when he moved to Leipzig in 1723, he was leaving a court at which music had been fostered with great enthusiasm and appreciation during the period after the royal wedding in December 1721.

Thus, it comes as no surprise that music making continued in a lively fashion after April 1723. Bach came over from Leipzig to take part as often as he could, and vocal compositions as in the preceding works were well to the fore. We spoke earlier of this when we discussed Bach's return visits to his former domain. Attention should be drawn at this point to just one cantata from the period before 1728. It was performed on Oct. 20, 1726 (18th Sunday After Trinity), on the occasion of the "Exalted Attendance at Church of Her Serene Highness our Most Gracious Princess."[73] To celebrate the birth of the heir to the throne, born Sept. 12, 1726, of Leopold's second marriage, Bach had sent to Köthen his printed Opus No. 1, the First Partita for harpsichord, together with a congratulatory poem.[74] On the occasion of the first attendance at church of the young wife of the sovereign, he was evidently, by composing a cantata, making up for the fact that he had missed both the birth and the baptism of the heir. Sadly, this has been lost. Whether or not Bach attended the performance of his work in person is likewise a matter for conjecture, though this, too, may well have been the case.

Chapter 10

By far the most important visit, however, that Bach made to Köthen from Leipzig, was that in connection with the funeral service for the dead Prince Leopold. Again, there was a performance of vocal music composed by Bach, as we know from the research of Rust and Spitta.[75] This particular work stood alone, as long as virtually nothing was known of Bach's vocal works composed for the Köthen court, which may perhaps explain why it has been subjected to so many widely varying interpretations. In fact, it follows on organically from the Köthen tradition of vocal music making. At the same time, fresh research in this field has brought most valuable material to light and has considerably enriched our understanding of these works. The situation at the time was as follows. Leopold of Köthen died on Nov. 19, 1728, not yet 34. The atmosphere at court was as sad as may be imagined, for in the summer of that year the royal couple had undertaken a long journey to visit other courts; on their return to the royal palace of Köthen, however, they found that both children from the prince's second marriage, the Crown Prince Emanuel Ludwig, and the Princess Leopoldina Charlotta, who had been born on Sept. 3, 1727, had died during their absence. Then, early in the morning of Nov. 19, the prince himself had passed away, leaving behind a widow with a 6-year-old stepdaughter, Princess Gisela Agnes, born in 1722 of Leopold's first marriage. Since no male heir existed, the crown passed into the hands of the deceased's brother, August of Köthen, with whom, as is clear from many signs, Leopold's widow did not enjoy the most cordial of relationships. Her sorrow was so great that she could not bear to be present at her husband's funeral ceremony when it took place early the following year. That music should be performed at this ceremony was undoubtedly decided on immediately after Leopold's death, and this is perfectly understandable when one considers the dead prince's love of the art. In that case, however, the "honorary Kapellmeister," who even from as far away as Leipzig had come to Köthen on so many occasions for various activities, had to both compose and direct the funeral music. In the event, Bach created for this occasion a four-part funeral cantata, the libretto of which was written by Picander and published in the third volume of the latter's verse. The music itself has not been preserved. Probably, however, Wilhelm Rust has produced sufficient evidence to show that it was largely based on music from the *St. Matthew*

Passion, with which we are familiar. The opening chorus, as Rust has also pointed out, was taken from the funeral ode for the Electress Christiane Eberhardine of 1727.[76] I shall show that this was not the only movement from this work to be transferred to the Köthen composition. In fact, the opening chorus of the second part of the Köthen funeral music, which is repeated at the end of that section, is, as far as we can judge, the only passage in this work not used elsewhere in Bach's compositions; in other words, it was most probably an original piece. Rust has provided the evidence for this conclusion. According to him, the Köthen funeral music came about in the following way. Bach extracted certain passages from the already completed *St. Matthew Passion* and the funeral ode, rearranged them, and provided a new libretto to adapt the pieces for use at a burial ceremony. If we accept that interpretation, Arnold Schering's attempt to reverse the relationship between the Passion and the funeral cantata (in his view, the Köthen work came first and the corresponding movements in the *St. Matthew Passion* were the parodies) must be regarded as a failure.[E42] The most recent research into the Köthen documents confirms that this is indeed the case. As a result, these studies have at the same time gained great significance for the history of the *St. Matthew Passion* itself.

If we begin by examining the genesis of the funeral music, an entry in the Köthen household accounts becomes highly significant. It reads:

> 1728.   *Nov. 27*. Payment to the musician Spiess for the copying of
> musical scores and copperplate engraving and completing the
> necessary formalities ....4.18 Thalers

We can picture the situation at the time. Prince Leopold had died on Nov. 19, and the court was in deep mourning. Orchestra and choir were silent. Only eight days after the prince's death, however, sums of money were already being allocated for musical purposes—that is, if we take the reference to "completing the necessary formalities" to mean that Spiess was to gain final approval for the work in connection with copying of scores and the copperplate engraving. There is no doubt that this entry referred to the preparation of music for the prince's funeral. The solemn interment in the royal vault beneath the Köthen Jakobikirche was postponed until early in the new year. During the winter months, Leopold's mortal remains were kept for the time being in the court chapel. Even so, work began immediately on the music that was to accompany the actual burial ceremony. First and foremost, this entailed the production of the performance materials. Sparse though they are, the references in the household accounts are concrete evidence that this matter was in hand.

If the duplication of the individual parts was already well under way, a score must have been in existence, and since the efforts of an additional copyist were called for, with sums of money being set aside for the purpose, a considerable volume of material must have been involved. Otherwise, the full-time copyist attached to the court orchestra would have coped on his own. All this is fully compatible with what is known of Bach's Köthen funeral composition. At this point we should recall Bach's technique when producing parodies of earlier musical scores. Our studies of the source materials have provided us with an accurate picture of the process.[77]

Once the new libretto was complete, the first stage of the parody was for Bach to organize the production of new scores, generally by a copyist. The latter was given the score of the original work and would have no difficulty in merely copying out the unaltered instrumental parts. For the vocal parts, however, he received, in addition to the old score, a new libretto, the strophic form of which precisely matched the original text, word for word and syllable for syllable. He would enter the new libretto below the stave lines. This was the raw material that Bach would give a final polish, in most instances contenting himself with improving the vocal lines, in order to achieve the best possible setting of the textual revisions. A full score of the parody was produced only if the new composition was intended for regular, repeated use, e.g., as a normal ingredient of the church's musical calendar.

Having briefly reminded ourselves of this procedure, we can now picture vividly the situation at Köthen during the second half of November 1728. On the death of the sovereign, a messenger was hastily dispatched to Leipzig to inform Bach of the sad news and to commission the composer, who had, after all, been a very close friend of the deceased, to produce music for the funeral ceremony with all speed. The first step was for the libretto to be written in Leipzig. To this end Bach contacted the fluent Picander, informing him that, with the exception of certain passages of the funeral ode, he intended to make use of several movements from the recently completed but as yet unperformed[E43] *Passio secundum Evangelistam Matthaeum*, in this or that particular grouping or sequence, and that he would require a parody of the text. In addition, the movements within each section of the work would have to be linked by means of recitatives to be specially written for the purpose. Picander was no great poet, but he was able to manage tasks of this kind, and in a short time at that. Thus, probably as a joint effort on the part of librettist and composer, the text of the funeral cantata was produced. Undoubtedly, Bach would have composed the music for the recitatives straightaway and forwarded all the materials to Köthen, where it is known they were present on Nov. 27. These consisted of the two original scores for the funeral ode and for the *St.*

Matthew Passion, Picander's libretto, and the recitatives composed by Bach. These last additions were undoubtedly written in the composer's own hand, as we know was his custom in such instances. Original materials produced in this way, e.g., as in the case of the cantata *Auf, schmetternde Töne der muntern Trompeten* [BWV 207a], which was a second parody of *Schleicht, spielende Wellen* [BWV 206], have come down to us.[78] The individual parts could now be produced, though of course not yet completely. The chorus, intended both to open and to conclude the second part of the work, was certainly missing at this stage, since this particular passage could not have been a parody, that is, it had to be an original composition. In both character and manner of composition, this chorus stands out from the rest of the work. It would have been composed later and forwarded separately. This again is very significant, since its text was the very passage from the Bible that Consistorial Councillor Christian Friedel took as the basis for the sermon he gave at the funeral service on March 24, 1729.[79] The wish of the Köthen court and the clergyman Friedel, no doubt emphatically expressed in 1728, to the effect that the text of the funeral sermon should form part of the music that accompanied the ceremony, ran counter to Bach's custom in works of this kind. I remind the reader of the motet *Jesu, meine Freude*. To replace a text in a parody required, as we know from examples in Bach's Masses, profound changes in the original score, as well as work on the part of the copyist that could be carried out only under the constant eye of the composer. This explains why Bach wrote the choral movement based on Psalm 68:21, which begins and ends the second part, as an original piece and why he was only later able to forward it to Köthen. The copying out of the instrumental and vocal parts of this number must likewise have taken place at a later date, and these, as we know from many examples of Bach's manuscripts, were then inserted in the otherwise complete scores. I am convinced that a full score of this funeral piece was never completed. This would have necessitated an immense, and at the same time entirely pointless, effort. From Bach's point of view, he could not make use of the work again, nor could the Köthen orchestra. Bach was not in the habit of writing full scores unless he had good reason to do so. Furthermore, the Köthen orchestra was soon to be substantially reduced by Leopold's successor.

It is incumbent on me at this point to produce the evidence for my statements concerning the funeral service, the officiating clergy, and the text of the sermon. Here I must briefly digress from my description of the preparations for the funeral ceremony to return to the contents of the Anhalt State Archive, in particular to the third group of documents to which I alluded earlier. These relate to specific events in the royal household, births, marriages, death, acts of homage, and so forth. These very comprehensive archive facsimiles have to my knowledge yet to be examined from the point of view that interests me, namely, the performance of music at Köthen. For the most part they are in this respect unproductive, since the great mass of the archives deposited in the collection consists of official court notices of events in the royal household that were sent to other European courts. In the case of the betrothals, negotiations in connection with dowries, among other things, play a prominent part. The sole interesting exception here, as far as I can ascertain, is the document relating to the funeral ceremony of Prince Leopold that took place on March 23–24, 1729.[80] Here we learn, down to the very last detail, how the prescribed ceremony took place. Later, I shall mention some of the most important aspects of that occasion when I describe the actual funeral ceremony. To lend color to that portrayal, the following details will have to suffice. Everything, every single item of the funeral arrangements, was specified with the utmost precision beforehand—the order of precedence of the state, ecclesiastical, and municipal dignitaries in the funeral cortege; the movements this procession was to execute at various points along the route; the manner in which those taking part were to take up their positions; how many of the accompanying footmen were to bear wax torches; how many torches soaked in pitch; what measures were to be adopted for the safety of the public; what precautions might be taken to prevent fire (one can imagine, of course, that the entire population turned out to witness the spectacle); even the sequence of dishes with which the guests were regaled and the arrangements for laying out the crockery on the palace tables—all this information has come down to us. Among all these details, which literally regulated the progression of the ceremony at every stage, we discover the arrangements for the divine services, including the name of the preacher and an indication of the text of his sermon.

The most interesting and undoubtedly most valuable discovery, however, is the copy of the original printed text of our great funeral composition, the title of which runs as follows:[81]

> *Funeral music most humbly performed at the Memorial Service for the erstwhile Most Serene Prince and Master, Lord Leopold, Prince of Anhalt, Duke of Saxony, Engern and Westphalia, Count of Ascania, Lord of Bernburg and Zerbst etc. in the Reformed Municipal Cathedral Church of Köthen by Johann Sebastian Bach, former Kapellmeister to His Serene Highness of Most Blessed Memory. Printed at Köthen by Johann Christoph Schondorff.* (8 unsigned folio sides)

The text of the movements that start on the second page, the reverse of the first side, merits our special attention because it differs markedly from the only version known hitherto, that handed down in Picander's collected verse.[82] The divergence may be explained with the aid of a handwritten copy of the first three parts of the work that also came to light in the fascicle from the Köthen archives mentioned earlier.[83] Here, however, we clearly have the version that was already in existence in Köthen by Nov. 27, 1728. The fact that the fourth and last part of the work is absent from this manuscript may be explained in one of two ways. Either Bach did in fact in the first instance send the three parts only, and the fourth was forwarded later, or, and this seems to me to be the more likely explanation, the last part of the manuscript was written in a different hand and could not easily be matched with the other parts, with the result that it could later become detached and be lost. I favor this interpretation because such a chain of events would have been highly understandable, given the short time available in November, i.e., that numerous different hands were involved in the production of the fair copy intended for the court. In the top right-hand corner of the manuscript, added later by a different hand, we find the following note:

> The words of these verses have been printed here in their corrected form.

Thus, the text Picander composed and sent to Köthen, as part of the process of "completing the necessary formalities" mentioned in the household accounts for Nov. 27, 1728, perhaps in this instance the checking of the printed proofs, was not allowed to go forward unaltered. The corrections undertaken, however, as the comparison of the two versions below bears out, were without exception improvements.[84] They are partly connected with details of language and style, but in one case the substance of a whole passage was changed and a completely new text furnished. (This fact alone would suffice to reduce Schering's thesis to an absurdity.) The one major change concerns the conclusion of the first part, which consists of a repeated sequence of recitative and aria. In Picander's original text, the second of these two recitatives ran as follows:

Ach ja!
Wenn Tränen oder Blut,
Hochsel'ger Leopold,
Dich von dem Tode könnten retten,
So wären tausend Herzen da,
Die Dir und uns zu gut
Vor Dich ihr Blut gegeben hätten.
O wärest Du uns nicht so lieb und hold
In Deinem Regiment geblieben,
So dürften wir uns nicht
So sehr um Dich betrüben.

Recast, this became:

Ach ja!
Dein Scheiden geht uns nah,
Hochsel'ger Leopold.
Und die wir Dich mit Schmerzen klagen,
Daß unser Sonnenstrahl vergeht,
Der unserm Land so hold
Mit heitern Blicken aufgegangen.
O Jammerriß! der uns so früh entsteht,
Der unser Herz mit bangem Zagen
Wie das gebeugte Haupt mit schwarzem Flor umfangen.

Neither wording is particularly successful from a linguistic point of view. In the second version, however, the exaggerated, one might almost say Byzantine, tone is replaced by one that is far more personal. A further point of interest in this comparison is the exact formal concurrence of the two librettos, which may be explained by the fact that they were written to conform to an already established musical score. In other words, the recitative had been delivered to Köthen before the textual revision was undertaken, which in fact happened in the case of all the recitative numbers. In this instance, Picander, who evidently was not in agreement with the corrections his libretto had suffered, unceremoniously left out the last four parts of the first section of the work when the libretto came to be published in his collected verse. For this reason, its full extent and actual wording have been imperfectly known until now.

Nevertheless, in other instances the poet included in his collected works verses in their original form, irrespective of the fact that the corrected versions, while not affecting the content, were clearly improvements on the originals. As an example of this I cite the "Aria for 2 Choirs"--(1) "Die Sterblichen" (The mortal ones), (2) "Die Auserwählten" (The elect)--which brings the second part of the funeral cantata to an end. The original wording, as we have it in the manuscript and the printed version of 1732, is as follows:

1. Geh, Leopold, zu Deiner Ruh,
   2. Und schlummre nur ein wenig ein.
1. Unsre Ruh,
   So sonst niemand außer Du,
   Wird nun zugleich mit Dir begraben.
   2. Der Geist soll sich im Himmel laben
      Und königlich am Glanze sein.

In the corrected version this became:

    1. Geh, Leopold, zu Deiner Ruh,
        2. Und schlummre nur ein wenig ein.
    1. Nun lebst Du
       In der schönsten Himmelsruh.
       Wird gleich der müde Leib begraben,
        2. Der Geist soll sich im Himmel laben
         Und königlich am Glanze sein.

I chose this second example precisely because it illuminates particularly clearly the relationship between this work and the *St. Matthew Passion*. One sees immediately that the music of "Ich will bei meinem Jesu wachen" from the *St. Matthew Passion* belongs to both texts. As we noted earlier, Schering believed that this piece was originally composed for inclusion in the Köthen work, and that it is the Passion that contains the parody. In view of the extreme awkwardness of the text of "Geh, Leopold," a clear instance of the difficulties that arise when a fresh libretto is applied to an already existing composition, this would have been highly improbable, even if we are to take only the text we know from the 1732 printed version. In fact, the two recently discovered sources, the manuscript and the original printed score, enable us to recognize how the work came to be written down to the last detail. In the short space of time between the 19th and 27th of November, 1728, i.e., between the date of Leopold's death and the delivery of the libretto of the funeral cantata to Köthen, work had to be carried out in great haste. The text produced bore all the marks of a librettist resorting to parody; the alterations that were made indicate that its faults were immediately apparent and were corrected accordingly. The scores, however, including those of the recitatives, had to remain intact, in other words to retain the form in which they had been sent from Leipzig.

    We now return to the final section of the first part of the work mentioned earlier, to the four pieces that have been discovered only recently:

Rec. "Wie wenn der Blitze Grausamkeit"
Aria "Zage nur, du treues Land"
Rec. "Ach ja! Dein Scheiden geht uns nah"
Aria "Komm wieder, teurer Fürstengeist"

Close examination of these texts reveals that the first of the two arias was a parody of "Blute nur," taken from the *St. Matthew Passion*. The aria that concludes the section, however, was the final chorus of the funeral ode [BWV 198, 10] of 1727 with a new libretto. Its original text had been as follows:

Doch, Königin, Du stirbest nicht,
Man weiß, was man an Dir besessen,
Die Nachwelt wird Dich nicht vergessen,
Bis dieser Weltbau einst zerbricht.
Ihr Dichter, schreibt, wir wollens lesen,
Sie ist der Tugend Eigentum,
Der Untertanen Lust und Ruhm,
Der Königinnen Preis gewesen.

I now give the corresponding wording used in the Köthen funeral music
as it finally appeared in the original printed version:

Komm wieder, teurer Fürstengeist,
Beseele die erstarrten Glieder
Mit einem neuen Leben wieder,
Das ewig und unsterblich heißt.
Die Jugend rühmt, die Alten preisen:
Daß unser Land und ihre Zeit
Soviele Gnad und Gütigkeit
Von unserm Fürsten aufzuweisen.

These lines may be superimposed on Bach's score with complete success,
as may be illustrated by the following extract from the second part of the
chorus:

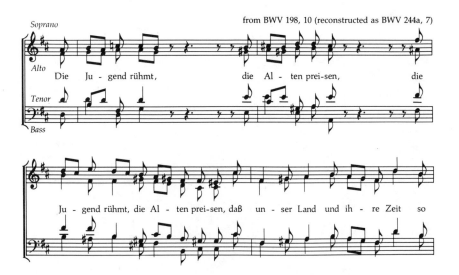

More concise, more dignified than in the parody version, almost as if carved in stone or fashioned in bronze, the poetry of Gottsched's original version comes across as the whole chorus sings its hymn of praise in unison. Furthermore, the new words of the libretto, particularly the reference to the young folk, who were of course represented by the members of the Lutheran school choir, are entirely appropriate to the music. This movement rounds off the first part of the Köthen composition beautifully; it had begun with the opening chorus from the same funeral ode of 1727. Of similar significance is the assertion, which is now possible after the discovery of the complete original libretto, that the Köthen funeral cantata as a whole contained 24 numbers, 14 of which were ensemble pieces. The point is that 24 and 14 have a symbolic meaning, the first with reference to Revelation 4:4 and 10, the second in connection with the composer's own name, BACH.[E44]

Chapter 11

We may, however, go a stage further. The discoveries we have made reveal that Bach contributed not one but two compositions to the Köthen funeral ceremonies. Of the second of these we do not know the musical setting, the text, or the author of the latter. Nor do we know when Bach completed the work or when he sent it to Köthen. Nevertheless, we are able to show that it did exist and that it was performed at Köthen. The documents in both the relevant sections of the Anhalt State Archives are in agreement on this point. I give below the text of the entry in question as it appears in the household accounts:

> 1729.   *March 25.* Payment to erstwhile engaged Kapellmeister Bach, his wife and son from Leipzig, likewise the musicians from Halle, Merseburg, Zerbst, Dessau, and Güsten, who on the evening of March 23 at the interment and on March 24 at the burial service, assisted with the music for the funeral of His Serene Highness Prince Leopold of Blessed Memory. In settlement, including board etc.................. 230 Thalers.[85]

Here we have it clearly stated that Kapellmeister Bach and other artists who were summoned to Köthen, both on the evening of March 23, i.e., at the actual burial ceremony, and at the funeral sermon held the following morning, i.e., at the great service held in the Jakobikirche, had performed "Musiquen" for which they were paid. The records in the relevant volume of documents relating to this event are in complete accord. I quote verbatim the most detailed of these.[86] In connection with the evening burial ceremony, the record states:

> At the royal funeral of the lifeless body of His Serene Lord and Sovereign, Prince Leopold, Prince of Anhalt, Duke of Saxony, Engern and Westphalia:
>
> 1. All bells in the royal residence and throughout the land were rung on the evening of Wednesday, March 23, from 9 to 10 o'clock.
>
> 2. The mortal remains of His Highness of Blessed Memory reached the Reformed Municipal Church towards 10 o'clock. There was a considerable following behind the funeral carriage.

3. Thereafter funeral music was performed for some time, while the assembled company entered to take their designated seats in the church, which was beautifully illumined, though draped in black throughout.

4. The Royal Consistorial Councillor Christian Friedel walked between the Communion table and the body of the sovereign and said a prayer that made reference to the distressing occasion.

5. The hymn "Nun laßt uns den Leib begraben" was sung as the body of the sovereign was laid to rest in the royal vault.

6. The Blessing was said and

7. with the singing of the hymn "Hertzl. lieb hab ich dich, o Herr" the funeral ceremony was brought to an end at 2 o'clock in the morning.

Against my assertion concerning the existence of a separate composition created for this nocturnal burial ceremony, it could be objected that it would also have been possible for the very extensive work with which we are familiar, which consists largely of Picander's libretto, and the funeral ode and *St. Matthew Passion* scores, to have been divided up in such a way that the first two parts were performed during the evening and the final two the following morning. This view, however, is contradicted by the wording of the newly discovered libretto printed in Köthen by Löffler for use on the day, which states unequivocally that all four parts were heard on March 24 at the one evening funeral service. We should further take note of the liturgical arrangements laid down for this "Commemorative Sermon." On this subject, the record states:

Again, on March 24

1. All the bells were rung, on three occasions, at 7, 8, and 9 o'clock in the morning.

2. The funeral service began in the Lutheran Church with the singing of Psalm 16, "Alle Menschen müssen sterben."

3. Psalm 90 and further funeral hymns were sung until the arrival of the illustrious relatives of the deceased.

4. Music was performed.

5. The hymn "Freu dich sehr, o meine Seele" was sung.

6. The sermon in memory of the sovereign was delivered on the text of Psalm 68:21, "Wir haben einen Gott, der da hilft, und einen Herrn, der vom Tode errettet."

7. At the conclusion of the sermon, general dedication of the text and a musical performance appropriate to the theme.

8. Details of the prince's life and circumstances were read out, and the illustrious relatives, servants, and all the subjects of the deceased were comforted.

9. The above concluded with a short prayer and the Lord's Prayer.
10. Music was performed.
11. The Blessing.
12. The chorales "Herr Jesu Christ, wahr'r Mensch und Gott" and "Hertzlich thut mich verlangen" (stanzas 9–11) were sung, where-upon each and every one returned home.[87]

The above details enable us to see exactly how performances of the two sets of funeral music formed part of the services on March 23 and 24. During the first of these, Bach's music was heard as the funeral procession entered the Jakobikirche, apparently "for some time," meaning that the performance lasted throughout that part of the ceremony. It would be a mistake to deduce from the mention at the end of the report that the service ended at two o'clock in the morning that the ceremony lasted four hours; this would only have been possible if Bach's music had continued for a considerable length of time, since the remainder of the liturgy would have lasted half an hour at the most. According to the descriptions we have of the events of that evening, which have come down to us in considerable numbers (to excess almost, and that does not include the documentary report in the archives), the ceremony began at 10 o'clock in the evening in the palace chapel, where the coffin had been placed and from which point it was then conveyed to the municipal church. (We even hear of the difficulties of transportation due to the confined space in the palace). The torchlight procession wound its way through the streets to the Jakobikirche; bearing in mind the elaborate character of this part of the ceremony, we must allow a considerable period to elapse, probably three hours at least. Nevertheless, Bach's lost composition must have been a substantial and important work, and we shall return to it later. First of all, however, we shall examine the description of the second funeral service, the "Com-memorative Sermon" of the morning of March 24.

Here we learn that a parallel service was held in the Lutheran Agnuskirche, a fact of which we were previously unaware. There the cer-emony began with chorales, while in the Reformed Cathedral Church psalms were sung. The report does not say how the service at the Agnu-skirche continued. At the Jakobikirche, the first Psalm closed with the words:

For Thou wilt not leave My soul in hell, neither wilt Thou suffer Thine holy One to see corruption. Thou wilt show Me the path of life; in Thy presence is fullness of joy; at Thy right hand there are pleasures for evermore. (Psalm 16:10–11)

This was followed by Psalm 90. During the singing the royal family assem-bled. The congregation sang the hymn:

> Freu dich sehr, o meine Seele,
> Und vergiß all Not und Qual,

which preceded the sermon, based on Psalm 68:21. Here the record states that at the "conclusion of the sermon" there was "a musical performance appropriate to the theme"; we recognize the second part of Bach's work, which began and ended with a chorus based on the words of the psalm. The details of the deceased's life were read; the relatives, servants, and rest of the congregation "comforted"; prayers were said, ending with the Lord's Prayer (this was a staunch Reformed Church, remember) and then came the third part of the "music." Though it is not stated specifically, we may safely assume that the fourth part of the music was performed as the congregation left the church.[88] This is clear from the libretto of this part, which includes the words "Wir gehn nach unsern Hütten hin" (We retire to our dwelling places). Thus, the end of the "Musicieren" balanced its opening, which had accompanied the entry of the cortege into the church the previous evening.

The focus of attention in this great work is the second part, in the midst of which—and this is no coincidence—stands the aria, the music of which to the words "Aus Liebe" forms the centerpiece of the second part of the *St. Matthew Passion*. Examined from the musical aspect, these parts of the composition, in spite of the fact that they are for the most part parodies, display an astonishingly compact unity of structure. In addition, we have the reference to the rather intimate circumstances at the Köthen court and its musicians. The orchestra's first violinist, *Premier Cammer Musicus* Spiess, was the first of the solo instrumentalists to be heard (the aria "Erhalte mich," which is the "Erbarme dich" of the *St. Matthew Passion*). The former royal singer, Anna Magdalena Bach, sang the soprano solo "Mit Freuden" ("Aus Liebe" in the *St. Matthew Passion*). In the third part of the work there followed the solo performed on the viola da gamba, the prince's favorite instrument, played by the orchestra's solo gambist Abel, perhaps using the deceased's very own instrument (aria "Laß, Leopold"—*St. Matthew Passion:* "Komm, süßes Kreuz"). At the end of the third part, the solo oboist, Herr Rose, offered his sovereign a farewell greeting (aria "Geh, Leopold, zu deiner Ruh"—*St. Matthew Passion:* "Ich will bei meinem Jesu wachen"). The fact that the fourth part of Bach's work, intended to accompany the "comforted" congregation as it made its way home, contained two passages in the major key, "Mache dich, mein Herze rein" and "Ich will dir mein Herze schenken," both of which also produce a decidedly soothing effect in the Passion, is in keeping with the task the finale was meant to perform. Thus the four parts of the composition form a coherent whole aesthetically, conceptually, and on the human plane;

furthermore, they are so closely interwoven with the funeral service as such that neither may be separated from the other within the overall framework.[89]

Here we have the evidence for the existence of a previous composition by Bach for the nocturnal funeral ceremony. The fact that it has been lost, something of which we became aware only during the last century, is a matter for the deepest regret. In support of my remarks in this connection, I go back to a much-quoted reference in Forkel's biography of Bach, a passage that has hitherto been a constant puzzle and has given rise to much shaking of heads:

> Among the many compositions that he had completed in Leipzig, written for a particular occasion, I am mindful of two funeral cantatas, the one intended for the burial ceremony of his beloved Prince Leopold of Köthen, the other performed at the funeral oration on the death of the Queen of Poland and Electress of Saxony Christiane Eberhardine, which took place in the Paulinerkirche at Leipzig. The first contains double choruses of uncommon splendor and the most moving impact, the second has admittedly only single choruses, but these are so attractive that whoever begins to play them through, cannot fail to finish them. It was composed in October 1727.[90]

As long as it was thought that only one Bach composition had existed for the Köthen funeral ceremony, these remarks by Forkel caused those researching in the field considerable difficulty. The point is that what the eminent Göttingen scholar says about the work with which he was familiar does not tally with the four-part composition with a libretto by Picander. "Double choruses of uncommon splendor"? There is only one double chorus in the funeral cantata known to us—the revised final number of the St. Matthew Passion. Even if the lost setting of Psalm 68:21 was supposed to have a double chorus, in other words, for there to have been in reality several eight-part vocal numbers in this composition, we should have been faced with other difficulties. If the truth is that Bach's setting of the Picander verses is intended here, we should have to level the charge of superficiality at Forkel. He would in that case have completely overlooked the fact that almost every movement in this work was identical with material from the St. Matthew Passion. Furthermore, two great choruses likewise occur in the funeral ode of 1727, on which he lavishes praise in the same breath as he acclaims the Köthen funeral cantata, in particular its choral numbers. In fact, Johann Nikolaus Forkel has not escaped censure in this very connection. He has been accused of careless and overhasty work.[91] Today we can recognize the injustice of such criticism. It must be said again that it is utterly improbable that the music performed at the funeral sermon of March 24 was ever written down as a complete score and therefore could have been at the disposal of Bach's Göttingen biographer Forkel. When Forkel speaks of a composition by Bach for the funeral of Prince Leopold, we should take him quite literally; he had in mind the lost work performed at night when the last respects were being paid to the mortal remains of the dead prince. Forkel's admiration for this piece, undoubtedly an original composition, serves only to increase our deep regret that it has not survived into our own time.

Chapter 12

The attempts at clarification and assessments contained in the previous chapter have brought us face to face with a number of issues broached earlier that are now our chief concern, namely, the form and stylistic character of Bach's compositions for the Köthen court. Important though the external circumstances of Bach's life and the composer's personal experiences may be, what matters for us in the final analysis is the actual work of this supreme master craftsman. It must already have become clear that new light has been shed on his creative output during the years 1717–23 and after, insofar as this was connected with his office as Kapellmeister at Köthen, as a result of the researches described in this study. In this summary, three points need to be emphasized:

1. Bach's creative activity during this period was far more extensive than was formerly supposed. Many compositions written at this time must have gone astray. From an artistic point of view, his life during those years can hardly be described as a period of leisure or even one of comparative leisure.

2. The works he did compose were entirely bound up with the realities of life at the Köthen court, including the constraints that this environment imposed. Bach's output at that time was not the product of an untrammeled imagination, inspired solely by the master's artistic intuition. It was, rather, unmistakably commissioned, i.e., written to order. In this respect the work of the Köthen period was no different from that at other times in Johann Sebastian's life.

3. The vocal compositions, both secular and sacred, were far more prominent than has been hitherto supposed and than the surviving compositions would lead us to believe.

Nevertheless, it must be stressed that, as distinct from the preceding period at Weimar and the one that followed at Leipzig, secular instrumental compositions were very much in the foreground during the Köthen years. The concertos, the orchestral suites, and the great clavier works we owe to Köthen;[E45] they impart a very special character to this era of Bach's creativity. Alongside these, and in their way no less significant, are the newly revealed vocal works. It is the parallelism between the two genres, the instrumental and the vocal works, that seems to me to constitute the true character of this period.[92] It is therefore all the more important for us to get to know the vocal works in this group as well as we possibly can.

Let me begin with a general observation that has importance for our overall assessment. The first face-to-face meeting between Bach and Prince Leopold for which documentary evidence exists took place in Weissenfels in February 1716.[E46] On that occasion the prince was encountering the Weimar Konzertmeister as a composer of vocal works. We need only bring to mind the soprano aria "Schafe können sicher weiden" (Sheep may safely graze) from Bach's Weissenfels hunting cantata to imagine the delight of the visitor from Köthen, himself a truly musical man, at meeting the composer. The very first work Bach presented to his new sovereign immediately on his arrival in Köthen was also a vocal composition, the charming serenade *Durchlauchtster Leopold*. Vocal music, unquestionably deriving exclusively from the pen of the court conductor, was performed every Jan. 1 and Dec. 10 and on frequent occasions in between. Whenever, in later years, the *Director Musices* and Leipzig *Cantor Scholae Thomanae* paid a visit to Köthen, singers from outside were called on to facilitate the performance of vocal works. When in 1727 Prince Leopold was in Leipzig for the Jubilate Fair, he had the opportunity of hearing not only Bach's religious cantatas, but also his congratulatory music on the occasion of the birthday of Augustus the Strong.[93] Similarly, it was with two great vocal compositions that Bach paid his final respects to his exalted friend.

We must now address ourselves to the question of the form of these vocal works, since this issue is of the greatest significance for the development of Bach's vocal compositions as a whole. It was no accident that earlier I dealt with Bach's Köthen concertos in such detail, the reason being that the instrumentalists at his disposal participated in both the chamber music and the vocal works. Not only that, in both instances the composer allowed his musicians to speak the same language, as it were, incorporating the vocal passages into that formulation. The fact that the Lutheran school choir, the *tutti* vocalists, lacked both the talent and training for more artistically demanding singing was not allowed simply to act as a constraint on the composer's work. True genius that he was, Bach found ways around this external handicap; it became, in fact, a means of his artistic advancement. In the choral movements he treated the full four-part vocal ensemble in the same way as the ripienists in the concerto movements. This provided the background for the concerto players and the soloists—generally two in number—in the figuratively richly handled passages of the choruses. Thus evolved the transference of instrumental form to the vocal works, after the manner of the Vivaldi vocal concerto movements, that Bach was to bring to the pinnacle of perfection during the years he spent at Köthen. The extract from the chorus of the cantata *Der Himmel dacht auf Anhalts Ruhm und Glück* (see page 54) shows this clearly. There are plenty of other examples in the vocal works of the Köthen period. I have ascribed the original version of Cantata No. 184, *Erwünschtes Freudenlicht*, to New Year's Day, 1718. For the first time, Bach made use of the Lutheran school choir without at this stage asking anything too difficult of the group, as one may gauge from the following extract from the score, which contains everything sung by the choir in the main section of that particular movement:

In both passages, the choir repeats in harmony what the instruments had performed more elaborately. In the central section of the number, the *tutti* singers remain silent; here the vocal line is set for two voices only, the instruments resting as the duet is sung. They enter only in short intermezzo passages, their motifs taken from the *tutti* theme of the main part of the movement, as the following example shows:

Bach composed no choral movement of this simplicity in Weimar; there he had been able to give his fully professional choir far more exacting tasks to perform. It is this very simplicity of form, however, that brings out all the more clearly the true nature of the piece and allows us to recognize its unmistakable origins in the concerto movement.

The final number of the cantata *Die Zeit, die Tag und Jahre macht* displays a similar basic structure. This chorus, however, "Ergötzet auf Erden, erfreuet von oben," represents a further development from the one we have just examined. Here the full four-part ensemble is also used in the movement's central section, no longer singing in simple harmony. Now the vocal lines are freer, tending towards polyphony. Even so, the division of the singers into concerto soloists and ripienists and the respective tasks allotted to the two groups are conceived in a clearly concertante manner, as may be illustrated by the following small excerpt from the vocal material:

freu - et von o - ben,
Tutti Glück - se - li - ge Zei - ten, ver - gnü - get das Haus
freu - et von o - ben,

Reconstructed as BWV 134a (Meas. 73-85)

Bars 47 to 52 of the same chorus are more polyphonically structured, again
with four-part singing. We meet the technique in its most developed form
in the second movement of Cantata No. 145, *Auf, mein Herz, des Herren
Tag*, in the accompaniment to the libretto "So du mit deinem Munde
bekennest Jesum." We have placed the original version of this work in
Bach's last years at Köthen, by which time the overall competence of the
Lutheran school choir would have increased substantially under the direction of the court Kapellmeister.[E47]

The double solo parts in the choral movements that we have discussed
remind us that among Bach's instrumental concertos of these years the
double concertos were quite outstanding in their importance. The tasks
assigned to the instrumental soloists in the outer movements of these works
are fulfilled by the solo vocalists in the choruses. It is the same with the
middle movements of the concertos, where the ripienists are either not
heard or merely in the literal sense of the word accompany the music; here
again we meet analogous arrangements in the vocal works of Bach that we
have ascribed to those years. In the opening arias of cantatas [BWV] 202
(*Weichet nur...*) and 32 (*Liebster Jesu*) the oboe's expressively ranging can-
tilena blends with the soprano line in a way that is unmistakably similar
to the oboe's melodic intertwinings in the second movement of the first
Brandenburg Concerto or in the sensitively judged duet between the two
soloists in the Double Concerto for Violin and Oboe.

Brandenburg Concerto No.1, 2nd movement, from Meas. 23   from BWV 1046, 2

Weichet nur, betrübte Schatten, from Meas. 7

from BWV 202, 1

Schat - ten   be - trüb - - - - te

Schat - ten, Frost und Win - de__ geht zur__ Ruh

Liebster Jesu, mein Verlangen, from Meas. 11

from BWV 32, 1

Lieb - ster Je - su,_mein Ver-lan-gen, mein Ver-lan-gen, sa-ge mir, wo find ich dich

Liebster Jesu, mein Verlangen, from Meas. 41

from BWV 32, 1

mein Hort, er-freu - - - - - - e mich

In all these instances, the strings merely perform the harmonic accompaniment. In both arias too, Bach stipulates *adagio* and *largo* respectively, as in the central movement of the concerto. In this way, not only the outer movements of the concertos built around the antithesis between *tutti* and soloists but also the slow central movements, where the solo material appears in the very foreground, incorporate the concerto style into the vocal dialog of the Köthen cantatas.

Alongside the concerto, the suite is the second great form of cyclic instrumental composition that occupied Bach during those years. It too has a decisive effect on the Köthen vocal works. In the very first chapters of this study I drew attention to the frequent use of dance forms in Bach's vocal compositions of 1717–23. This is in fact one of the marked characteristics of these works. We took as our starting point for those earlier remarks the final movement of the serenade *Durchlauchtster Leopold*, which begins as follows:

Strings with 2 doubling Flutes · from BWV 173, 4

As I stressed at the time, the piece is headed "Al Tempo di Menuetto." What is striking in the minuet type of the aria "Jesu, deine Gnadenblicke" from Cantata No. 32 (see page 77 above) is that it is written in 3/8 time. It should be pointed out, however, that in many respects this work recalls the wedding cantata, *Weichet nur, betrübte Schatten* [BWV 202], which we have in a transcript made by Johannes Ringk in 1730, who, as Spitta remarked (see vol. 2, p. 463 [English version vol. 2, p. 633]), must have become acquainted with the work through his teacher Peter Kellner. From the latter's pen[E48] we have the copy of the harpsichord suite in A minor [BWV 818a] by Bach, which likewise dates from the Köthen era and whose minuet runs as follows:[94]

Harpsichord · Menuett from Suite BWV 818a

116

We find this type of composition in the minuet aria "Herr, so groß als dein Erhöhen" in the cantata *Ihr Häuser des Himmels* [BWV 193a] (see page 71 above). In the last movement of the Whitsuntide cantata *Erwünschtes Freudenlicht* (No. 184), which in its original form was performed in Köthen on New Year's Day, 1718, we discerned a complete gavotte. The concluding movement of the wedding cantata *Weichet nur, betrübte Schatten* is even so headed:

In the aria "Glück und Segen" of the cantata *Erwünschtes Freudenlicht* (see page 62 above) we encountered a polonaise. We described the third number of *Weichet nur, betrübte Schatten* [BWV 202], the aria "Sich üben im Lieben," as a *passepied* (see page 74 above); it is indeed representative of the type. We come across this cheerful, lively dance form particularly often in the Köthen vocal works, twice even in the New Year composition *Die Zeit, die Tag und Jahre macht* [BWV 134a]. From the aria "Auf! Auf! Sterbliche" the first oboe and basso continuo parts are quoted below:

Similarly, in the final choral number of this work, which is rounded off with a return to the same dance form, we find the following:

Outer (Violin + Oboes I, II and Continuo) Lines   from BWV 134, 6

Thus, both the genres, concerto and suite, are of outstanding importance for Bach's vocal works during the years 1717–23. It now comes as no surprise to discover thematic parallels and echoes in both the vocal and the instrumental compositions. Two further examples have already been cited, the affinity between certain thematic images in the cantata *Der Himmel dacht auf Anhalts Ruhm* [BWV 66a] and motifs from the main theme of the first movement in the fourth Brandenburg Concerto [BWV 1049] (see page 52 above), and the similarity of theme between the aria "Phöbus eilt mit schnellen Pferden" from the wedding cantata *Weichet nur* [BWV 202, 3] and the final movement of the Sonata for Violin and Harpsichord in G Major [BWV 1019, 5]. Such illustrations could be multiplied.[95]

The reverse, however, may likewise be detected, i.e., the influence of a vocal composition on an instrumental work, most clearly seen in the case of the transference of a soprano aria divested of its libretto to the likewise above-mentioned Sonata in G Major [BWV 1019a, 3]. In this case, the discovery of the piece's origin proves significant in that we recognize the remains of a vocal work composed by Bach at Köthen, and perhaps more important, because we see here the interrelationship between the composer's instrumental and vocal works of those years. This perfect synthesis of what was sung and what was performed instrumentally, the Bach style of blending vocal and instrumental as we have it witnessed here, must, in historical terms, be regarded as by far the most significant fruit of the years at Köthen. To perceive this in all its clarity only became possible when the evidence had been provided to show that, specifically during the period 1717–23, there emerged a substantial amount of vocal composition alongside the concertos, suites, sonatas, and other instrumental forms. But we cannot let it rest there. The enrichment of Bach's creative method at Köthen was also beneficial to his compositions written after he left the court, during the major epoch of his life's work that now began at Leipzig. These compositions too may be seen in a different perspective as we leave Köthen and follow Bach to Leipzig.

Chapter 13

Among the early Leipzig compositions, mention should first be made of the secular pastoral cantata *Entfliehet, verschwindet, entweichet, ihr Sorgen* [BWV 249a].[E49] The first three movements of this musical entertainment, written to celebrate the birthday of Duke Christian of Sachsen-Weissenfels on Feb. 23, 1725, consist of a reworked concerto grosso with solo violin and oboe, one of the many related pieces from the years 1717–23, most of which have been lost. The first two movements of the cantata appear in their instrumental, i.e., original, form only. The duet, however, which follows these in the birthday serenade, is the third movement of what was originally a purely instrumental work, now furnished with a libretto. The structure of the quartet number with which this work ends, as Spitta observed with an eye to the *Easter Oratorio* parody, resembles that of the French overture.[96] Whether or not this "finale" is a parody, as is the case with the opening numbers, or whether the transference is merely structural, will always remain a matter of conjecture.

The adoption of the purely instrumental elements of pieces of this kind, or the addition of a libretto to the whole or part of a work, occurs in Bach's compositions into the 1730s. To our knowledge, the composer made particularly liberal use of this form of transposition in the cantatas with organ obbligato written [*during the years 1725–27*].[97] [E50] Of these, the cantata *Geist und Seele* [BWV 35] was mentioned earlier. Cantata No. 146, *Wir müssen durch viel Trübsal*, contains two movements taken from the Clavier Concerto in D Minor [*Ed.: This cantata dates from May 12, 1726*]. The opening and middle numbers of a lost sister piece in E major were accommodated in Cantata No. 169, *Gott soll allein mein Herze haben* [*Ed.: of Oct. 20, 1726*], while the finale of the same source found its way into Cantata No. 49, *Ich geh und suche mit Verlangen* [*Ed.: from Nov. 3, 1726*]. It is well known that examples of this kind are frequent. Mention should be made, however, of the opening chorus of Cantata No. 110, *Unser Mund sei voll Lachens* [*Ed.: first performed on Dec. 25, 1725*], which, furnished only in the fugue section with a libretto, is identical with the overture to the fourth orchestral suite in D major [BWV 1069].[98] [E51]

Köthen works live on in the form of Leipzig religious cantatas in just the same way as Köthen secular cantatas were later refashioned into sacred works. It is significant that both forms of contrafact reached their peak at the same time, around the year 1730. The causes in both instances were related. Equally important, however, is the fact that forms developed in Köthen were also of lasting influence on the original compositions of the Leipzig period, particularly during the first decade. One or two examples will be cited to illustrate this.

Most probably on the day after Boxing Day, 1723, and at any rate during the very first years of Bach's time as Thomas Kantor, Cantata No. 64, *Sehet, welch eine Liebe,* received its first performance.[E52] The theme of the aria "Was die Welt in sich hält" from this work is quoted below:

As in the Köthen vocal works, we meet once again in this sacred cantata the pure form of the gavotte. If the work was first performed on Dec. 27, 1723, it must have been preceded on Christmas Day itself by the monumental Cantata No. 63, *Christen, ätzet diesen Tag in Metall und Marmorsteine.* Both of its outer movements are choruses of great stature; viewed architecturally, however, both are to be regarded as concerto movements. *Tutti* and solo sections alternate one with the other. The ensemble passages display a far richer figuration than we find in the Köthen cantatas. In Leipzig, the first choir of the Thomas School provided Bach with a highly proficient four-part ensemble, to which, from the outset, he could allocate far more demanding tasks than had been the case with the humble choristers of the Lutheran school at Köthen. Nevertheless, in the solo passages we feel we are back at the court of Prince Leopold. This is particularly true of the recitatives, all three containing freely declaimed passages alternating with firmer rhythms; the flavor of Köthen is just as prominent, even more so perhaps, in the two duets. The very fact that these numbers are for two vocal parts is a legacy of the 1717–23 period; in the later Leipzig cantatas, duets, as I remarked earlier, become very rare. The first duet of Cantata No. 63, performed in a slow tempo (Bach stipulated *adagio*), contains in the part for oboe or obbligato organ delicately fashioned passages reminiscent of those that the composer had written at Köthen, in both the central movements of the concertos and in cantatas, for *Cammer Musicus* Rose.[E53] In the second duet the solo first violin is heard above the rest of the strings, another Köthen trait. This movement is also of particular interest from the structural point of view. We cannot speak of a string accompaniment in the normal sense. Instead, the pronounced themes of the strings lend support to the structure of the piece as a whole, while the thread of the solo themes is suspended within this framework and borne by the vocal parts. Thus, once again, we find the concerto principle permeating the entire structure. Sections such as bars 53ff. provide a dialog between soloists (in this case, the singers) and the orchestral violins performing *piano*, which is a dynamic marking typical of the concerto:

Bars 114ff. appear to have been extracted from the central section of a double concerto movement:

As the soloists perform their theme, the orchestral instruments play the opening motif of the *tutti* theme *pianissimo* and transposed to the minor key. Furthermore, the fact that the orchestra at the conclusion of the dominant section at bar 132 returns with the main theme *forte* is in line with

Bach's technique in related concerto pieces, particularly in the final movements.

It is common to find single suite movements—dance forms—in Bach's cantatas composed during the early years in Leipzig. An example of this has been presented earlier, the aria "Was die Welt in sich hält" from Cantata No. 64. We also meet the overture in the religious works of this period, even linked to the chorale. The best-known example of this is the opening chorus of Cantata No. 20, *O Ewigkeit, du Donnerwort*. The first section of the melody is incorporated into the stately opening passage, the second into the fugued *vivace* section of the movement. The third and final section returns to the broad tempo and the opening thematic material. We know, however, of only one example of the complete form of a suite within a religious cantata. This is the festive cantata, which Bach composed on the occasion of the rededication of the restored church at Störmthal in the vicinity of Leipzig (Nov. 2, 1723), *Höchsterwünschtes Freudenfest* [BWV 194]. In contrast to the overturelike elaboration of Johann Rist's hymn "O Ewigkeit," discussed above, the vocal section is confined to the fugued central part of the opening movement. The stately introduction, which reappears at the conclusion of the piece, is essentially instrumental, although the chorus is heard for a mere 2½ bars at the very end. During the fugato, as in the Köthen suites,[E54] we have the alternation of *tutti* and solo performance. Bars 100–21[a] clearly stand out from the rest of the number:

124

The solo bass makes his appearance, to be accompanied for the first 12 bars by two (instead of three) oboes, while the rest of the orchestra remains silent. The four-part section that then follows and lasts as far as bar 121[a] is likewise performed by a reduced section of *Konzertisten* from the choir; not until the second quarter of bar 121, as the direction *forte* to the instrumentalists indicates, does the full choir reappear. Thus, once again we have a combination of the overture form and concertolike features.

Apart from the opening chorus, Cantata No. 194 has four other move-ments, two arias performed in each of its two parts, representing the dances that follow the suite overture. The first of these arias, "Was des Höchsten Glanz erfüllt," has a rondeau-like structure. The second, "Hilf, Gott, daß es uns gelingt," begins with the following instrumental prelude by the strings:

126

As was so often the case in the Köthen cantatas, the complete gavotte movement, presented purely instrumentally, precedes the entry of the vocal part. The third aria, which appears in the second part of the cantata, is a gigue. The only form of accompaniment is the basso continuo, beginning with the following ritornello, where the dance form is immediately recognizable:

The last of the solo movements is a vocal duet accompanied by two oboes. Again we may perceive a duet link with the vocal works of the years 1717–23. The entry of the vocal parts is once more preceded by the two wind instruments playing a dance form, on this occasion a minuet:

The fact that we have here a complete suite within a religious cantata, even allowing for the placing of the gigue in the penultimate instead of the conventional final position, has led many scholars to conclude that we are dealing with what was originally a purely instrumental composition, furnished only later with a libretto. Against this view it should be said that the surviving material does not point to a parody. The appearance of the original parts is explained perfectly satisfactorily if we assume that Bach used the piece later as a religious composition for the feast of Trinity in Leipzig. Moreover, libretto and score form a unified whole; one could not instance a single part of the work where, as is virtually always the case in parodies, one would have to conclude that the score was not originally composed to fit the libretto as we now have it. The keys in which the piece is written would argue against any form of parody. The overture is in B-flat major; of the four arias, however, only the first is in that key. The remainder are in E-flat major, G minor, and F major. Thus, if one were to regard the cantata as a piece of instrumental music, to which a libretto was added at a later date, one would have to assume transposition of most of the numbers, a view contradicted by the manner in which the instruments are handled. Furthermore, the single movement in a minor key and the gigue would be completely out of place within a suite in a major key.

Chapter 14

Turning once again to the years 1717–23, we see that Bach, even before his move to Leipzig, used dance forms within religious compositions, the original nature of which is not in doubt.[99] This brings us back to the vocal works that Bach composed before he finally left the service of Prince Leopold, three of which have so far been completely omitted from our considerations—cantatas [BWV] 22, *Jesus nahm zu sich die Zwölfe*, and [BWV] 23, *Du wahrer Gott und Davids Sohn*, and the *St. John Passion*. Admittedly, none of the three was written for performance in Köthen; they were composed with an eye to the post of Thomas Kantor in Leipzig.[E55] Since they emerged during Bach's period of office as court Kapellmeister at Anhalt-Köthen, however, they cannot be ignored here. We shall learn much of importance from them that is relevant to the issues concerning us.

I begin with Cantata No. 22, *Jesus nahm zu sich die Zwölfe*. It is generally acknowledged that this piece does not belong in the front rank of Bach's cantatas. Spitta's conjecture that with this trial composition—the work was offered as such on Quinquagesima Sunday in Leipzig—Bach had decided to adapt his style to the more lightweight taste of his audience in that city and therefore not to present the far more substantial but equally more demanding companion piece, the cantata *Du wahrer Gott und Davids Sohn*, as had been the original intention, lacks credibility.[E56] With the *St. John Passion*, performed a few weeks later on Good Friday of the same year, no such considerations were uppermost in his mind; instead, he gave the citizens of Leipzig a work that has few equals in the magnificence of its form and content.[E57] For this reason alone I share the view, originally put forward by Bernhard Friedrich Richter, that Bach composed Cantata No. 22 during his stay at Leipzig to accompany the libretto he saw there for the first time, in other words, that he was, to a certain extent, on probation. The best explanation would be that with the composition Bach was simply following on from what he had grown accustomed to at Köthen. Put bluntly, the work was of a very familiar type. The very choice of instruments, the fact that in the orchestra he makes use of one wind instrument, the oboe, alongside the strings and basso continuo, is a pattern that frequently recurs in the Köthen cantatas.[E58] The second aria of the cantata ("Mein Alles in Allem, mein ewiges Gut") is preeminently typical of Bach's method of composition at the time. The opening ritornello is quoted:

Unmistakably, this prelude and postlude has the form of a *passepied,* so often found in the Köthen cantatas. Of note, however, here, is the soloistic treatment of the first violin; exactly as in the Köthen compositions, with the same closely related figurations as in the congratulatory pieces, it stands out from the rest of the strings. Thus, both historically and formally, Cantata No. 22 forms a bridge between Bach's vocal works composed at Köthen and Leipzig.

We could make the same observation in connection with the two other, far more weighty religious pieces that Bach composed with Leipzig in mind while he was still employed and resident at Köthen, though already a candidate for the post of Kantor at the choir school of St. Thomas. Cantata No. 23, *Du wahrer Gott und Davids Sohn,* consists of only four movements, the first being a duet for soprano and alto with an obbligato accompaniment of two oboes. Thus, at the head of the works stands a vocal two-part solo movement such as we know from virtually all of the Köthen cantatas. A stylistic feature of Bach's vocal works of those years was the alternation of strictly measured recitatives with recitative sections in free rhythm. In Cantata No. 23 the entire recitative that constitutes the second movement is to be sung in accordance with the composer's inscription *a tempo*. In that this is also necessitated by the chorale "Christe, du Lamm Gottes," incorporated into the movement as a *cantus firmus*, with whose figured treatment the work comes to an end, we may say, with Bach's preceding cantatas in mind, that the master was using here the form of an arioso recitative in fixed rhythm, such as he frequently composed in Köthen, in order to be able to insert the chorale into the counterpoint against the recitative.

The chorus, which forms the third movement, requires treatment in greater depth. Its main theme is introduced by all the instruments, the two oboes, the strings, and the basso continuo, while the wind instruments are treated *colla parte* with the first violin, as follows:

Strings with doubling Oboes I, II   from BWV 23, 3

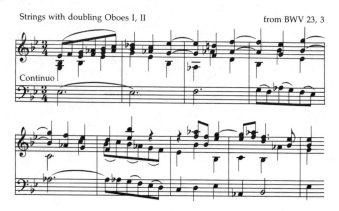

The chorus enters to take up the theme at the beginning of bar 9, initially without orchestral support (bars 9–17[a]). After another purely instrumental passage (bars 17–24[a]), singers and orchestra come together to perform the central musical theme quoted above. The latter recurs at various parts of the movement, sometimes purely vocally, sometimes purely instrumentally, transposed to other keys, even to the minor. In between these sections of the piece, however, we meet direct passages, accompanied either by the basso continuo or *piano* by other instruments. Thus, the overall arrangement appears as follows:

1–32[a] *Tutti* theme .... E flat major—B flat major
32–46[a] Solo theme

Thus, once again we have the typical concerto movement, transposed to the vocal sphere. Just how closely our piece is related to the form of the instrumental concerto is perhaps most clearly demonstrated by the following example from bars 61–77[a]:

It is known that the intended performance of the cantata *Du wahrer Gott und Davids Sohn* did not materialize at the Leipzig service on Estomihi Sunday, 1723.[100] We may be sure, however, that Bach did originally compose the work specifically for that date and ceremony. One distinctly recognizes that in this instance the court Kapellmeister, the creator of many instrumental concertos of the highest order, is composing a piece for the church. He carries over into this religious vocal music, the composition of which was to constitute Bach's main task should he become Thomas Kantor, the formal ingredients of his preceding works. In fact, the last great vocal compositions written at Köthen form a bridge to his activities in Leipzig. The cantatas that arose during the period immediately after he moved to that city can only be understood against the background of the Köthen works, particularly the vocal compositions.

I venture to regard the *St. John Passion*, surely the mightiest work of Bach's *oeuvre* before he transferred to Leipzig, as a fruit of his compositions for the orchestra at Köthen. In my own earlier publications I have expressed the opinion that the architecture of the *Passio Domini nostri Jesu Christi secundum Evangelistam Johannem* [BWV 245] may only be explained as a form that was primarily conceived instrumentally.[101] In doing so I drew on an insight by Spitta, who realized that in Bach's case forms that characterize an individual movement may be transferred to whole works. At that time I cited the Prelude to the English Suite in G Minor [BWV 808] as a parallel structure to that of the *St. John Passion*.[102] I in no way realized then what special significance the suite form had for Bach's vocal compositions, and what an important part Bach's works composed specifically at Köthen played in this respect. Today we must go a stage further, and to this end I give a brief outline of the structure of the Passion once again. Its focal point is the section in the second part that begins with the chorale "Ach, großer König, groß zu allen Zeiten" and ends with the other chorale, "In meines

Herzens Grunde." The chorale "Durch dein Gefängnis, Gottes Sohn" forms the keystone of this section. The pillars that support the edifice, however, are the *turba* movements, whose symmetrical grouping around the center of this great series of movements, which I have chosen to call "the inner heart" of the Passion, lends the work its artistic unity. Between these chorales are interspersed purely solo parts, the Gospel recitatives and its contemplation in freely expressive solos with poetic texts; as distinct from the *tutti* numbers, these latter retreat deliberately into the background. In this way, the structure of this heart of the work may be briefly summarized as follows:

> *Chorale: "Ach großer König"*
> *Tutti* "Nicht diesen, sondern Barabbam"
>　　　　Solo section (Gospel record and contemplation)
> *Tutti* "Sei gegrüßt, lieber Judenkönig"
>　　　　Solo section (record)
> *Tutti* "Kreuzige, kreuzige"
>　　　　Solo section (record)
> *Tutti* "Wir haben ein Gesetz"
>　　　　Solo section (record)
> *Chorale: "Durch dein Gefängnis"*
>　　　　Solo section (record)
> *Tutti* "Lässest du diesen los"
>　　　　Solo section (record)
> *Tutti* "Weg, weg mit dem, kreuzige"
>　　　　Solo section (record)
> *Tutti* "Wir haben keinen König"
>　　　　Solo section (record and contemplation)
> *Tutti* "Schreibe nicht: der Juden König"
> *Chorale: "In meines Herzens Grunde"*

The structures of the *turba* movements bracketed together here match one another musically in size or emphasis, and in the first two sections of each group ("Nicht diesen" and "Wir haben keinen König"), like those that bring them to a close ("Sei gegrüßet" and "Schreibe nicht"), they achieve a similar balance.

After all we have said about the importance of the form of the concerto for Bach's vocal compositions at that time, there can now be no doubt that the overall concept of the structure we have examined has derived from that of the instrumental concerto movement.[103] The fact that we may also detect an affinity with the above-mentioned suite prelude [BWV 808, 1] in no way contradicts this view, since in Bach's case concertante features (the alternation of *tutti* and solo parts) find their way into the suite, just as movements that are suitelike in character may occur in the concertos. This means that forms that were originally secular instrumental compositions survive in individual cantata numbers or possibly whole cantatas. They even shape the entire structure of one of Bach's greatest sacred works, for that is an appropriate description when applied to the *St. John Passion*.

We are then faced with a question, frequently raised and answered in various ways, some of them highly contradictory, but never so far to our complete satisfaction. This is the issue of the relationship between Bach's "secular" music and his "sacred" or "spiritual" compositions. The mere fact that we have been examining the Köthen period forces us to come to grips with this fundamental problem. As we are now aware, during those years Bach's output included a considerable number of vocal works produced alongside instrumental pieces; the two forms influenced each other, with the result that the finished works presented a perfect synthesis of vocal and instrumental features. Not only that, we realize—and the implications of this are far more profound—that of the vocal works that Bach wrote during the years 1717–23, a considerable proportion were religious cantatas and that they too are characterized by an inner fusion of instrumental and vocal forms.[E59] We may go a stage further. It is only through this realization that we may fully come to understand the vocal compositions intended for use at divine service in Leipzig, particularly those written during Bach's first decade in that city.

Chapter 15

In the preceding chapters I have used the term "secular compositions" as if its meaning was self-evident. But as soon as we try to go a stage further than the straightforward listing of examples in order to clarify what is understood by Bach's "secular" music, i.e., seek to define the term, we realize that it is purely negative in character, implying more or less the following: By "secular compositions" we mean those works by Bach written neither for the church, nor for purposes of divine service, nor written with any specifically religiously edifying purpose in mind. Behind such an interpretation lies an understanding of Bach that needs to be justified. Here it is of relatively little importance whether we tend to stress the one aspect or the other in our differentiation between "secular" and "religious" or "spiritual" compositions.

Some writers—and this happens time and time again for reasons that lack objectivity—see Bach first and foremost as a composer and artist who, whenever he had sufficient leisure time, i.e., during those periods when he was not tied by commissioned works and the limitations they imposed, allowed his soaring artistic imagination free rein to create the most sublime works that were essentially music for music's sake, pieces that, according to our definition, were predominantly "secular." Alongside these, the church compositions were mere occasional exercises, most probably no more than a means of earning a livelihood. According to this interpretation, the Köthen period becomes the high point of Bach's musical life. This was the generally accepted understanding of those years, but it is a view that has now been overturned. They were in fact an astonishing period of unremitting productive labor.[E60] The compositions he wrote were by no means the products of an untrammeled artistic imagination. The master was genuinely restricted by the commissions he received that had to be fulfilled by certain dates, more so than at any other time in his life. Nor did Bach have at his disposal a sizable stock of his own works that he could draw on, as was the case in later years, either for unchanged, or slightly revised, or completely parodied performance. In Köthen, everything had to be original, and at all times the composer had to pay the most careful heed to the performers at his command in the case of both the instrumental and the vocal works.

If, however, we view Bach from the other perspective, i.e., primarily as a composer of church music, who, it is conceded, produced many valuable "secular" pieces, we get into similar difficulties. Again it is the Köthen period as we know it that causes the problems. The reason is that until now this chapter of Bach's life was just as important in the minds of all those for whom he symbolized the very summit of Protestant music, in the sense that at Köthen the master, significantly for a short space of time, had found himself in a purely secular appointment and for that reason had confined himself to purely "secular" music. He had followed this course for scarcely more than half a decade and had then returned to the mainstream of his life's great work. The creator of secular instrumental compositions gave way to the supreme master of church cantatas, motets, Passions, the five-part Kyrie and Gloria, the *Symbolum Nicenum*, the six-part Sanctus, and finally the great chorale cantatas.[E61] Accordingly, Bach's life and work were divided into two parts, both chronologically and creatively. In our remarks on the Köthen works themselves we have shown that such a view is untenable.

To solve the problem that confronts us, we might proceed purely biographically, addressing our questions to Johann Sebastian Bach himself and seeking the answer to the question how he would wish his work to be regarded in the historical sources at our disposal. It is a well-known fact that we obtain no direct information from these. The extant letters in Bach's own hand, the meager reports of conversations with the composer, and the details that we possess about his style and method of teaching are unhelpful, if we expect them to reveal anything of the essential nature of his musical compositions.[104] (At least this curious reticence precludes the possibility of any kind of individualistic, humanist interpretation.) In the absence, then, of firsthand evidence, we must make do with the indirect sources. Three scholars, each deserving an honorable mention in the field of Bach research, Wilhelm Rust, Bernhard Friedrich Richter, and Rudolf Wustmann, have all, from their separate points of departure, made the point that it would be greatly advantageous to our understanding of the composer if we knew in which order he customarily stored the manuscripts of his works.[105] By the end of his life, he must have accumulated enormous quantities of manuscript material in his study. We may further assume that his compositions must have been arranged systematically, if only for the simple reason that Bach to a considerable extent used the works over and over again. I believe it is possible in broad terms to answer this question raised by Rust, Richter, and Wustmann and that there would be much of importance to be gained from doing so.

We begin with the first description of Bach's life of any substance to appear in print, the obituary composed jointly by his son Carl Philipp Emanuel and Johann Friedrich Agricola, which was published in 1754 in

Mizler's "Musicalische Bibliothek."[106] This "necrology" contains a summary, albeit carefully executed, list of the deceased's works. The manner
in which the compositions are grouped together here gives us a fair idea
of the order in which the works were arranged at the time of Bach's death.
In support of this conjecture I would cite the list of Johann Sebastian's
works that formed part of the estate of Carl Philipp Emanuel published
two years after the latter's death.[107] After the death of his father, Carl Philipp
Emanuel Bach had divided the legacy of manuscripts between himself and
Wilhelm Friedemann. Not everything that Bach's son, at that time a keyboard accompanist at the court of Frederick the Great, inherited was still
in existence at the time of his own death, though the bulk of the compositions remained. The description of the works contained in the above-
mentioned 1790 list of personal effects is considerably more detailed than
that of the 1754 obituary. Much had evidently become somewhat disor-
dered over the decades, particularly the works that Bach's son himself was
able to use. Whole sections of the works had been rearranged by 1790, yet
the basic pattern of the older catalog was still discernible. The executors
of C. P. E. Bach's estate had drawn up the 1790 list of effects. We can still
recognize today how they carried out the task of cataloging: They simply
went along the cabinets in which the scores were stored, noting down the
works in the order they stood. This reveals that 40 years after Johann
Sebastian's death, a considerable quantity of his manuscripts were still
being kept in the same order as that with which the composer himself was
familiar. The details from the two catalogs are of particular importance,
since they show no obvious division into "secular" and "religious or spiritual" works. In other words, Bach's study did not contain separate cup-
boards for the two groups of compositions; clearly the composer himself
did not make that distinction, which today is regarded as so fundamental.
    As far as I can judge, the distinction was initially made by the editors
of the first published complete edition of Bach's works [the Bach-Gesellschaft edition]. It was the normal procedure at that time for religious and
secular works to be bound together in separate volumes. Even here, however, the proposition was not entirely feasible, as the third volume, that
containing, among other things, the four parts of the *Klavier-Übung*, reflects. Bach had published the pieces assembled here under one and the
same title. Whereas the first two and the so-called fourth volumes (Bach
himself had refrained from numbering the last opus) are clearly secular,
i.e., nonreligious, in character, the third contains one of the master's greatest religious works. Thus, again seen from this historical point of view, the
fundamental division made today between "secular" and "religious" works
is untenable.
    Nevertheless, the attempt to draw this distinction continues to be

made, particularly from the religious quarter, where it is usually pointed out that the master's compositions that have come down to us and have been assembled in the great complete edition are for the most part works intended for the church. Immediately we have to ask whether the picture we gain from the extant works matches the original circumstances. From the 1754 obituary list alone we can see that considerable losses had been incurred since Bach's death, losses that, in terms of the quantity involved, we may only partially estimate. We can gain a much clearer picture of the extent to which the religious works have gone astray than is possible with the secular compositions. We read, for example, that in 1750 there were five annual cycles of "church pieces" (i.e., religious cantatas) in existence, and five Passions. Today we have about 190 religious cantatas and two Passions, and the discrepancy becomes clear. From the point of view of the nonreligious compositions, however, the situation is far less clear since the obituary merely lists both instrumental and vocal works in a very summary fashion and without reference to the quantities involved. This makes it difficult for us to gauge the amount of nonreligious compositions by Bach originally in existence. It must have been considerably greater than the complete edition indicates, since, in quantitative terms, the losses among the secular works far exceeded those among the sacred compositions. Research findings, particularly those of recent years, confirm this again and again. Among the Bach compositions that have come to light since the compilation of the great complete edition, either in manuscript form or having been shown to exist as a result of historical and literary analysis, the secular works are substantially in the majority. This is very much in keeping with the impression we received in our study of the Köthen period. Of course, the recent discoveries have included many cantatas, though only half of these were intended for the church. Next to the lost vocal compositions, there must also have been instrumental works—undoubtedly "secular" in character—on a considerable scale, of which only relatively few have survived. As far as the years at Leipzig are concerned, it has already been shown elsewhere that Bach's participation in public, nonreligious musical performance was far more extensive than, for example, Schering in the third volume of his *History of Leipzig Music* suggested.[108] We know of no part of Bach's life during which he was not producing "secular" compositions. In Arnstadt he had written his witty capriccio on the occasion of the departure of his brother Johann Jakob [BWV 992]. The years in Weimar gave rise, among other things, to the arrangements of the Italian instrumental concertos for harpsichord [BWV 972–87], together with the oldest surviving secular cantata, *Was mir behagt, ist nur die muntre Jagd* [BWV 208]. The Köthen era is exceptional, however, insofar as in those years nonreligious compositions decidedly took precedence over those for the church. That too is the reason why in this context we must face up to the secular-versus-spiritual issue.

This study has dwelt in some detail on Bach's parody technique. The procedure presents those who would "salvage the reputation" of the religious Bach with some considerable difficulties. The line that is usually adopted is as follows: They begin by pointing out, quite rightly, that the days of downgrading a composition simply because it was a parody are over. Bach himself and his contemporaries formed no such judgment. Furthermore, though I do not wish to suggest that in every case Bach's parodies were totally successful artistically,[109] it could be said that in many instances the revised version, and the new libretto that went with it, developed musical qualities that had lain dormant in the original to such a point that the parody, aesthetically speaking, represented a marked improvement. It is also pointed out, again quite correctly, that Bach's parodies did not always involve the transference of a secular piece into the religious sphere. Often a secular piece remained purely secular, a religious work equally exclusively religious. It may further be said that Bach, in terms of the methods adopted and the overall scope of the compositions, used the parody technique in different ways at different times. In general, after having reached something of a peak around the year 1730, this method of working receded into the background towards the end of Bach's life. Whereas, particularly during the early Leipzig years, the master would transform whole works into new ones by the addition of a fresh libretto, he gradually became, as we now know, more cautious. The parodying of recitatives can be detected until 1726. Bach discontinued the practice after that date, preferring to write new recitative numbers; in other words, he parodied only the choruses, arias, etc., on those occasions when entire sections were removed from older compositions. The next stage, whenever he wanted to reuse former materials to create a new work, was for him to extract passages from various pieces, instead of a single original, choosing his sources with great care in order to provide new libretti with the most appropriate scores. Typical examples of this procedure are the *Christmas Oratorio* and the short Masses. In contrast with the parodies of the Köthen cantatas discussed above, these were not simply revised versions of previous works; here the parody passages derived from various earlier sources.[E62]

All this is quite true. But if, by arguing in this way, the intention is somehow to minimize the problems posed by the parodies, we become aware of the unsatisfactory nature of what is basically an unsound apologia. Even if the attempt to play down the issue of the parodies were to succeed, that would still not mean that the question that concerns us has been answered. The conclusions we reached in our analysis of Bach's Köthen works make it specifically clear that there is much more to this phenomenon of parodying previous works. Compositions by Bach originally created for the church, including some of his greatest works, e.g., the *St. John Passion*, contain within them features of musical forms conceived and developed in the secular sphere. This may be explained by reference to the homogeneity of the baroque style, imposing its form and fashion on every sphere of life, including dress, furniture, and the works of art that accompanied the liturgy. In their grand design as much as in their surface ornamentation, castles, palaces, and churches convincingly displayed this unity of form. It is precisely this facility that the baroque possessed—of being able to grasp and shape existence as a whole—that revealed it as a genuinely original style, perhaps the last of its kind.

No one would dispute that Bach, in terms of the history of artistic style, belongs to the baroque. It is a view, however, that is so commonly held that the question whether there is not something intrinsic and important that places the composer outside the baroque is never discussed. We need to reexamine what sets Bach apart from this "style" and where the dividing line runs. This is necessary because this question is of paramount importance to the problem of the relationship between the secular and the religious in his work. Attempting to sum up in general terms the essential nature of that epoch in the history of art, we can say that one of its main features was the glorification of man as the *homo divinus*. Affirmation of human existence and an intensely powerful affirmation of the world in which we live dominate everything. Suffering, privation, and death are not the central themes of baroque macabre art. In the shape of the macabre these form at best a repulsive and deterrent counterpart at the very periphery of the movement. It is no coincidence that Leibniz regarded our world as one of the best imaginable. It was a view that was reflected in the choice of subject matter in both secular and Christian art. The Martyr, the Crucified One, is not the focus of our attention, but the Victor, Christ as a heroic figure. He who overcame all suffering to journey heavenwards is more important to the artist than the man who descended into the depths of a lost world, drank from the bitterest of cups, and was finally crucified as a criminal. Mankind, represented by its greatest figures, its mighty ones and its saints, participates in the glorification. Favorite subjects of portrayal are the apotheoses of princes and the assumption into heaven of the truly devout. Linked with this came a tendency to revere the ancient world, in the fine arts just as much as in baroque music, which added to the glorification of that age through its most original achievement, opera. Whenever Biblical themes were chosen, they derived predominantly from the Old Testament, again largely influenced by the heroic ideal. Hercules and Julius Caesar, Samson and Judas Maccabaeus are placed side by side, and even the image of the Messiah is conceived and formed in this heroic sense.

I am conscious that the above remarks in no way represent a complete characterization of what is meant by the baroque. The details I have noted, however, do constitute the most distinctive features of that style. Yet none of these can be reconciled with our image of Bach. The *homo divinus*, either mighty or saintly, appears as a central figure in none of his works. Of course, there are important features that link Leibniz and Bach.[110] The characteristic optimism of the Leibnizian view of the world, however, is not shared by the composer. Bach's world is one that has strayed from the path of God, the apostate world of sinners, but also that saved by Jesus Christ. Of course, Bach also created splendid Easter compositions. Nevertheless, if we were to select one theme as central to the composer's work, it would have to be the cross and Christ Crucified. It is no coincidence that the avowal "Crucifixus pro nobis" forms the centerpiece of the artistic structure of Bach's setting of the *Symbolum Nicenum* of the *Mass in B Minor* [BWV 232]. Nor do I think it a chance occurrence that among all of Bach's Easter compositions, Cantata No. 4, *Christ lag in Todesbanden*, is by far the most significant. This is not only due to the magnificent words of Luther's Easter chorale, Bach's setting of which is "through-composed," but also to the subject matter that celebrates both Good Friday and Easter and describes the "veritable Easter lamb" as "roasted high upon the cross in hot love." It is likewise no coincidence that the Passions themselves represent the very pinnacle of Bach's creativity. The association of the name Bach solely with the *St. Matthew Passion* throughout the middle decades of the 19th century, a historically understandable diminution of the composer's stature, does in fact contain a central truth. Whenever the Thomas Kantor, either in the cantatas or the organ works, composed hymns of atonement, he made use of the most carefully elaborated forms. Both in the third part of the *Klavier-Übung* and in the late[E63] Cantata No. 38, *Aus tiefer Not*, based on Luther's free adaptation of Psalm 130, the musical setting seems to be modeled on the style of Pachelbel.

The world is that which has strayed from God's true path. Through grace alone can the godless be accepted as justified before God, since Christ died for the sins of mankind. From this perspective alone is Bach's unmistakable, peculiarly close relationship with death intelligible; it pervades the whole of his work, not merely the compositions of the later years. In other words, it cannot be seen as a form of resignation; in Bach's case that would be unthinkable for he was one of the most vital of men. It has even less to do with those baroque images of death that seek to excite horror and loathing.

How indicative it is that Bach—quite by contrast with Handel, for example—had no serious interest in the ancient world. Only rarely, and then simply following the taste of the time, does he treat themes from antiquity. There is no suggestion of any kind of hero-worshiping; instead we have a healthy sense of humor, not only in small occasional pieces of a private nature, as in the Köthen wedding cantata *Weichet nur, betrübte Schatten* [BWV 202] with its delightful miniature version of the "swift steeds" of Phoebus. It is also true of Bach's cantatas composed for public performance or for celebrations connected with persons in high positions. Neither in the "Streit zwischen Phöbus und Pan" [BWV 201], nor in the "Zufriedengestellter Aeolus" [BWV 205], nor in any of the other related works is subject matter taken from the world of the ancients treated really seriously. The characteristically tragical element that we find in the baroque treatment of the ancient world is entirely absent. There is likewise little suggestion of any hero worship and none of the deification of the sovereigns celebrated elsewhere in Bach's compositions.[111] This reluctance is very closely linked to Bach's total disinterest in the opera. Even the historical events of the Old Testament exert no attraction as subject matter for his works. When he does set the words of the Old Testament to music, we have passages taken from the psalms or the prophets, seen from the point of view of the Christian, as in a hymn. Bach's Lutheranism, which is most clearly expressed in the composer's founding his entire work on the chorale, decisively outweighs his involvement in any of the intellectual associations of the baroque.

Chapter 16

Before delving deeper into the significance of the preceding remarks for an understanding of the relationship between the secular and the religious or spiritual elements in Bach's work, these need to be further clarified with the aid of a concrete example that at the same time will return us to the composer's years at Köthen: the *St. John Passion* [BWV 245]. We should first inquire into its sources. It is well known that for the production of the libretto Bach used the poetry of Hamburg City Councillor C. H. Brockes, *Der für die Sünde der Welt gemarterte und sterbende Jesus, aus den vier Evangelisten in gebundener Rede vorgestellet* (Jesus tortured and crucified for the sins of the world, based on the four Gospels and told in verse).[112] Here, however, he differed fundamentally from other librettists of the time who had used this text, including Telemann, Keiser, and Handel. These simply "through-composed" the Brockes text as it stood. It is true that Bach leaned heavily on Brockes, but he did so critically and selectively, reshaping the story in the process. The versified account of the Passion in Brockes's work is replaced by the unaltered Biblical text (John 18–19, with interpolations from Matthew 26:75 and 27:51–52). In both Bach and Brockes we find free-versed sections, Bach preferring here to follow the example of his Hamburg model. However, the texts were substantially refashioned and not only linguistically. What is much more important is that the arioso movements and the arias take on a completely new meaning. No longer are they, as in Brockes, components of the actions placed in the mouths of the Biblical characters; rather, they are the meditations of the devout believer on the word of the gospels, effectively stripped of their dramatic element. The chorale, which in Brockes and his followers at best did no more than impart a dignified framework, now becomes an integral part of the work as a whole. It is the response of the congregation to the received Word of God. In place of an oratorio, a sequence of scenes presented on an imaginary stage, we have a religious work of art with its own individual style forming part of the divine service. The negative aspect of what we know to have been an act of cooperation between Bach and Christian Friedrich Hunold now turns out to be highly significant. Probably the Köthen court conductor was setting to music cantata texts written by the poet from Halle, though this is not the full extent of Hunold's importance as far as the history of music is concerned. Even before his connection with Bach, even in fact before this relationship was known about, he had his place. His poem "Der blutige und sterbende Jesus" represented the first transference of madrigal verse to the realm of Passion composition.[113] Thus, Hunold may be regarded as the originator of the Passion oratorio. Despite the long years of collaboration with this author, however, Bach made no use of the above text. Probably he considered Brockes's work a better point of departure, as the Passion began to take shape in his mind.

This oratorio text, however, is not the only source material originating in Hamburg that Bach drew on during his last winter in Köthen while he was composing the Passion intended for Leipzig.[E64] Alongside it, we have a second, hitherto unheeded source, the *St. John Passion* that Handel had composed in 1704 to a libretto by J. G. Postel.[114] [E65] A comparison of the two Passions, one by the 19-year-old Handel and the other by the 38-year-old Bach, is extraordinarily illuminating. Of course, this should not extend as far as the artistic merit of the two compositions. Aesthetically speaking, it would be unfair to judge one of the earliest, as yet immature, pieces by Handel against a Bach masterpiece. Even so, it is probably permissible to compare the approach adopted towards the two Passion settings, because in this respect that of the young Handel does not differ intrinsically from Bach's later treatment of the subject.

It is in addition far more fruitful to get Bach and Handel/ Postel side by side than to compare Bach's *St. John Passion* with Brockes's version, since Postel also presents the account of the suffering and death of Jesus through the words of the Fourth Gospel. (The fact that the Hamburg librettist chose to include both chapter 18 and chapter 19, whereas Bach confined himself only to the latter of these, makes no material difference.) Moreover, in this instance, both textually and musically, Bach's work harks back to the Hamburg model. Not only did Bach make use of Postel's verse, but he also received inspiration from Handel's music.[E66]

We should first examine the librettos of the two works. For a long time, scholars have been searching for the origin of the words of the chorale that stands at the very heart of the central section of Bach's *St. John Passion*. It occurs in precisely the same place in Postel as in Bach, i.e., after the line from John 19:12: "Von dem an trachtete Pilatus, wie er ihn losließe" (From thenceforth Pilate sought to release Him). It appears as the following aria text:

> Durch dein Gefängnis, Gottes Sohn,
> Muß uns die Freiheit kommen.
> Dein Kerker ist der Gnadenthron,
> Die Freistatt aller Frommen;
> Denn gingst du nicht die Knechtschaft ein,
> Müßt unsre Knechtschaft ewig sein.

In other words, Bach alters only one word. Instead of "Muß uns die Freiheit kommen" (Freedom *must* come to us), we have "Ist uns die Freiheit kommen" (Freedom *has* come to us). In doing so, he transforms the meaning of the passage. No longer does deliverance lie in the future; it is now an accomplished fact. Thus the verse is sung not dramatically, in order to reflect the situation in the gospel, but in a spirit of reverent contemplation, from the heart of a Christian of the present day. (The boldness Bach displayed in this superimposition of the chorale melody on a text originally devised as an aria should likewise not go unnoticed here.)

Thus, we have clear evidence that Bach was familiar with the Postel libretto. The extent to which he borrowed from Postel exceeds that of any other of the textual sources he drew on in arriving at the text of his Passion. From the source materials discovered and analyzed by Rust, Spitta, and Wustmann, Bach adopted little more than certain conceptual, linguistic, and structural features that he then reshaped to create his new forms. He does the same with the Postel text elsewhere, e.g., in one of the arias that belong only to the original version of the Bach Passion and in consequence are not normally discussed. The aria in Bach's version [BWV 245c] was worded as follows:

> Ach, windet euch nicht so, geplagte Seelen,
> Bei eurer Kreuzesangst und Qual.
> Könnt ihr die unermessne Zahl
> Der harten Geißelschläge zählen,
> So zählet auch die Menge eurer Sünden,
> Ihr werdet diese größer finden.

It comes after the sentence from the Biblical record: "Da nahm Pilatus Jesum und geißelte ihn" (Then Pilate took Jesus and scourged Him—John 19:1). In Postel's text at this point we find:

> Unsre Bosheit ohne Zahl
> Fühlt der Heiland, der Gerechte,
> Mehr als selbst der frechen Knechte
> Peitschenstreich und Geißelqual.
> Klag, o Mensch, weil du verschuldet,
> Daß selbst Gott die Geißel duldet.

The conceptual link is clear, as is the linguistic dependence of the Bach libretto on that of Postel, which extends to the recurrence of the rhyme "Zahl-Qual."[E67] Hitherto the source of the final chorus of Bach's *St. John Passion*, in addition to the Brockes verse:

> Sein ausgesperrter Arm und sein geschlossenes Auge
> Sperrt dir den Himmel auf und schließt die Hölle zu

was reckoned to be the last movement of the Schleizer Passion, with the lines:

Ruht, ihr heiligsten Gebeine,
Ruhet unter diesem Steine
Bis zum frohen Oster-Tag,
Da ich euch empfangen mag,
Wo ich nachmals nicht mehr weine.

But the final movement of the Postel text probably also influenced Bach:

Schlafe wohl nach deinem Leiden!
Ruhe sanft nach hartem Streit!
Weil dein Tod uns Himmelsfreuden,
Weil dein Kampf uns Sieg bereit't.

A final instance of parallelism between the two librettos, by far the most significant, will be discussed later. In this final comparison, not only Postel's verse but also Handel's setting is significant. In the meantime, it will be shown that Bach both knew Handel's composition and was influenced by it. With this in mind, we must examine the feature that is common to both works, namely the gospel text. In their settings of the Biblical passages, both held to the tradition whereby the straightforward narrative sections were given to the Evangelist, a tenor; the sections of direct speech by individual persons to the so-called "soliloquents," who were drawn as solo voices from the crowd or *turba*, i.e., the chorus. In Handel's case the words of the soliloquents are throughout treated arioso, occasionally accompanied by the basso continuo, but for the most part with further instrumental support.

The role of the Evangelist is quite different. With four exceptions, the part is cast in *secco* recitative throughout. These four exceptions deserve individual mention. The first is the inscription on the cross, "Jesus von Nazareth, der Juden König" (Jesus of Nazareth, the King of the Jews—John 19:19). Here Handel stipulates *adagio*. The treatment of the vocal part is decidedly arioso and is further distinguished by the repetition of single words. The three remaining parts of the Biblical text that receive special treatment in the role of the Evangelist are the following quotations taken from the Old Testament:

John 19:24

"Sie haben meine Kleider unter sich geteilet und haben über meinen Rock das Los geworfen" (Ps. 22:19) (They parted My raiment among them, and for My vesture they did cast lots).

John 19:36

"Ihr sollt ihm kein Bein zerbrechen" (Ex.12:46) (A bone of Him shall not be broken).

John 19:37

"Sie werden sehen, in welchen sie gestochen haben" (Zech. 12:10) (They shall look on Him whom they pierced).

Handel underlines the allusion to the fulfilled prophecy by the entry of the strings above the continuo in strictly notated rhythm. In the two other instances Old Testament prophecy is highlighted not by the use of accompanying instruments but by altering the treatment of the continuo line, which changes from sustained chords into a strict and regular quaver movement, once again indicating a vocal performance that is no longer freely declaimed but delivered in a fixed rhythm. Again, in the setting of John 19:36 we come across the repetition of individual words.

We know from the Köthen cantatas that at that time Bach was fond of the transition from free to strict rhythmical delivery within the recitative.[E68] When we now establish, however, that within the lines of the Evangelist in Bach's *St. John Passion* precisely the same passages as in Handel's version are made to stand out from all the other Biblical quotations (Bach prescribes *adagio* at the four points), then this feature likewise clearly points to influence from the Handel model. This is the more likely since it has been possible to show clearly that Bach knew the Postel libretto, which, as far as we know, only Handel had set to music.

Thus we can demonstrate that there are both textual and musical links between the earlier Handel Passion and Bach's own composition. We can show this to be the case once again from one of the most important passages in Bach's *St. John Passion*, namely the aria "Est ist vollbracht." Until now the origin of its text was unknown. As the following juxtaposition of the two extracts illustrates, it clearly derives from Postel's libretto:

Bach

Es ist vollbracht!
O Trost für die gekränkten Seelen.
Die Trauernacht
Läßt mich die letzte Stunde zählen.
Der Held aus Juda siegt mit Macht
Und schließt den Kampf! Es ist vollbracht!

Postel

O großes Werk,
Im Paradies schon angefangen!
O Riesenstärk,

Die Christus läßt den Sieg erlangen!
Daß nach dem Streit in Siegespracht
Er sprechen kann: Es ist vollbracht!

Both stanzas stand at the same point in the gospel record, after the Lord's
final words on the cross (John 19:30). Taken together with the exact structural concurrence of the two texts, this is sufficient to establish Bach's
dependence on Postel. There is a further significant observation that arises
from a comparison of this movement in each Passion and the one that
immediately follows it. In Bach's commentary for solo bass, interspersed
with chorale excerpts, "Mein teurer Heiland, laß dich fragen," there is an
allusion to Christ's last words:

Mein teurer Heiland, laß dich fragen,
Da du nunmehr ans Kreuz geschlagen
Und selbst gesagt "Es ist vollbracht,"
Bin ich vom Sterben frei gemacht?

The text of this passage derives from Brockes. The curious conceptual
parallels with the preceding alto aria, however, allow us to infer that there
was more than one source for the two passages. With Postel's verse we
have a second possibility at our disposal, and in this instance Bach's attitude
towards his model is particularly instructive. Postel speaks of "Riesenstärk"
(gigantic strength) and "Siegeskraft" (victorious power). In Bach, too, there
are references to the hero and his victory, but his phraseology is Biblical
rather than secular, reminiscent of Rev. 5:6. Both passages, Bach's and
Postel's, lead up to Christ's declaration. Bach's, however, places these
words at the head of his piece and in so doing allows them to dominate
the entire text of the aria.

How Postel's words were intended to be understood may be seen from
Handel's setting, to which we now turn.[115] His gospel recitative is from
the very beginning characteristic. The key is E-flat major, and we should
not overlook this fact. At that time, Handel was living and collaborating
very closely with Mattheson, who nine years later (1713), in the second
chapter of his *Neu eröffnetes Orchester,* under the heading "Von der mu-
sicalischen Tohne Eigenschaft und Würckung in Ausdrückung der Affec-
ten" tried to characterize the different keys in a manner that unquestionably
would have held good for the 19-year-old composer. Here we read: "E-
flat major contains much that is impassioned and emotional; it eschews all
that is earnest or grave, but at the same time is, so to speak, the archenemy
of opulence."

It is enlightening to consider this description of the key with regard
to Handel's recitative. The vocal part is presented in a great, emotionally
powerful, resonant line. The very first phrase contains a repeated leap of

an octave and spans the entire range of an 11th:

Es ist＿ voll - bracht! ＿＿＿＿

The tempo is devised in note values of four different lengths. The text is repeated twice and at its second appearance ends with a leap of a ninth.

Es ist voll-bracht! ＿＿＿＿＿＿＿＿＿＿＿＿

The punctuated rhythm, an expression of royal pomp and splendor, which we heard earlier in the first phrase, completely dominates the descending line. The section draws to a close majestically, with a series of simple, affirmative figures—once again spanning a ninth—and ends with a perfect cadence in E-flat major.

Es ist＿ voll - bracht!

A hero meets his death in triumph, his final words charged with energy and the confidence of victory.

The theme is taken up in the aria. Both the key and the timbre of the soloist remain the same. Both formally and conceptually, the theme follows on from the previous passages:

Grave

O gro-ßes Werk! ＿

At the mention of "Riesenstärk" and its "Siege," however, the ceremonial, regal rhythm appears in all its majesty:

Die Chri- stus läßt den Sieg er - lan - - - - -

gen

The aria is in two parts, the first accompanied only by the basso continuo, the second bringing the entry of the strings. Now we hear as the vocal theme an exact repetition of the melody sung arioso in the preceding Biblical recitative. It is heard twice, both opening and concluding this aria section. In the process we see how the arioso theme of the gospel recitative is developed in the aria both conceptually and structurally; indeed, the first part of the aria is derived completely from it. The connection between the two sections may be shown as follows:

A. The Gospel Text: "Es ist vollbracht" .... Bass, Strings, Continuo
B. 1st Part of Aria: "O großes Werk!" .... Bass, Continuo
C. 2d Part of Aria:
    1. "Es is vollbracht"
    2. "daß nach dem Streit . . ." } .... Basso, Strings, Continuo
    · 3. "Es ist vollbracht."

The instrumental accompaniment plays an important part in the presentation of C as three sections. Indeed, it highlights the division, because in the section termed C2 only separate, free-standing chords support the vocal line, whereas in C1 and C3 the harmonies of the orchestra and basso continuo are heard continuously. Here the form of the instrumental accompaniment in sections A, C1, and C3 is clearly related, as is evident from the following comparison:

The final section brings a complete return to the arioso. In this section, the young Handel succeeded in creating a tightly knit and clearly constructed entity. The Biblical text and its expressive contemplation are woven together into a coherent whole, the one interpreting the other. Christ's final words express the "gigantic strength" of the hero.

    When we call to mind these characteristics of the Handel composition, the enormous distance between his work and the world of Bach becomes clear. At the same time, it becomes all the more necessary to perceive the affinities. Bach's aria is also in two parts, the concluding repetition of the ritornello from the first section merely rounding off the piece. Again in Bach the instrumentation in the two parts of the aria is different, the strings occurring only in the latter section. Another similarity is the way in which the main theme of the number flows from the words of Christ sung in the preceding passage. Here again the finale of the aria faithfully returns to the sequence of notes in the gospel recitative. The curious upturn in the otherwise descending line:

seems likewise to hark back to the Handel original, as do the punctuating accompanying rhythms that we meet, not only in the instrumental, but also the vocal parts:

Thus there exists, in terms of formal appearance, a close relationship between the two works. Their basic stance, however, is entirely different. Of course Bach's aria also speaks of victory, both in the music and in the libretto. In the second part, where the bar is headed *Alla breve*,[E69] we are plunged into the very midst of the fight. And what a terrible battle it is! Luther called it a "wondrous battle," because the true Victor succumbs before the eyes of the world. His sovereignty is masked in His downfall, His heavenly triumph concealed in earthly defeat. His journey on earth ends in total catastrophe as the middle section of the aria finishes tellingly on a diminished seventh chord.

True we hear the punctuated regal rhythm, but only mutedly, with not the least sense of triumph or even emotion.

The key of the aria is B minor. Even if in Bach's case we must be very cautious in our general assessment of his choice of key, we should not overlook this B minor, contrasting as it does with Handel's E-flat major. It is no coincidence that the aria "Erbarme dich" or the first "Kyrie eleison" of 1733 are in this key. Nor is it a coincidence that the last fugue of Book I of the *Wohltemperirtes Clavier* [BWV 869], to name one of the greatest of the Köthen works, should also display this strange key that seems so full of deep emotion. It is a key, however, that well matches the aria's theme. The line in which Christ's last words are sung has a dying fall; visible life is extinguished. Of the Lord it is said "Und neigte das Haupt und verschied" (And He bowed His head and gave up the ghost).

The word of the Scriptures is proclaimed and belongs to the faith. The message must then, of course, be taken up by those who would hear. Yet it is not proclaimed aggressively; it does not demand or seek to arouse belief. Both key and vocal register in Bach's aria differ from those of the previous musical setting of this part of the Scriptures. This is not a musical presentation of a religious drama; rather we find ourselves participating in a divine service that, in accordance with Luther's famous definition, takes the form of a dialog, on the one side the Word of God, on the other the believer's response.

Even as a young man, Handel was a dramatist through and through; not long after his *St. John Passion* he was to experience with *Almira* his first great operatic success. He belongs foursquare in the baroque philosophical camp, where man and the powerful reality of life on earth are glorified. Even in death on the cross at Golgotha man is portrayed as being *heroic*. With Bach it is quite different. He proclaims the incomprehensible mystery—God's victory is gained by surrendering to the forces of a godless world, through His death in our stead. Perhaps nowhere else is the dividing line that separates Bach from the very essence of that element of baroque thinking as clearly drawn as it is here. That is true, however, not only of the particular number, nor even of this particular work; it holds good for the whole of Bach's creative output. Of course, secular forms mingle with those that are religious or spiritual in content. Works, however, that were originally secularly conceived, acquire a new—one has to say their true—purpose when they enter the religious sphere.

This applies also to the grand design of the centerpiece of the *St. John Passion* referred to above (see page 133). In purely structural terms it may be derived from older, entirely secular compositions. There too Bach had used chiastic forms. Where the chiasmus is fundamental to the structure of a work, however, at whose center stands the cross of Christ, we cannot ignore the fact that in Christian symbolism the X always represents both the cross and Christ Himself and reminds us that He died on it to redeem the world. Only in this way can we understand why Bach chose precisely the third stanza of Valerius Herberger's hymn "Valet will ich dir geben" (I would bid you farewell) to stand at the end of his great chiasmus. It tells of both—the cross and the name of Christ:

In meines Herzens Grunde
Dein Nam' und Kreuz allein
Funkelt all' Zeit und Stunde.

(Deep in my heart
Your name and cross alone
Shine eternally.)

The name that brings salvation to those who hear it and the cross as the symbol of redemption combine to form the subject matter of the congregation's declaration of faith. We may pursue this line of investigation further, down to the last detail of the Passion's structure, and of this, in conclusion, I wish to quote just one more example. I have in mind the thematic relationship between the motifs of the two alto arias in the work. The phrase we hear in the second part:

has already occurred in the first, at the entrance of the solo voice:

This musical affinity between the two movements aids our understanding of their meaning when taken together: "Es ist vollbracht," "von den Stricken meiner Sünden mich zu entbinden" (It is finished [in order] to release me from the bonds of my sins). Secular form (the aria) and instrumental form (the concerto) come together as a means of religious proclamation and belief.

With that we return to the other important religious composition that Bach wrote at the end of the Köthen period, the cantata *Du wahrer Gott und Davids Sohn* ([BWV] 23). We are already familiar with the choral movement "Aller Augen warten, Herr, du allmächt'ger Gott, auf dich" in concerto form. We should not overlook the fact that the bass line of the *tutti* theme:

is derived from the melody of the Passion chorale "Christe, du Lamm Gottes," which dominates the whole cantata. Similarly, of the duet that opens the work we are able to say that it shares the characteristics of the Köthen cantatas in that here we find, once again, a movement scored for two vocal soloists. At the same time, in view of the subject matter of the text, the very fact that the piece is written for two parts acquires symbolic meaning. The explanation is that, just as in the famous *B Minor Mass* duets, "Christe eleison," "Domine Deus," or "Et in unum Dominum Jesum Christum," the vocal scoring makes a symbolic statement concerning the Lord, who is here addressed. At one and the same time, He is "wahrer Gott" (true God) and "Davids Sohn" (the Son of David), i.e., true Man. In such expressions, insofar as they resort to symbolism, Bach's method dates back to ancient church tradition, where the forms of a particular spoken language serve allegorically to bring out the religious content of a piece of music.

Chapter 17

One of the most remarkable misjudgments of historical fact occurred recently when the incorporation of secular elements in music written for the church, as happens in Bach, was held to be an indication of an especially progressive cast of mind.[116] The days are long since past when the melody of H. L. Hassler's love song "Mein Gmüt ist mir verwirret" could safely be transferred to a hymn, or to quote another example, when the confessional song "Auf meinen lieben Gott" in church hymnals could be preceded by the words "To the tune of *Venus, du und dein Kind*" without causing the slightest offense. As things have developed, we have witnessed an increasingly distinct division between "religious" and "secular" music. In this context, there exists from within Bach's very own family circle a document that has been preserved and which I quote:

> If it is indeed true that there will remain a place for moderate music in the church, especially since the late D. Dannhauer regarded it as an ornament to the divine service, a view that does not meet with the approval of all theologians, it is at the same time a well-known fact that very often the performances are excessive. One might well agree with Moses when he says: "Ye take too much upon you, ye sons of Levi" (Num. 16:7). The reason is that this music often sounds so very worldly and jolly that it is more befitting a dance floor or an opera than the divine service. The last thing, in the opinion of many pious folk, that such singing should suitably accompany is the Passion of Christ. Fifty or more years ago, it was the custom on Palm Sunday for the organ to remain silent in church, and there was no music making at all on that day because it signified the beginning of Holy Week. Now, however, with the story of the Passion, which hitherto was sung so finely *de simplici et plano*, in a straightforward, reverent manner, they have even begun to set the occasion to music in the most elaborate artistic fashion, using many different kinds of instruments. From time to time they incorporate a verse from a Passion hymn and the whole congregation joins in the singing, after which the instruments are again heard in company. When this Passion music was performed for the first time in a distinguished city, by 12 violins, numerous oboes, bassoons, and other instruments, many were amazed and did not know what to make of it. On another occasion in a court chapel, many high ministers and noble ladies were together assembled and were singing the first Passion hymn from their books in a

spirit of great devotion. When the theatrical music struck up, all these persons were greatly astonished, looked at each other and said, "What shall become of this?" An elderly dowager warned, "Take heed, my children! It is like being at a comic opera." All were most heartily displeased and raised just complaint. There are, it must be conceded, certain spirits who find pleasure in such idle matters, especially when they are of a sanguine temperament and inclined towards sensuality. Such people stoutly defend these great musical performances in church and regard those who think otherwise as capricious or miserable souls, or as facetious, as if they alone possessed the wisdom of Solomon and that the rest lacked understanding. Oh, how good it would be for the Christian church if we were to preserve that early devotional simplicity in the sermons, prayers, and hymns that make up our divine service. If some of those early Christians were to rise again and join our congregations, only to hear an organ thundering out its music, together with so many other instruments, I do not believe that they would recognize us as Christians and their own successors.

The above passage, which is occasionally referred to but rarely quoted *in extenso*, has not, as far as I can ascertain, been studied in depth. It originates from Christian Gerber's *Geschichte der Kirchen-Ceremonien in Sachsen* (Dresden and Leipzig, 1732). It has been directly associated with the *St. Matthew Passion*, which was performed three years before Gerber's book appeared,[E70] and has been used to show the extent of the resistance and the lack of appreciation that the Thomas Kantor had to face. There are considerable objections to this view. Gerber makes no mention of a specific place, referring only to "a distinguished city." This would more likely point not to Leipzig, which was a progressive commercial center and university town, but to Dresden, the official residence of the elector and king, seat of the authorities and social focus of the nobility. The phrase "many high ministers" likewise clearly suggests a seat of government, i.e., Dresden. The "elderly dowager" was amazed when the elaborated Passion was heard there "for the first time." In Leipzig, however, this had been performed in the Thomaskirche as early as 1721 by Bach's predecessor, Johann Kuhnau. Bach himself had presented his *St. John Passion* [*in both 1724 and 1725*].[E71] In other words, the passage is being strained to the limit if we try to relate the circumstances it describes to Leipzig in the year 1729 and to a particular performance of Bach's *St. Matthew Passion*.[117]

Beyond these circumstantial details, however, the criticism that Gerber was making has a more general significance. Spitta made reference to this author in the context of the attacks on the apparent "secularization" of church music resulting from the introduction of the Neumeister cantata form.[118] He described Gerber as a "serious-minded" man. More to the point is the fact that Gerber was regarded by his contemporaries as a Pietist, and undoubtedly correctly. [His biographer] F. Blankmeister describes him as a "country clergyman of the Spener school."[119] This explains the reference to "the late D. Dannhauer" that occurs at the beginning of the passage. Johann Konrad Dannhauer (1603–66), professor of theology, minister, preacher, and head of the church convention in Strasbourg, who had among other things taken part as dogmatician against the syncretism of the Calixt school, had been Spener's teacher and had been called "beatus Dannhawerus" and "pater meus in Christo" by him.[120] To Spener's pupils it must have been painful to hear from a man for whom their teacher had such high respect views on the provision of music in the divine service with which they as Pietists (particularly those of the second generation) no longer agreed. Gerber himself made that very point when he wrote that Dannhauer's view "does not meet with the approval of all theologians." Here we have the key to an understanding of the whole of Gerber's criticism. His words express the Pietist ideal, the yearning for a return to simple devoutness and the unceremonious forms of divine service practiced by the first Christians. The opposite view, however, the orthodox view, leans on the Biblical reference to the music in Solomon's temple, richly endowed with instruments as it was.

Thus, if Gerber's critical remarks really do refer to Bach's Passions, which I consider out of the question, the Thomas Kantor would have faced the same kind of opposition he had encountered earlier in his year of office at Mühlhausen. At that time, he had chosen to avoid the controversy between the new Pietist movement and the orthodox church by moving to Weimar, the home of traditional Lutheranism. In that city it was by no means regarded as secularization to introduce the modern cantata form as fostered in the verses of men such as Erdmann Neumeister or Salomo Franck; it is no coincidence that both of these were defenders of the orthodox cause. Bach was following their course, i.e., the orthodox course, when in both his church cantatas and the Passions he made use of forms of the recitative and *Da Capo* aria taken from the modern secular sphere. He was convinced that to do so was in no way a question of secularization; on the contrary, when he assumed the position of Thomas Kantor, he explicitly undertook to avoid any such tendency. In the formal document of May 5, 1723, accepting the post, he signed the following explicit statement:

Whereas the worshipful council of this town of Leipzig has appointed me to observe the conditions set out below . . . (7) In the maintenance of good order in those churches, to arrange the music so that it does not last too long and to write it in such a way as to avoid all semblance of opera, in order that the congregation may be more encouraged to true religious devotion, . . . I do hereby pledge to carry out faithfully the above conditions, under pain of forfeiture of my post.

It would be tantamount to accusing Bach of deliberate duplicity to draw any conclusion from the above other than that the composer was utterly convinced that his music entailed no form of secularization in the spirit of the objections raised by the Pietists. On the other hand, we cannot overlook the fact that two months before Bach had signed this document, on Good Friday (March 26) 1723 his *Passio secundum Evangelistam Johannem* had been performed at St. Thomas.[E72] When I compared Bach's *St. John Passion* with that of the young Handel earlier, I showed how he had dissociated himself from the dramatic tendencies of the baroque style of religious music. It is, however, only in this particular context that the implications of Bach's behavior at that time become patently clear.

In this connection must be mentioned the fact that there is not a single known instance during his 27 years in office in Leipzig of the consistory or the clergy objecting to any form of secularization in the Kantor's sacred composition. On the contrary, we can be fairly certain that the chief pastor of the Thomaskirche, Christian Weiß, had been involved in the drafts of the texts of Bach's cantatas, including the recitatives and the arias,[121] in the same way as we have proof that the composer's texts had received the express approval of the consistory.[122] In the religious disputes of the day, the Leipzig theologians were unequivocally on the side of orthodoxy. The orthodox church fostered richly elaborated *Figuralmusik* as part of the divine service and had no objection to its being interspersed with artistic forms deriving from music outside the church.

Thus, the question that now finally concerns us, namely the relationship between the "worldly" or "secular" in Bach and the "spiritual" or "religious" elements may be answered only in terms of the composer's Lutheranism. In the final analysis, it is a theological issue, and we must start from the Lutheran understanding of "the world." An open attitude towards the world is one of the most distinctive characteristics of Luther the Reformer himself, of the Reformation he initiated, and of its form of divine service. This is only possible because the statements about the world contained in the first article of faith are nowhere distinct from the religious stance of the second and third articles. The *justificatio impii* that the cross holds is at the very center of all things. The death and resurrection of Christ are the safeguard and guarantee of all salvation. The same Christ, however, whose coming the Christian world awaits, is already now, albeit very obscurely, Lord of the world. No area is removed from His rule, just as conversely there are no parts of the earth that do not need His justifying grace. If this is in both aspects taken seriously, any attempt to render that which is worldly absolute, even less any religious glorification of the secular, is out of the question. On the other hand, in the so-called "religious" or church sphere, there can be no dimension that is not dependent on the forgiveness of sins. The church and the world thus confront the Middle Ages and secularism in an entirely different relationship one to the other. Then, there was no glorification of the world. The Lutheran knew that he was not "of the world," that he nevertheless lived in it and could never be absolved from his ties with it. Despite this peculiarly close connection, however, there remains an essential difference between the two dimensions "world" and "church." They are not simply two sides of the same coin. The irreversibility of the relationship between the two spheres makes this quite clear. In the person of Jesus Christ, God has entered our realm, the world of man, but the reverse can never occur. Through His mercy God can become man; a deification of man, however, is not possible. Bach's view of the world may be grasped only from this basic tenet of Lutheranism. The world remains the world; indeed only then may it be fully comprehended in its essential worldliness and taken seriously; but as such it is part of God's scheme of salvation.

It is on this foundation that Bach bases his understanding of the "secular" in his music. We meet it in perhaps its most vivid depiction in the setting of the *Symbolum Nicenum* [BWV 232^{III}], one of his greatest religious works, whose structure may be outlined as follows:

```
 ┌ Chorus: "Credo in unum Deum"
 └ Chorus: "Patrem omnipotentem"
 ┌--- Solo: "Et in unum Dominum"
 │    Chorus: "Incarnatus"
 │    Chorus: "Crucifixus"
 │    Chorus: "Resurrexit"
 └--- Solo: "Et in Spiritum Sanctum"
 ┌ Chorus: "Confiteor unum baptisma"
 └ Chorus: "Expecto resurrectionem."
```

The chiastic, cyclical structure in the sequence of movements here is an unmistakable successor to the central core arrangement, which developed in Köthen in the second part of the *St. John Passion*.[E73] Taken from a purely artistic point of view, the Credo composition of 1733 represents a simplification, a monumentalization of the architecture of the Passion composed a decade earlier. At the same time, however, the essential element, the symbolic content, is far more clearly illustrated; it is in keeping with the Lutheran creed, which places Christ at its very center. If we wanted to identify the exact—one might also say—the mathematical center of the

Bach setting of the Credo, we should find that it is formed by the word "Crucifixus." The chiastic, i.e. cruciform, structure of the whole underlines this central message. Christ crucified is the center and salvation of the whole world.

What is true here of this religious composition applies *mutatis mutandis* to the whole of Bach's work. The further addition of the letters J. J. (*Jesu juva*) above scores not intended for church use is no empty formula. The composer was acting here in accordance with the words of the apostle: "Whatsoever ye do in word or deed, do all in the name of the Lord Jesus" (Col. 3:17). It is only against such a background that we may in Bach's case as a true Lutheran come to understand his "secular" forms and his transference of nonreligious passages to sacred music. Once again the irreversibility of the relationship between secular and religious music is ultimately to be interpreted theologically. When Bach occasionally refashions works composed for nonreligious purposes into church pieces but never reuses religious compositions outside the divine service, this too should be seen as an expression of the irreversibility of the world/church relationship characteristic of the teachings of Lutheranism.[E74]

If we inquire about the "secular" Bach's relationship to the "religious" Bach, we are in effect asking about Bach the Lutheran. The point is that the so-called "secular" Bach is in reality the whole man. All investigations into the composer's theological position only become fully meaningful through this realization. Not only does our understanding of the Thomas Kantor in terms of the history of thought depend on the answers to these questions, but also our conclusions as to the very legitimacy of his music as church music. If the relevant research were to reveal that Johann Sebastian was decisively influenced by Pietism, then the question of the legitimacy of his religious works would scarcely be relevant. It is also true that in Bach's case certain influences deriving from Pietism are indisputable. Yet these are no more pronounced in Bach than they are in Neumeister and Franck, who in this connection represent the two most important librettists used by the composer. In none of these instances are Pietist influences of decisive importance in any work as a whole. No less significant are all the studies that deal with Bach's relationship to the Age of the Enlightenment and rationalism. Most recently Walter Blankenburg has drawn our attention to this issue.[123] In order to prove Bach's links with the thought of the Enlightenment, Blankenburg points to features of his music that he believes bring the composer closely in line to the thought of Leibniz. Discussion of this subject has scarcely got off the ground yet. What I find particularly arguable here is the very close identification of Leibnizian thought with that of the Enlightenment as such. Nevertheless, we have no need to be too sophisticated in trying to answer the question we have posed. The key to the understanding of the Enlightenment and rationalism, in precise contrast to Lutheranism, is the increasingly marked autonomy of the first article of faith in comparison with the second. Paul Gerhardt, the thoroughgoing Lutheran, sings:

Geh aus, mein Herz, und suche Freud

(Go out, my heart, and seek joy)

or:

Die güldne Sonne
Voll Freu und Wonne
Bringt unsern Grenzen
Mit ihrem Glänzen
Ein herzerquickendes liebliches Licht.

(The golden sun
Full of joy and rapture
Brings to our confines
With its brilliance
A lovely heart-warming light).

This means that the poet is well aware of the splendors of creation, but none of his songs, not even those in which the name of Jesus is not mentioned at all, may be dissociated from the statement:

Ist Gott für mich, so trete
Gleich alles wider mich.

(If God is for me,
Then let everything straightway stand against me).

In other words, in none of his songs may the context be divorced from Lutheranism's central tenet, the belief in justification through faith alone. Contrast this with the verse of the rationalist Gellert (who for a short time collaborated with Bach in Leipzig):

Wie groß ist des Allmächtgen Güte.

(How great is the goodness of Almighty God).

The very mention of "Almighty God" enables us to appreciate the gulf between Gellert's view and that of the older Lutheranism. The divide becomes truly apparent, however, when we perceive how the world of the first article of faith is treated relatively independently of that of the second. When we then ask in which of the two camps Bach belongs, there can be no doubt as to the answer. He belongs firmly on the side of Lutheranism, not rationalism, nor even the Enlightenment. He lives in a world inwardly closed, as yet undivided into spiritual and secular spheres, a world that is

162

nourished by the very essence of the Lutheran Reformation belief.

This examination of the composer's Köthen years has brought me face to face with the question of the "secular" Bach with particular urgency. It is to be hoped that we have pointed the way towards a proper resolution of the question. Insofar as there is a problem that remains unresolved, it should be addressed not to Bach but to ourselves, to the inhabitants of the 20th century. The contemporary significance of the issue that has concerned us will then become clear. The complete unity of existence that for Bach was utterly self-evident no longer exists for modern man. As he confronts reality he finds himself permanently faced by a double danger. Either man seeks to escape from the alleged narrowness of the church into an illusory freedom where inevitably worldliness is rendered absolute and glorious. Or he, as a "devout person," believes that he can withdraw from the world and all its horrors by retreating, as he fondly imagines, into the enclosed domain of "the religious life," if only for the duration of a divine service or some "spiritual" musical performance. Profounder thinkers have long since recognized that both are impossible. Johann Sebastian Bach, the very Bach whom our preoccupation with his life at Köthen has taught us to know so well, provides the great alternative to the inwardly torn nature of modern existence. Our age will arrive at a truer understanding of his work the more it seeks to find the very roots of his creativity and his existence. This study has shown with the utmost clarity that in purely historical terms there remains much to be done. From what I have written, however, it is equally undeniable that these historical insights may become our possession only as a result of thorough theological thought, and that if there is to be a really new and deeper understanding of Bach, it must stem from a spiritual renewal that starts within ourselves.

Chapter 18

Supplementary Material

(Editorial)

The imperial principality of Anhalt had been founded in 1218 when King Friedrich of Germany, soon to become Emperor Friedrich II, conferred on Prince Heinrich *Pinguis*, a son of the Saxon elector Bernhard I, an area of land that had previously been partly in Saxony and partly in Brandenburg, giving him its title as Prince of Anhalt.

The principality was twice partitioned (reapportioned among brothers by negotiation)—in 1252 and 1586. From 1586 to the period of Bach's Köthen activities, the princes of Anhalt-Köthen were:

1586–1650   *Ludwig I* (June 17, 1579—June 7, 1650)

1650–1665   *Wilhelm Ludwig I* (Aug. 3, 1633—April 13, 1665)
            (Wilhelm Ludwig, who was married for less than
            two years before his death, left no direct heir;
            Köthen now passed to another branch of the An-
            halt family, the princes of Anhalt-Plötzgau.)

1665–1669   *Leberecht I* (April 8, 1622—Nov. 7, 1669)
            (He also died without issue, so that the Principality
            of Anhalt-Köthen-Plötzgau passed to his only sur-
            viving brother.)

1669–1670   *Emanuel I* (Oct. 6, 1631—Nov. 8, 1670)
            (There was now a short intermission, pending the
            birth of Emanuel's posthumously born [and only]
            heir.)

1671–1704	*Emanuel Leberecht I* (May 20, 1671—May 30, 1704) (However, since Emanuel Leberecht only came of age in 1692, his own rule was shorter than that of the regents who acted for him until then.)
1704–1728	*Leopold I* (Nov. 29, 1694, Old Style—Nov. 19, 1728, New Style) (Leopold also succeeded nominally long before he did effectively; he came of age on Dec. 10, 1715. He also left no male issue, so that the principality passed to his brother.)
1728–1755	*August Ludwig I* (June 9, 1697, Old Style—Aug. 6,1755, New Style)

The princely house of Anhalt-Köthen continued until 1847— 130 years after J. S. Bach's appointment. There had first been a resident prince in the time of Albrecht I (who ruled 1310—16), the second ruler after the first partition.

Anhalt was, throughout its history, quite an extensive area, but its dominions included no really large town; the principality was divided into quite small *Kreise* (districts identifiable to the imperial administration), each of which had its titular prince or court; there was no effective capital and for much of the time no senior line of princes. This situation gave each prince some degree of autonomy. Some distinguished themselves as academics and clerics, like Georg III of Plötzgau (June 14, 1507—Oct. 17, 1552), whom an early 18th-century English historian neatly described as "a learned Prince, and a great advancer of Luther's Reformation, of which he was a Minister, and reckoned amongst the Reformers; was Provost of the Cathedral of Magdeburg, and preached before the Emperor Charles V."[E75] Others served as soldiers; in Bach's time, the ruling prince of Anhalt-Dessau, confusingly another Leopold I, was "General of the King of Prussia's Forces, and Colonel of a Regiment of Foot."[E76] Earlier Leopold of Köthen's great-uncle and predecessor, Leberecht I (born 1622), had served in both the Swedish and the Venetian armies. However, Anhalt was not especially prosperous economically, and its princes had always been too disparate in intention, as well as too complacent in international outlook, to hold much political sway. They found themselves—as their subjects generally did—in a position that was a part of an old, established order; until serious injustice or burdening taxation afflicted the inhabitants of the small German states, they would feel little cause to question it, let alone to challenge it.

Leopold I of Anhalt-Köthen deserves careful attention as an example of this kind of despot. We know that he had a supervised upbringing centered in Köthen and Berlin, where he attended the academy and that he had followed this by pursuing a short Italian tour—a clear indication that the military life was not for him. We have been led to suppose that his mother, Gisela Agnes, princess *emerita* and imperial countess of Nienburg, was responsible for this prudent, if conventional, upbringing, but we know also that she had not converted him from Calvinism to Lutheranism (possibly she had not tried) and that, despite having a delightful town house of her own in Köthen, she actually died in Nienburg in 1740.

Great significance has been attached to Bach's reference to Leopold I in his letter to Georg Erdmann of Oct. 28, 1730: "Daselbst hatte einen gnädigen und *Music* so wohl liebenden als kennenden Fürsten; bey welchem auch vermeinete meine Lebenszeit zu beschliessen" (The place had a prince who was gracious, and in *music* as enthusiastic as he was knowledgeable; I expected, indeed, to end my days in his service). However, the letter continues in a spirit of considered criticism. Leopold is described ironically as a "Serenissimus" whose marriage had rendered his attitude to music "etwas laulicht" (somewhat lukewarm), only implying that the princess herself, "apparently an *amusa*," was somewhat directly responsible for this. The usual interpretation has been that the prince was somewhat easily influenced, both by his own inclination towards music and by his first wife, who apparently was uninterested in matters of taste.

This may well not have been the case. Leopold, his father, and his mother all give an impression of having been forceful people who did not look readily to others to decide on their priorities. The apparent religious tolerance exercised by Emanuel Leberecht was a compromise between the entrenched positions instilled into the outlook of both himself and his consort by their strongly polarized educations. Leopold's continuation of this tolerance did not mean that his subjects were at peace with one another, however much they may have been able to be at peace with their own consciences; there was an openly hostile attitude between the clergy of the Jakobikirche and the Agnuskirche that might on occasion lead to barely disguised conflict between those at court, even including Gisela Agnes and the princes themselves.[E77] When Bach's deputy, Josef Spiess, found himself in financial difficulties and was unable to pay his bills, Leopold pronounced that, in the future, Spiess's salary should be paid directly to his wife—a judgment that was probably just but was also calculated to embarrass and to humiliate; yet earlier in the same year, Leopold had made a gift to him of 20 Thalers towards the purchase of a jerkin of "drap d'or" as a reward for supervising the remaining portion of the Kapelle while he and six of his musicians had been visiting Karlsbad.[E78]

As far as matters artistic and cultural were concerned, there is not much evidence of dedicated interest other than music, but that which there is must be considered surprising if we compare Leopold to his Anhalt cousins; Henrietta Friderica of Anhalt-Bernburg was certainly not Anhalt's only *amusa*. Leopold and his brother laid the foundations of quite an impressive library that included philosophically and intellectually challenging material.[E79] In July 1718, a theatrical troupe under Johann Ferdinand Becker visited the palace, acting on a specially constructed stage in the large conservatory in the palace garden; the same facility was used early in 1719 when a group presenting (Italian or French?) comedies also visited Köthen. The first visit resulted in a payment to Becker of 170 Thalers—nearly one half of Bach's annual wage of 400 Thalers.[E80] In 1720, Leopold redecorated the residential portions of his palace—and very probably refurnished the royal suite of rooms in the south wing (the "Ludwigsbau") in preparation for the arrival of his first princess—but there were no major alterations to the palace buildings during his reign—nor, indeed, during some 40 years on either side of it.[E81]

One reason for this was undoubtedly his generosity towards music; he attracted an excellent core of good musicians to Köthen and saw to it that they were supplied with adequate support materially (new instruments were bought; music was efficiently copied and bound) and artistically through the regular importing of stimulating external musicians to play with—and possibly sometimes to—them. Recent research in the Köthen archives has identified a number of hitherto unknown participants in the music making of Leopold's court.[E82] Some certainly worked with Bach; others may have done so.

By the time that Bach arrived in Köthen in December 1717, the total musical complement of the Kapelle was around 16, excluding the Kapellmeister:

1. SPIESS, Josef (?–1730, Köthen). Premier Kammer Musikus and first violinist. He was active in Köthen from 1714 until his death; from 1710 to 1713 he had been Kammer Musikus

and violinist at the court of Prince Friedrich Wilhelm of Prussia, who dissolved the Kapelle on his accession as Friedrich Wilhelm I (on Feb. 25, 1713).

2. MARCUS (MARX), Martin Friedrich (?–?). Kammer Musikus and second violinist/violist. He was active in Köthen from 1714 until June 20, 1722, when he was succeeded by Christian Ernst Rolle (no. 20 below). Markus had served at the Prussian court with Spiess; he probably left because he felt that his prospects in Köthen were not good, owing to the development of Emanuel Heinrich Gottlieb Freytag and the prevailing attitude toward music at court after Leopold's first marriage.

3. FREYTAG, Emanuel Heinrich Gottlieb (1698–1779, place of birth unknown, died Köthen March 28). Kammer Musikus from late April 1721 and violinist from Oct. 17, 1716. Son of Johann Freytag (no. 15 below). On Bach's recommendation, he was sent to Berlin between mid-1720 (date not specified) and the end of April 1721 to complete his musical training. By the time of the disbanding of the Kapelle at Köthen in 1754, Emanuel Freytag was its acting Kapellmeister.

4. ABEL, Christian Ferdinand (1682–1761, born Hannover, died Köthen April 3). Kammer Musikus and gambist. He was in the musical military service of Charles XII of Sweden before his appointment at Köthen in 1714. A Lutheran, he retained contact with Bach after 1723, probably partly through his own distinguished son Karl Friedrich (1723–87). Abel's military background and his specialty of playing the viola da gamba (on which instrument he instructed the prince) probably indicate abilities of a professional level on other string and possibly wind or keyboard instruments.

5. LINIGKE, Christian Bernhard (1673–1750?, place of birth unknown, buried Köthen Jan. 3, 1751). Kammer Musikus and violoncellist. Like Abel, he was born into a musical family, in his case from the Brandenburg area. He played at the Berlin court alongside Spiess, Marcus, and others, but followed them to Köthen later; his appointment is first recorded in March 1716. He remained in Köthen until his death. He was a practicing Lutheran and attended the Agnuskirche alongside the Bach family.

6. FREYTAG, Johann Heinrich (?–1720, died in Köthen on Aug. 1). Kammer Musikus and flutist. Son of Johann Freytag (no.

15 below). Johann Heinrich Freytag joined the Kapelle in 1716.

7. WÜRDIG, Johann Gottlieb (?–1728, buried in Köthen on Sept. 19). Kammer Musikus and recorder player (also a player of other instruments?). Würdig trained and/or started his musical life as a Stadtpfeiffer, which profession he combined from 1714 with that of participating in the Köthen Hofkapelle as a flutist; on Jan. 2, 1717, he succeeded Johann Georg Bahn as senior town musician but was almost immediately incorporated into the Kapelle as a Kammer Musikus. Although a Calvinist, Würdig was paid to play in the Agnuskirche around 1722.

8. ROSE, Johann Ludwig (?–post-1754, place of birth and death unknown). Kammer Musikus and oboist. Rose may, with Torlée, have had French, possibly Huguenot émigré, origins. He played in Friedrich Wilhelm's Kapelle until its dissolution in 1713 and joined the Köthen Kapelle in 1714. He settled in Köthen, attending the Lutheran church; he probably stayed in Köthen after the dissolving of the Kapelle in 1753 and died there. He instructed Leopold's pages in fencing.

9. TORLÉE, Johann Christoph (?–?). Kammer Musikus and bassoonist. Torlée, like Rose, may have had French antecedents. Also like Rose, Torlée had belonged to Friedrich Wilhelm's Berlin ensemble until 1713 and had been listed as a Köthen Kammer Musikus from 1714. In 1716 he provided lodgings for Abel (no. 4 above), who was already married and had two daughters, which implies that he may have had independent resources. He was probably of the Lutheran persuasion.

10. KREYSER, Johann Christian (?–post-1754; between 1713 and 1754 at the minimum resident in Köthen). Copyist and chapel organist (i.e., keyboard player). Since Kreyser relinquished some of his duties early in December 1717, yet was once again Hoforganist at the dissolving of the Kapelle in 1754, we cannot be sure that he worked with Bach at all; however, his mention as a "Musicus" in Stricker's 1714 ensemble implies that he played in the Kapelle in some capacity, besides attending to his two salaried duties. Since he was appointed to the post of chapel organist in Leopold's and subsequently August Ludwig's households, he was almost certainly a Calvinist.

11. GÖBEL, Johann Bernhard (?–?, in Köthen before 1717 and

until at least 1737). Copyist. He was a minor official of the Jakobikirche before his appointment early in December 1717. He had relinquished his post by June 1718. He was, in turn, succeeded by Johann Bernhard Bach. Göbel served for a considerable time as "vierter Schulcollege" in the Calvinist school attached to the Köthen Jakobikirche; there is no record of his having any instrumental ability.

12. SCHREIBER, Johann Ludwig (?–1723, died in Köthen on March 28). Trumpeter. His origins are unknown, and it is possible that he developed his skill from military experience. According to the late Ernst König (*BJ* 1979, p. 162), Schreiber was already installed in his post when Krahl (no. 13 below) was appointed. We have no certain knowledge as to which of these two trumpeters (if either) was the inspiration for Bach's demanding part in Brandenburg Concerto No. 2 (BWV 1047). Schreiber was of the Calvinist persuasion; he was buried on March 31, 1723.

13. KRAHL, Johann Christoph (?–1745, died in Köthen). Trumpeter. Krahl's appointment to the Köthen ensemble appears to have started in 1714, probably after Schreiber's. Their salaries were equal. Krahl's wife was a Lutheran; she sat next to Anna Magdalena in the Agnuskirche (we should not forget that Magdalena's father was a trumpeter also). However, in Köthen there was no such designation as Kammer Trompeter or Hoftrompeter (as there was in Weissenfels at the same period), and the salaries paid to both Schreiber and Krahl were comparatively low. The precise date of Krahl's death has not been discovered.

14. UNGER, Anton (?–post-1725). Timpanist. Unger's origins are necessarily obscure because his surname is common. He was both court timpanist and the tenant-innkeeper of Köthen's *Grosser Gasthof*, an important hotel in the town square where the town council banqueted and distinguished visitors to the town—including temporarily engaged musicians—were boarded.

15. FREYTAG, Johann (?–ca. 1742). Hofmusikus and ripienist. Father of Johann Heinrich and Emanuel Heinrich Gottlieb (nos. 6 and 3 above). He was presumably a string player who participated only in the larger works performed by the Kapelle.

16. HARBORDT, Wilhelm Andreas (?–?). Hofmusikus and ripien-

ist. He was granted formal dismissal on Jan. 19, 1718, which has led some writers to conclude that he and Bach did not favorably impress one another, but lack of information must render this conclusion speculative; similar arguments apply to the short tenancy of Johann Bernhard Göbel's post as copyist (no. 11 above).

17. WEBER, Adam Ludwig (?–?). Stadtpfeiffer and ripienist. His participation in the Kapelle was recorded in 1716, which indicates that he, like Würdig, would have been available to Bach; he was paid more than either Harbordt or Johann Freytag between July 1717 and June 1718.

This list does not include any singers, yet Bach's predecessor, August Reinhard Stricker, had composed a large number of vocal works, and later the Monjou sisters, possibly succeeded by the Wilken (Wülcken) sisters, were engaged to sing at court, presumably with the Kapelle.

Further resident musicians attached to the Köthen household or available to the Kapelle between 1718 and 1729 included the following:

18. BACH, Johann Bernhard (1700–43; born Ohrdruf Nov. 24, died Ohrdruf June 12). Copyist, keyboard player, violinist. He served an unofficial apprenticeship with his uncle Johann Sebastian in Weimar and at Köthen, living with the family just as the young Sebastian had with his own father. His official task as copyist only lasted a few months (from June to, at the latest, December 1718), but he was in Köthen and ready at hand to assist Bach between December 1717 and March 1719. Apprentices, who were not usually paid for work but were supposed to be supported by their masters, may well have augmented the Hofkapelle here as elsewhere.

19. GOTTSCHALK, Emanuel Leberecht (?–1727, died in Köthen on Sept. 1). Until 1714 organist of the Agnuskirche. Copyist and Kammer Musikus (from 1719). Gottschalk was also one of Prince Leopold's personal servants from 1714; in this capacity, he was sent with Bach to bring the large harpsichord from Berlin in March 1719.

20. ROLLE, Christian Ernst (?–1739, born in Halle, died in Neubrandenburg). Organist from 1714 and probably assisted in the Kapelle before 1722. He left Köthen in 1728 for an ap-

pointment as organist in Neubrandenburg. He probably played the viola also.

21. VETTER, Carl Friedrich (1688–?, born in Leipzig on Feb. 23, last reported in Blankenburg/Harz in 1727). Kammer Musikus. Copyist and possibly singer from August 1719 until the summer of 1720. We cannot identify his instrumental specialty.

22. FISCHER, Johann Valentin (?–?). Kammer Musikus and violinist/violist briefly employed by Leopold in 1719.

23. APITZ, Johann Levin (?–?). Oboist. Pupil of Johann Ludwig Rose ca. 1720.

24. ROSE junior (?–?). Oboist. He was paid to play before the prince on Oct. 18, 1724, as one of a series of "visiting" oboists (see author's note 30); it seems likely that these oboists were hoping to become engaged by the Köthen Kapelle, so he may well have been available earlier on an occasional honorary basis alongside his father.

25. SCHULTZE, Johann Caspar (?–1750, born at Langensalza, buried in Köthen on Jan. 3, 1751). Kantor of the Agnuskirche from 1717. The extent of Schultze's instrumental ability—as well as his availability and acceptability to the princely court—remains unknown. However, it is quite likely that he did collaborate with Bach, especially in church music for the Agnuskirche.

In addition to the listed musicians—some of whom may not have associated with Bach to any great extent, but others of whom certainly did—there were probably a few others of whom we are not presently aware. The little palace in Köthen was quite small—especially in comparison to the solid, heavier style of building cultivated in Weissenfels, Gotha, and Zerbst; even the Weimar Augustusburg was larger. One result of this was that in Köthen a number of those who served in the palace lived outside it in the town; such soldiers, craftsmen, and servants were quite often specialists, although some (like the oboist Rose, who instructed the pages in fencing as another of his duties) may have fulfilled more than one function. However, unlike Weimar and Weissenfels, this apparently meant that there were few musicians who doubled as lackeys, cooks, secretaries or coachmen. While at Weissenfels we must search through the palace accounts carefully to identify hidden musicians, and at Weimar the skilled oboist, violinist, and cellist

Gregor Eylenstein remained unidentified in modern times because at court his importance as a secretary was regarded as higher than his significance as a musician, in Köthen musicians—at least the instrumentalists—are probably not often hidden behind other titles.

Where this may have happened is with regard to singers—in particular female ones. We know that Monjou, the father of the two singing daughters first mentioned in print by Mattheson, was Master of the Pages in Köthen and that his daughters returned to Berlin after singing before the queen of Prussia, Sophia Dorothea, in 1722. Probably they were servants of the prince or of his first wife in addition. The register of communicants of the Agnuskirche makes it clear that the Wilken family was likewise settled in Köthen for a time; the first mention (probably referring to Anna Magdalena) is of a "Mar. Magd. Wilken" who took Communion on Trinity, June 15, 1721; the last mention of the family is of "Susanna Maria Wilkin" on Trinity 2, June 14, 1722 (this latter date excludes Anna Magdalena, since she had by now married Bach and obviously would stay in Köthen; she, of course, was paid a distinct salary). Between mid-June 1721 and mid-June 1722, the following members of the Wilken family are recorded as having taken Communion:

Sus. Marg. Wilkin (Susanna Maria?)	twice (?)
Dor. Wilken	
Johann Andr. Wilke	twice
Cathar./Cathar. Mar. Wilken	twice
Judica Cath. Elis. Wilkin	

Even allowing for some erracticism regarding the exact names of short-term residents, these records clearly indicate the presence of at least Anna Magdalena's father and two sisters or other relations. The dates are well spaced; no two members of the family are reported to have taken Communion on the same day.

It is recorded that the musicians who were paid to participate in the funeral music of Leopold I on March 23 and 24, 1729, included Bach himself, his wife, his son (presumably Wilhelm Friedemann, now aged 18), and musicians from "Halle, Merseburg, Zerbst, Dessau, and Güsten." It seems probable that those from Merseburg and Halle were distinguished enough to warrant invitation, and since Christian Friedrich Linigke was still a member of the Köthen Hofkapelle, it seems quite likely that his supposed relation, "Konzertmeister Lienigke aus Merseburg" (see author's note 28), was in attendance. It also seems that the usual practice was for male singers to be imported from Halle—the nearest large town with a strong choral tradition. The musicians from Anhalt-Zerbst (where Johann Friedrich Fasch had been Kapellmeister from 1722), Anhalt-Dessau, and Güsten (a small town in the eastern part of the *Köthnisch Ambt Warmsdorf*) were very probably sent out of respectful remembrance by Leopold's fellow rulers and subordinates; we do not know who these musicians were nor whether Köthen musicians had been sent to participate in memorial services for Prince Victor Amadeus of Anhalt-Bernburg (d. Feb. 14, 1718) or his heir (and Leopold's first father-in-law), Prince Karl Friedrich (d. April 21, 1721).

In *Bach: eine Bildbiographie,* first published in 1960,[E83] Werner Neumann quotes Johann Mattheson as follows:

> The Kapellmeister of Köthen is a learned court official and a composer of the highest order. He is responsible for supervising, arranging, and composing sacred as well as secular music at the court of an emperor, a king, or a noble prince and for the direction of its performance to the glory of God, the pleasure of his master, and the benefit of the entire court. At times he has between 50 and 100 musicians at his command.[E84]

Neumann continues: "So grand an establishment was well beyond the means of the miniature court of Anhalt-Köthen. The young prince stretched his budget to the limit when he increased the orchestra to 18 players."[E85] However, opinionated though Johann Mattheson may seem to have been concerning musical theories and judgments, we do him no justice if we misinterpret his comments. He nowhere states that the musical resources of the Köthen Kapelle were ordinarily so strong. Neumann seems to have missed the point.

Mattheson must have meant that in the event of a visit to Anhalt by the emperor, the king of either Prussia or Poland (the latter being by rights Anhalt's ruler as elector of Saxony), or other princes or dukes, it fell to the lot of the most distinguished local Kapellmeister to furnish any music required for the occasion; this would have been Bach's responsibility between 1717 and 1729, except that from 1722 the Kapellmeister of Anhalt-Zerbst was Johann Friedrich Fasch, who was less distinguished than Bach but more readily available after May 1723. In the event of a ceremonial visit to the minor principality of Anhalt-Köthen (which did not, apparently, occur), Bach would certainly have been expected to assemble an impressive musical ensemble from the area, train it, and provide it with music appropriate to such an occasion. In practice, the military preoccupations of the contemporary prince of Anhalt-Dessau (Leopold I of Dessau, "der alte Dessauer," field marshall of Prussia) and the considerable age of the contemporary princes of Anhalt-Zerbst and Anhalt-Bernburg[E86] would not have fostered a strong tradition of music making elsewhere in Anhalt during Bach's Köthen service. It is possible, however, that Mattheson's comment concerning the maximum resources that the Köthen Kapellmeister might direct was based on reports of a specific occasion that did involve Bach, Leopold of Köthen, members of the Weissenfels Hofkapelle, and musicians from Leipzig. This was the homage cantata *Entfernet euch, ihr heitern Sterne!* [BWV Anh. 9], performed on May 12, 1727, before Elector-King Augustus "the Strong"; this cantata, in which the stars of heaven (representing the princes and dukes of Greater Saxony, the governor of Leipzig, and other musical patrons) bow in homage to the king of the heavens (Augustus), celebrated the birthday of the king during his visit to Leipzig. The music is lost, although some of it may be reconstructible. However, an account of the performance published in 1728 stated that there were more than 40 musicians involved in a torchlit performance, which included the *Alumni* (boarding choral scholars) from the Thomasschule and students of Leipzig University.[E87] Most significant is the title used by an eyewitness to describe Bach on this occasion: rather than *Cantor u. Director Musicis,* Christoph Ernst Sicul referred to the composer and director of the music as "Capell-Meister und Stadt-Cantor, Hr. Johann Sebastian Bach."[E88] There is also the possibility that the funeral of Leopold I, where we know that Bach directed an ensemble drawn from various places (see above), provided a second occasion on which Bach, as Kapellmeister "von Haus aus" to Köthen, directed an ensemble totaling more than 50 performers; Mattheson might well have received eyewitness accounts of this event, possibly from performers who had taken part.

Nevertheless, the occasions on which Bach enjoyed the facility of such large ensembles as these were completely exceptional, both during the time of his employment in Köthen and throughout his life. It is rather more irritating to have to admit that there are also many uncertainties regarding normal, day-to-day music making in the Köthen Court. It has been claimed that there were weekly concerts in the Schloss and that these may even have been a regular feature every weekend. This invites the question as to who attended them, besides Leopold I. Presumably his brother and successor,

August Ludwig, and his (often forgotten) younger, unmarried sister, Christiane Charlotte (Jan. 12, 1702—Jan. 27, 1745), were also likely to attend, along with other important members of the privy council and the princely household. However, the town also boasted the Neue Schloss (Wallstrasse 31 and the adjacent two houses today), where some or all of the family except Leopold himself may have lived, especially after Leopold's first marriage in 1720. It is, of course, quite possible that music was made here in the larger rooms. This New Palace was essentially a rather luxurious town house, but since it had been adapted to its new purpose only around 1710, it was probably more comfortable than the late 17th-century Ludwigsbau, the residential wing of the main palace.

The exact arrangement of the main Köthen palace (Schloss) and its gardens in the time of J. S. Bach is not recorded today; however, there is rather more certainty concerning its state around 1720 than there is for some other periods, and we are fortunate in that the main hall (and music room) has been restored to a state that will be acoustically very similar to that which Bach experienced. In this restored state, it retains the mirrors that adorned it from its earliest days. This *Spiegelsaal* (hall of mirrors) was already known as such by 1602 and is therefore based on Italian models rather than on Versailles. Possibly the modern, heavily gilded and marbled restoration does not represent this splendid cradle of Bach's music with absolute authenticity; we know that Prince Leopold's successor, August Ludwig, had both the chapel (today the so-called *Bach-Saal*) and the *Spiegelsaal* redecorated with elaborate gilded ornamentation in the 1730s. However, if in Leopold's reign the room was less brilliant and slightly more formal in its appearance than it is today (see the cover photograph), it will still have retained its elegance, its comfortably spacious proportions, and its warm but responsive acoustics.

The *Spiegelsaal* occupies the topmost floor beneath the roof and between the two towers of the south wing of the Schloss (see Illustration 1); it occupies the full width of the Ludwigsbau, which is here symmetrical, so that there are two corresponding gables halfway along either of the long walls, which are also ventilated by symmetrically arranged windows. The ceiling is divided into three rectangular portions, separated by slightly arched beams; each of the three divisions is concave, those to the east being arched and that to the west being pointed. In all, the dimensions are about 50 feet long by 19 feet wide by 14 feet (maximum) high. The walls as restored are largely marble and mirror-faced. It seems likely that the floor was originally of wooden finish and that it was carpeted. Possibly there were tapestries over parts of the walls, curtains, and less but more luxurious seating than we find there today.

This is easily the largest room that existed in the Schloss (and very probably, apart from the churches, in Köthen) in Bach's time. It was not simply a music room; it was also the throne room, where the prince would sit to preside over his privy council, to sit in judgment as the legal administrator of his subjects, and to give audiences to distinguished visitors and those of his subjects whose petitions interested him. The throne was possibly also used by the prince when he listened to music.

In common with most prosperous Germans of his day, and with virtually all of the nobility, Leopold lived and slept on what Germans and Americans call the "second story" of his palace; the rooms he occupied are today defended by a strong wooden glazed gallery, which was added to the building in the 19th century—probably the midcentury. The internal arrangement of these living quarters is by no means preserved. The architectural structure of the building implies that there were two large rooms (or pairs of smaller rooms) below the *Spiegelsaal*, at least two more at either end of the wing, and several more easily accessible in the western side of the rectangular building. The Ludwigsbau very probably had an external gallery similar to that depicted on the most famous drawing of the Schloss, the work of an anonymous artist working around 1830 (see Illustration 2). Further evidence regarding the exact layout of the palace building may be gained by comparing a plan (Illustration 3) with Merian's engraving of the palace and its gardens (Illustration 4). The low building, which housed the pages, was demolished only in the early 19th century to make way for the Ferdinandsbau at the east end of the north wing; today the Ferdinandsbau contains the Naumann Museum of Ornithology.

It is probable, indeed likely, that music was played and heard in some of the prince's less imposing quarters; there will have been "withdrawing" rooms, a formal dining room, and possibly a room set aside for music in which the prince himself practiced on the viola da gamba and where he received his instruction from *Kammer-Violdagambist* Friedrich Abel. Such a room would be most likely to contain a harpsichord, and some of Bach's Köthen keyboard music might well have first been played to anybody outside the Bach family in such a room. But the obvious suitability of the *Spiegelsaal* for any music on a less than intimate scale must have proved attractive to all concerned.

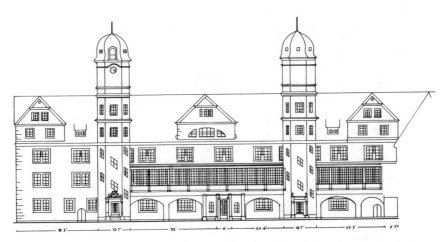

Illustration 1—Inner face of the southern wing, the "Ludwigsbau," of the Köther Schloss as it appeared in 1935, after *Die Kunstdenkmäler des Landes Anhalt: Landkreis Dessau-Köthen*, 1. Teil, ed. Haetge and Harksen (Burg bei Magdeburg, 1943). Drawing by Lorraine Toney, 1984.

Illustration 2—The Schloss, Köthen, seen from the east. Anonymous drawing from ca. 1830. The "Ferdinandsbau" (i.e., the close end of the north wing, with its distinctive tower and gabling) was new when the drawing was prepared; building had started on it in 1823. Source: Werner Neumann, *Auf den Lebenswegen Johann Sebastian Bachs* (Berlin: Verlag der Nation, 1953), 111.

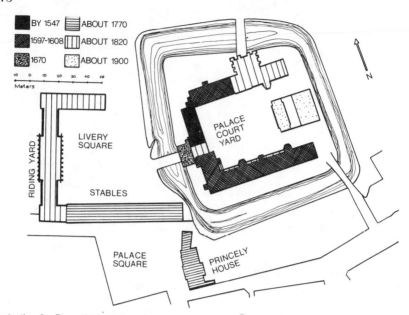

Illustration 3—Plan of the Köthen Schloss as it was in 1943 (before the destruction through bombing of most of the oldest—black-shaded—area). Drawn by Lorraine Toney, after *Die Kunstdenkmäler des Landes Anhalt,* ed. Haetge and Harksen (see Illustration 1).

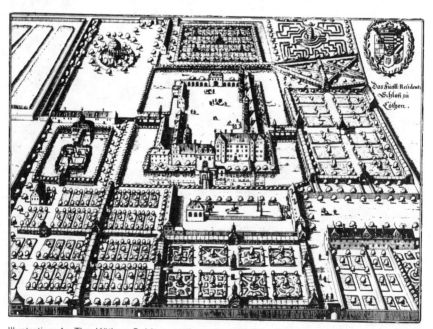

Illustration 4—The Köthen Schloss and gardens in the mid-17th century. An engraving published in Matthias Merian's *Topographia,* 1650.

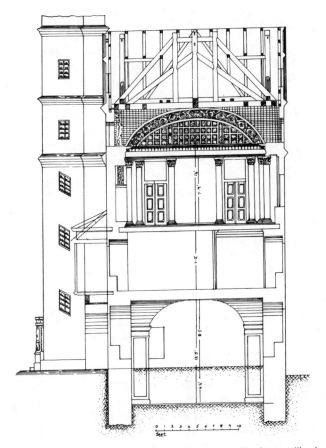

Illustration 5—Section drawing through the south wing or "Ludwigsbau" of the Köthen Schloss, after Büttner, *Anhalts Bau- und Kunstdenkmäler* (Dessau and Leipzig, 1892); redrawn by Lorraine Toney.

Before we leave consideration of the Schloss, a few further points should be made. First, the palace is not today exactly as it is depicted in the pictures we know so well and the plan supplied as Illustration 3. The oldest part of the building was damaged during World War II and has been demolished; there is a woodcut portraying it in Wäschke's 1907 article on the Hofkapelle, which happily deals with so much besides its stated subject.[E89] Second, there is a plan dating from around 1760[E90] that reveals that the formal gardens shown in Merian's engraving had been somewhat adapted, and much of the elaborate water gardens, besides the little maze and many of the small buildings, had gone by then; however, tiny traces from Merian's time may be identified here and there even today. Third, the building marked "about 1900" on Illustration 3 is a complete eyesore; never can police-dog kennels have been so poorly sited, and if it was not erected for that purpose, then there is nothing about it that indicates a higher one. Fourth, the building is very well worth a visit, and a great deal more could be made of it, bearing in mind its architectural distinction as well as its Bach associations. However, like many palaces throughout the world, it owes its very preservation to the fact that it has been put to multiple use for over 100 years; parts are probably totally inaccessible to the public, and parts have been so altered in recent times that they are not worthy of our internal inspection. But there is much—and, indeed, a whole impression—that is usefully memorable.

The questions that arise most naturally out of a visit to Köthen tend to concern Leopold rather than Bach. We are led to ask to what extent Leopold stayed at the Schloss, how far he entertained his relations and other acquaintances there, how often he was away, and how much things changed as a result of his two marriages. But we are led to ask these questions *through* Bach; it was his internal involvement in the life of this little court that made Köthen a household name for musicians throughout the world, whereas far fewer individuals today will have heard of Zerbst, Bernburg, or Wörlitz. As for Bach himself, Köthen was far less prominent than either Weimar or Leipzig commercially and administratively. His significance among those serving Leopold was very high, but it was only of importance that this was so within the immediate locality. There is abundant evidence that Bach was stimulated as a composer by contact with other musicians and encounters with new musical styles, and if, as seems probable, his duties kept him from such stimuli as a Kapellmeister, then we need search little further for an artistic reason—alongside various practical ones—for his wishing to move to Hamburg or Leipzig.

Be that as it may, the music that Bach composed in Köthen shows no trace whatsoever of such inner conflicts as may have disturbed its creator while he was composing it. Like Mozart later, Bach was professional enough to be able to avoid letting any untoward emotional feeling disturb the appropriate expression of his music, and as with Mozart, the range and depth of feeling within this music is quite remarkable.

A list of works that are known to have their origins at Köthen forms Appendix C below.[E91] If the reader compares it with the list of supposed Köthen compositions compiled by Wolfgang Schmieder in his 1950 thematic catalog,[E92] it is clear that this list has become much shorter than it was formerly. Not only the quantity but the balance of the various compositional genres within it has changed somewhat. A great deal of keyboard music and quite a high proportion of Bach's instrumental chamber music is today attached rather more firmly to earlier or, more frequently, later periods (notably the years between 1726 and 1739); some of the music is more realistically described as "of unknown provenance, but composed before about 1745." This paring down of the Köthen works, which has resulted from studies of sources rather than of stylistic and thematic ingredients of the music itself, has also diminished any impression that we might have gained formerly of a recognizable "Köthen style."[E93] The certainly datable works, such as the first part of Das Wohltemperierte Clavier, the Sei Soli for unaccompanied violin, the Brandenburg Concertos, and the Inventionen und Sinfonien convey an impression of consistent stylistic resource and flexibility such as we also find among Bach's late Weimar and late Leipzig compositions. What we have of the Köthen music seems to be an anthology that represents perhaps the best of what was once a far larger collection of Bach's music. Some of this remainder is without doubt totally lost, but other parts of it will survive unrecognized in contexts and later versions that we associate with Leipzig. Friedrich Smend was one of the first modern scholars to make this estimation, because he was one of the first commentators of all time to sit back and reflect on the quantity of music that Bach must have composed or prepared for performance as a regular duty between 1718 and early 1723.

The foregoing "background survey" of Bach's life in Köthen helps us to understand how it is that so much of Bach's Köthen music did become lost. First, Bach's music was composed expressly for Prince Leopold; it was his to keep since he had paid for its composition, its copying, its binding, and its actual performance. Despite modern writers' assumptions to the contrary, Leopold probably never and Bach himself possibly seldom participated—especially in subordinate roles—in the public court music making; Bach, as a string and keyboard player, would be dispensable from the performances of most kinds of music. He was probably allowed to take with him to Leipzig his difficult keyboard music (or some of it), his very difficult violin solos, and a few concertos, mainly for the violin, in score. These would have been manageable in the two cartloads of goods with which the family is supposed to have traveled to Leipzig (an important detail, since Bach already must have owned a number of instruments). How far Bach's music continued to be played after he left Köthen cannot be estimated, but it was probably regarded as difficult to play, and its most likely champion, Leopold, died only five and a half years later. It is also possible that the performing materials were less carefully kept when the composer was no longer present to supervise their use. Leopold and August Ludwig may have imported printed part-music of a more immediately fashionable nature, and the music library of performing materials—at least that of Bach's music—may have been dispersed or divided up when the Kapelle was disbanded in 1754.[E94]

Although Bach left Köthen in a position of honor and almost of congratulation—whereas he had left Weimar in disgrace—the music that he had composed in the former is probably very largely lost because it was not much copied; that from the latter is probably quite well preserved simply because Bach was much more active as a teacher in Weimar, and first- and secondhand copies of his music were plentiful enough to enable it to reach mid-18th-century collectors. The copying work of his colleague and relation J. G. Walther was also of invaluable service to the preservation of Bach's Weimar music, especially that for organ and domestic keyboards. At Köthen, Bach's only serious student was Johann Bernhard Bach of Ohrdruf, whose copying duties were partly taken up with part-writing for the Kapelle's own library. Besides, he had worked with Bach in Weimar, and it has so far proved impossible positively to identify his script. He returned with any copies he owned to Thuringia, where he died young, so that he could not have added anything to a national Anhalt Bach circle. Such a circle never developed, and as a result of this historically unsurprising fact, some considerable quantity of Bach's music from Köthen will have failed to reach any posterity, let alone an admiring one.

We should perhaps do well to remind ourselves that it seems from all of the available evidence that the last person to have been surprised by this lack of "recognition" would have been the composer himself. The achievement of fame seems to have had a low priority for one whose entire career was so evidently dedicated to the service of God through the practical service of man. Even the comparatively worldly Hamburg musician Johann Mattheson, quoted above, had acknowledged that the responsibilities of the Köthen Kapellmeister were the supervising, creation, preparation, and performance of music at court "to the glory of God, the pleasure of (the prince), and the benefit of the entire court."

Author's Notes

1. In Weimar Bach was first and foremost court organist, then chamber musician, and from 1714 on Konzertmeister—a somewhat unspecific title. This last office at the same time provided a direct link with the church, since with it went the obligation to provide church music on a regular basis, i.e., cantatas for divine service. The office of Thomas Kantor at Leipzig, on the other hand, was primarily educational, as is clear from the document signed by Bach on taking office in Leipzig on April 19, 1723. In this document he had first of all written the words: "Whereas the worshipful council of this city of Leipzig has appointed me, the undersigned, to the vacant office of Kantor at St. Thomas Church . . . ." He altered this by erasing the word "Church" and substituting "School" (cf. the excellent fascimile reproduction of this document in *J. S. Bach: Sein Leben und Werk*, published by Leipzig City Council [1950], Plate VI). In Leipzig, however, Bach was not only Kantor of the Thomas School, but also *Director Musices, Director Chori Musici Lipsiensis,* i.e., musical director of the city. In this capacity he was in charge of the city's guild musicians, Stadtpfeiffer and Kunstgeiger. Notwithstanding numerous duties unconnected with religion, however, his greatest task was to furnish music for divine service on a range of occasions at the city's churches.
2. Wolfgang Schmieder, on pp. 651–53 of his *Thematisch-systematisches Verzeichnis der musikalischen Werke von Johann Sebastian Bach* (Leipzig: Breitkopf and Härtel, 1950), has compiled a list of works composed at Köthen. If we compare these with compositions from other periods of creativity of similar duration, there are, in purely quantitative terms, fewer works. From this the conclusion has been drawn that the years 1717–23 must have represented a period of comparative "leisure" for Bach. See, for example, Walther Vetter, *Der Kapellmeister Bach* (Potsdam, 1950), 163, 206, and elsewhere. On the other hand, one might also have concluded that a relatively large number of the works Bach composed at Köthen are neither preserved nor recorded. The fact that we have scarcely more than half of the works that formed his total creative output is continually ignored. Vetter's reference to a "noticeable decline" in Bach's output of cantatas during the years 1725–27 (p. 255) is based on a similar misconception. (For a full treatment of Vetter's book see primarily note 5 below.)
3. Bach gives this title only on the first part of the *Wohltemperirtes Klavier*, which was composed in Köthen.
4. Bach was also concerned with nonreligious instrumental compositions in Weimar. These include the concertos based on Italian and other models (Schmieder, nos. 972–87). Nevertheless, in his Weimar instrumental compositions, music for the organ, i.e., for the church, is dominant.
5. I am in agreement with Walther Vetter when he expresses the view that the Köthen period is not to be regarded as a separate episode and that the fruits of those years acted as an integrating factor in the whole of the composer's later works. Vetter's book, *Der Kapellmeister Bach: Versuch einer Deutung Bachs auf Grund seines Wirkens als Kapellmeister in Köthen* (Potsdam: Akadem. Verlagsanstalt Athemaion, 1950), 404 pp., by far the most detailed treatment of our theme, is influenced throughout by this concept and therefore requires detailed comment. He critically reappraises the traditional view, reaching overall conclusions that deviate markedly from the conventional ones. He set out to correct the notion, prevalent in contemporary thinking, that the "Thomas Kantor" is the essential Bach; Vetter seeks to give the Kapellmeister Bach his due. There is much in Vetter's work that may be read with great profit, e.g., his

comments on the Brandenburg Concertos, his treatment of the passages that the *Klavierbüchlein* for Friedemann Bach has in common with the *Wohltemperiertes Clavier*, and his remarks on the subject of the reuse of instrumental movements in the church cantatas, among other things.

There is nothing intrinsically new in what Vetter has to say about Bach's work in Köthen itself. He too regards the years 1717–23 unequivocally, exclusively almost, as a period devoted to instrumental rather than church music. At that time the master, quite by contrast with the years that followed in Leipzig, had sufficient leisure time to follow the dictates of his own genius. Of Bach's vocal works from those years he deals only with *Durchlauchtster Leopold* and the cantata *Wer sich selbst erhöhet*, which in my view dates from a much later period (see note 43). He ignores the discovery of the cantatas based on Hunold's texts.

Already there must be doubts. They arise at a number of points throughout Vetter's work, in both a musical and a historical sense. The statement that Bach was appointed visiting Kapellmeister at the court of Weissenfels in 1733 (instead of 1723) may be due to a printer's error and is of no consequence. There are, however, far more serious mistakes, e.g., the assessment of Bach's application for the post of organist at St. James in Hamburg (pp. 164f.). If Vetter had consulted the original documents and Seiffert's exemplary interpretation of these (*Arch. f. Musikw.* 3 [1921]: 123ff.), he would have realized that Terry's view, which he adopts, was founded on that commentator's defective knowledge of the language of German officialdom in the 18th century. Likewise, the notion that the Weimar years (1708–17) were free from the troubled circumstances of Mühlhausen (1707–08), as typified by the doctrinal feud between G. C. Eilmar and J. A. Frohne, or the well-known aggravations of Leipzig is erroneous. Vetter was not aware of the tensions that existed between Dukes Wilhelm Ernst and Ernst August, which must have been extremely trying for Bach and undoubtedly influenced the events leading to the composer's move to Köthen (on this point see Reinh. Jauernig, "J. S. Bach in Weimar," *Joh. Seb. Bach in Thüringen* [Weimar, 1950], 49–106). To give one more example: Just how little his interpretation of the controversy between J. A. Scheibe and J. A. Birnbaum matches the facts may be gauged from Arnold Schmitz's description in *Die Bildlichkeit der wortgebundenen Musik Bachs* (Mainz: Schott, 1950), 37ff.

This brings us to Vetter's strictly musical comments. Here again we continually find ourselves at odds with the views expressed, as the following examples illustrate. We can hardly accept his characterization of the Fantasia and Fugue in G Minor ("the epitome of human insouciance," "carefree," "romping music, joyously conscious of its power"—p. 194). Even less credible is Vetter's opinion that the heading "Adagio" in the final bars of the chorus "Fecit potentiam" from the *Magnificat* "merely warns against an acceleration of tempo" (p. 334).

His verdict on the *Musical Offering* is entirely new (pp. 305ff.). Vetter argues that its theme is basically atypical of Bach. It abounds with an "ingenious, nervous subjectivism" and a "ringing sensibility that gets lost in the agonized chromaticism." King Frederick the Great, "when he was preparing for Bach's visit . . . had botched it together" from material "that was, so to speak, in the air at the time," and he "knew full well" that music of that kind was "out of keeping with Bach's mature style." Thus, "somewhat cynically" he had given the master "this nut to crack." Vetter relates that Bach refused to extemporize a fugue on the theme and, in doing so, demonstrated "manliness and fearlessness." On his return to Leipzig, however, he "paid the competent amateur leanings of the king a second compliment"; he sent him the *Musical Offering* with its trio sonata and six-part fugue. But that was not Bach's final word. From the theme that Frederick had set arose that of the *Art of the Fugue*, the "sublime mystery play in music." Thus, from "the whim," "the king's witticism," there evolved the main idea of one of the greatest works of art of the western world. This section of Vetter's work is headed "Mediocrity [*Das Unzulängliche*] becomes a momentous event."

We shall leave aside the misconception of Goethe's notion of *das Unzulängliche* (by which the poet meant "the heights of unattainability"), and we shall also overlook our historical objections (all sources unanimously agree that Bach performed the *thema regium* in Potsdam ex tempore as a three-part fugue!).

Despite the problems it raises, we shall try to imagine that the king was familiar with Bach's later works and their stylistic features. For the time being, at any rate, we shall let Vetter's view on the main theme of the *Musical Offering* stand, difficult though that may be. Let us, however, draw the logical conclusions from such an interpretation. No one would dispute that Bach could immediately discern the inadequacies—in Vetter's (not Goethe's) sense "mediocrity"—of any musical concept. The "nut he was given to crack" by the "sarcastic misanthropist" he calls a "splendid," a "right royal theme," and in doing so reciprocated Frederick's "petty cynicism." Thus, according to Vetter's interpretation, Bach's universally acclaimed *Musical Offering* was composed in a context of knowing smiles and mutual mockery!

Enough of these examples. Probably the reader has long since wanted to know the connection between Bach's later works in particular and those of the Köthen era. In fact, we have here one of the essential features of Vetter's overall view of Bach's work. I myself believe that there exists a marked contrast between Bach's Leipzig compositions and those he wrote at Köthen; at least that is the case if we take his output during the years immediately after 1723 into consideration. Admittedly, the influence of Köthen did not entirely disappear during Bach's first 10 years as Thomas Kantor, though it did recede into the background. However, according to Vetter, "In the long run Leipzig could not displace Köthen" (pp. 251–52). The last decade of Bach's life was thus a spiritual return to Leopold's court. It is clear from what I have written in this study that I do not subscribe to this view.

I must, however, contradict more forcefully and fundamentally what Vetter has to say on the subject of Bach's religious beliefs and his attitude towards the churches and the various denominations. Vetter asserts that the fact that Bach placed himself in the service of a prince who held Reformed [Calvinistic] beliefs is evidence of the composer's supradenominational standpoint. As proof Vetter cites Bach's reading of Pfeifer's work *Anticalvinismus!* This is supposed to demonstrate the composer's "unprejudiced steadfastness," which obliged him "to examine critically even the beliefs of others that he did not share" (p. 142). Somewhat curiously in his quest, Bach did not avail himself of the Calvinist writings at his disposal in Köthen. Instead he chose to read their fiercest critics. Bach, Vetter maintains, adopted a similar stance towards the Roman Catholic Church. When he treated in some detail an originally medieval melody, *Christ ist erstanden,* its "denominational independence would have particularly endeared it to Bach" (p. 106). The use of quotations from the altar intonation of the Credo and the Confiteor is similarly assessed. On hearing the *Tonus Peregrinus* (Psalm Tone IX) in Bach's *Magnificat,* Vetter asserts that Bach, untrammeled by any narrow religious restraints, uses here a form that is "Catholic, by nature" (p. 333). Does Vetter really not know that this tune is a stock item in Lutheran church music? Or does he somehow regard the latter church as supradenominational? He takes as decisive evidence for his belief in Bach's supradenominational stance the fact that the *Mass in B Minor* displays a "formal, spiritual, and musical affiliation to Catholicism" (p. 91).

It is clear from such utterances that Vetter has no understanding of the theological issues connected with Bach's work. Sadly, however, he ventures time and time again into theological territory. For example, he interprets the final bars of the chorus "Fecit potentiam" from the *Magnificat* as follows: "The Supreme Being punishes only those who are, to the very depths of their being, proud; those who, through human weakness, are occasionally arrogant obtain mercy" (p. 336). Vetter believes with this—one is forced to say—piece of banality that he has discovered a "typically profound exegesis of this Biblical passage on Bach's part"! In other words, Vetter is totally unaware of what is at stake in the controversy between Pietism and orthodoxy. Admittedly, he does not go as far as Harry Goldschmid, who says *expressis verbis* in his guide to the *Deutsche Bach-Ausstellung* (German Bach exhibition) (Leipzig, 1950), 29: "With Pietism, the old protest movement of the bourgeoisie against the prevailing feudal order, which had

been buried beneath the ruins of the Thirty Years' War, found a new lease on life."
Vetter, however, is moving in the same direction when he tries to associate the orthodox/
Pietist antithesis with the terms "conservative" and "liberal" (p. 66). We find similar
idiosyncratic notions in the liturgical field. Still on the *Magnificat*, e.g., Vetter writes:
"Bach adds the doxology to its 10 verses" (p. 330). It should be obvious that the Gloria
Patri would be added to a composition included among the psalms for divine service.
Astonishingly, Vetter describes the movement "Suscepit Israel" of this work as a "trio
for female voices"!

Regrettable though such howlers may be in an assessment of Protestant church
music, the nontheologian may be inclined to overlook this. The situation is different,
however, when we come to Vetter's general attitude to the church, religious services,
and theology as such. He allows no opportunity to pass to voice a low opinion on all
issues connected with the church and to distance Bach's work as far as possible from
the religious sphere.

In quantitative terms, too, Vetter is anxious to scale down the number of religious
compositions within Bach's total output. We may forgive Forkel for not including Bach's
organ works among his religious compositions. Referring to this omission, however,
Vetter (p. 41) adds, "We would do well to remember this," and pursuing the point,
he reaches the remarkable conclusion that Bach produced an ever-decreasing amount
of music for the church—a score or so of cantatas (p. 73)—during his decade at Weimar.
According to Vetter, a section of the Leipzig cantatas were not written for the church
either. A "sizable number" were composed "not for the church but for his wife and
children" (p. 276). Unfortunately, Vetter names none of these. Other works, such as
Wer sich selbst erhöhet (p. 122), "go beyond the bounds of religious music."

Time and time again, anything connected with the church is treated with con-
tempt—"bigotry" and "hypocrisy" (pp. 146, 278), "pastoral bickering" (p. 70), "religious
blinkers" (p. 306), "denominational carping" and "ecclesiastical hairsplitting" (pp. 264,
294), etc. Even the song of the tobacco pipe from Anna Magdalena's second *Klavierbüchlein* induces Vetter to take a swipe at the vicar, though on this occasion his in-
voluntary humor enables us to forgive him: "The heat of hell is paraphrased in such a
way that it may have sent a shiver down the spines of the denominational zealots" (p.
156). When he describes Bach's conflict with the University of Leipzig, Vetter goes
out of his way to make a dig at the theological faculty, even though it was not involved
in the controversy any more than the other faculties nor is it mentioned anywhere in
the source documents: "Bach may have known full well that the faculty of theology did
not primarily allow itself to be swayed by artistic considerations" (p. 156). We find a
similar distortion in the brochure *Johann Sebastian Bach* by Karl Laux and published
by the Cultural League for the Democratic Renewal of Germany (Leipzig: Offizin Haag-
Drugulin, 1950), 24, though in this instance it comes as no surprise: "Bach quarreled
with the theological faculty on the subject of divine service at the university church."
This brochure, in its own words, was intended to prepare its readers for the ceremony
on July 28, 1950. [*Translator's note*: This was the bicentennial of Bach's death.] It
contained sets of notes for eight concert programs consisting exclusively of secular
compositions by Bach. Despite the fact that it was published in April 1950, Vetter's
book, which came out three months later, is described and warmly recommended (p.
19). Recounting Bach's work as Thomas Kantor, Laux says: "He was at loggerheads
with the clergy of St. Nicholas Church" (p. 24). In only one of his Leipzig disputes did
Bach have a man of the church as his adversary, and that was his quarrel with a
subdeacon, in other words, a clergyman in a subordinate position. The superintendent,
the chief pastor at St. Thomas Church, and the consistory never placed obstacles in
Bach's way; the conflicts and altercations that Bach had to endure in Leipzig were,
with the one exception of the case cited above, with the secular authorities. Otto
Berthold reached the same conclusion in his work, *Das Leben in der Thomasschule
zur Bachzeit--J. S. Bach: Das Schaffen des Meisters im Spiegel einer Stadt* (Leipzig,
1950), 44: "Bach had few difficulties with the representatives of the church." Arnold
Schering reached a similar conclusion (*Musikgeschichte Leipzigs* 3 [1941]: 28). After

his account of the dispute with Gaudlitz, he writes: "As for the rest, there is no known instance of a preacher or any other clergyman ever interfering in Bach's work as a composer." It is important in this context to realize that the great majority of Bach's works during his 27 years at Leipzig were composed for a religious purpose and were commissioned by the church. Schering speaks of a "period of trouble-free creative activity" (ibid.). Of course, the younger Ernesti had studied theology, a point Vetter stresses whenever he mentions his name, but the tension between Bach and the young man derived not from the religious sphere but from the problems of managing the school. According to Vetter, Bach, by contrast with the "denominational zealots," stood above the petty denominations, the "sects" (p. 295), and could not conceivably be regarded as a representative of a "long since obsolete religious belief." Bach wrote "for Jew and Christian alike, and when Hindus and Moslems find their way towards his works, they will be equally accessible" (p. 356). Without doubt, and this Vetter himself admits, Bach's compositions are informed by religious belief, but not what Luther meant by the term, the very opposite in fact. Bach's belief is directed towards "the attributes and potentialities of man, of which the material world can offer no proof" (p. 354). Thus, in a choice of words that has highly contemporary overtones, Vetter states: "In this context, and perhaps not only here, there is nothing to stop us from placing Bach on the same level as any other great social thinker."

The enthusiasm with which *Neues Deutschland,* the organ of the Central Committee of the Socialist Unity Party (SED), greeted Vetter's book (Aug. 1, 1950) has in the meantime, however, given way to a much more sober verdict, albeit from the same ideological standpoint. Cf. the detailed discussion of this work published by Georg Knepler under the title "Bachdeutung und Wissenschaft" in the monthly periodical of the Cultural League for the Democratic Renewal of Germany, *Aufbau* 6, no. 11 (1950): 1114–17. [*Translator's note*: By this time (1950) the SED had become a straightforward Marxist-Leninist party in total control, under the aegis of the Soviet authorities, of the affairs of East Germany.] Nevertheless, Vetter is given credit for having "assembled important materials that allow the reader to construct a bridge towards a modern interpretation of Bach." In this very context, however, it is remarkable how far Vetter goes out of his way in his preface to his work to maintain that it is not a book that has been written to order and that it derives exclusively from his own conscience. (For further references to Vetter's publication see notes 2, 13, 14, 31, 41, 46, 72, 89, 92, 98).

6. Cf. nos. 5 and 6 of my series of booklets, *J. S. Bach: Kirchenkantaten* (Berlin: Christl. Zeitschriftenverlag, 1948; 2d edition, 1950.)

7. Charles Sandford Terry, *Joh. Seb. Bach*, 1st German edition (Leipzig: Inselverlag, 1929), p. 138. A secular cantata was performed during the marriage feast, the libretto of which, "Diana, Amor, Apollo, Ilmene," had been written by Salomo Franck. Diana's aria, which stands at the head of this work, begins with the words "Edles Jagen! Meine Lust." The complete text may be found in Salomo Franck, *Heliconische Ehren-, Liebes- und Trauer-Fackeln* (Weimar and Jena, 1718), pp. 100–05. Sadly, we have not been able to verify whether Bach or someone else composed this musical entertainment. In the same volume of verse by Franck we find (pp. 55–59) the text of a secular cantata, *Amor, die Treue und die Beständigkeit*, the presentation copy of which may be found in the Thuringian State Library in Weimar and which begins with Amor's aria, "Brich Titan, brich an." The work was "musically performed" on May 18, 1716, to celebrate the birthday of Duchess Eleonore Wilhelmine of Saxe-Weimar. It is also possible in this instance, though we cannot prove it, that Bach was the composer. I am grateful to Dr. Alfred Dürr for drawing my attention to these texts.

8. We find the following entries in the household accounts of the principality of Anhalt-Köthen for the year 1717:

> 1717. *Dec. 29.* The newly arrived Kapellmeister J. S.Bach receives 33⅓ Thalers monthly and has received this salary since Aug. 1.
>
> *Aug. 7.* To the same to defray removal expenses: 50 Thalers.

9. The document relating to Bach's discharge of April 13, 1723, may be found in Terry, *Bach*, German edition (1929), p. 168. [*Translator's note: 2d revised English edition (1933), p. 146.*]

10. Bach retained this title in the announcement of his funeral dated July 31, 1750: "There has passed to rest and now sleeps blessedly in the sight of God the right worthy and venerable Johann Sebastian Bach, court composer to His Majesty the King of Poland and Serene Highness and Elector of Saxony, Kapellmeister to His Highness the Prince of Anhalt-Köthen, and Kantor of St. Thomas School in this city. In St. Thomas's churchyard and in accordance with the rites and usages of the Christian church, his body hath this day been committed to the earth. Announced again on the next day of mourning after July 31, 1750." (Cf. facsimile in Heinrich Reimann, *Johann Sebastian Bach* [Berlin: Schles. Verlagsanst., 1912], p. 31).

11. Philipp Spitta, *J. S. Bach* (Leipzig, 1873–80), 1:716.

12. Rudolf Bunge, "Johann Sebastian Bachs Kapelle zu Cöthen und deren nachgelassene Instrumente: Nach urkundlichen Quellen," *BJ*, 1905, pp. 14–47).

13. Wäschke (Director of Archives), "Die Hofkapelle in Cöthen unter Joh. Seb. Bach," *Zerbster Jahrbuch* 3 (1907): 31–40. Remarkably Vetter (see note 5) makes no reference to this significant work in his book.

14. *Joh. Seb. Bach, 1685–1750, und sein Wirken in Cöthen 1717–1723*, Schriftenreihe des Köthener Heimatmuseums, Heft 1 (Köthen: Heimatmuseum, 1925). Vetter makes no mention of this study either.

15. Terry, pp. 134–74 [119–46 in the English revised edition (1933)].

16. Ibid., pp. 144–45 [122–23 in the English revised edition (1933)].

17. Terry, on the subject of the Köthen collection of musical scores, p. 141. I have already discussed Terry's account of Bach's journey to Hamburg in the autumn of 1720 (see note 5). Terry is seriously at fault when he places the first Leipzig performance of Cantata No. 61, *Nun komm, der Heiden Heiland*, in December 1717 and makes it contemporaneous with Bach's inspection of the organ in the Paulinerkirche (p. 144). In Leipzig, religious figural music was performed in Advent on the First Sunday in Advent only. But in 1717 this fell on Nov. 28, i.e., when Bach was still under arrest in Weimar. Bernhard Paumgartner rectified this error (*Bach* [Zürich, 1950], pp. 320f.). He correctly placed the performance at the First Sunday in Advent, 1722 (p. 338). His supposition that Bach also participated as organist in that performance is, however, very wide of the mark. [*Ed.: In 1985 we believe that Paumgartner was also incorrect; Cantata 61, first performed in Weimar on Dec. 22, 1714, was very probably first heard in Leipzig on Nov. 28, 1723.*]

18. Facsimile of a page of the "Protocolle," *BJ*, 1905, p. 23, and Bethge-Götze, p. 21.

19. Spitta, German edition, 2:958. [*Ed.: Cf. Bach-Dokumente (Leipzig and Kassel, 1969), 2:498ff.*]

20. In the household accounts we have the following entries in this connection:

> 1719. *Oct. 13.* To the same (J. S. Bach) for having held rehearsal in his house and maintaining the harpsichord in good order from Dec. 10, 1718, to Dec. 10, 1719: 12 Thalers.
>
> 1721. *Jan. 21.* To the same (J. S. Bach) for having held a musical rehearsal in his house and maintaining the harpsichord in good order from Dec. 10, 1719, to Dec. 10, 1720: 12 Thalers.

In other words, the sum for the maintenance of the keyboard instruments was included in the fee paid for the hire of Bach's house, which was used for rehearsals. Bach also received additional small payment, e.g., on Sept. 12, 1722, 1 Thaler for the repair of a harpsichord; and on Dec. 30, 1722, and March 20, 1723, for the renewal of harpsichord quills, 1 Thaler, 80 Groschen, and 1 Thaler respectively.

21. This sum consists of the following payments made to the bookbinder Günther junior:

> 1719. *July 8:* 16 Thalers; July 12: 16 Groschen; Sept. 4: 2 Thalers, 12

Groschen; Sept. 22: 12 Groschen; Sept. 26: 8 Groschen; Oct. 14: 4 Thalers.

1720.   *Jan. 15:* 10 Groschen; March 16: 1 Thaler, 18 Groschen; March 25: 1 Thaler; April 22: 18 Groschen; May 25: 1 Thaler, 15 Groschen.

In the case of the entry of July 12, 1719 (16 Groschen), we have "for 8 musical items," and for that of Oct. 14, 1719 (4 Thalers), "48 items." From this we may deduce that the cost of binding a score was always 2 Groschen.

22.   From this alone we can recognize how much more extensive Bach's creative activity at Köthen was than may be inferred solely from the surviving compositions.

23.   Leopold was born on Nov. 28, 1694 (Julian Calendar). After the Gregorian Calendar was introduced, the birthday celebration was put forward to Dec. 10. Compare here the incorrect statements in Terry (p. 138 n. 1, and elsewhere).

24.   The printing costs for the "Carmina" seem to be virtually complete from the beginning of 1719. Since the price remains constant (2 Thalers) it is clear that on each occasion there were two texts. The following entry expressly mentions two Carmina:

1720.   *April 21.* To Löffler for printing 2 New Year Carmina for the court orchestra: 2 Thalers.

In the years 1721 (entry of Jan. 1), 1722 (entries of April 3 and Nov. 28), and 1723 (entry of April 3), payments were made directly to Bach to be forwarded to the printer.

That the cultivation of vocal music, to which alone the production of printed Carmina refers, was even more lavish than the itemized records of expenditure on the royal orchestra indicate, is evident from the fact that the costs for additional printed texts are listed under other headings in the household accounts, generally without specific reference to what was being printed. Nevertheless, individual entries here suggest that these included the libretti of vocal music performed at court. I give the following examples:

1719.   *Dec. 30.* To the printer Löffler for printing excise forms, kitchen accounts, and materials for the orchestra: 11 Thalers (contained under heading No. 10 in the household accounts).

1722.   *Jan. 5.* To the printer Löffler for printing Carmina for the orchestra, title page of the sermon of the mystery of the Incarnation given by Daniel Sachs, also for customs and excise forms: 14 Thalers (contained under heading No. 10 in the household accounts).

1724.   *Jan. 13.* To the printer Löffler for printing soldiers' passes, excise forms, cellar accounts, music for the New Year Carmina, etc.: 10 Thalers, 12 Groschen (contained under heading No. 19 in the household accounts).

We may see from this last entry that the cultivation of vocal music continued after Bach ceased to be active as Kapellmeister *[Ed.: in a resident capacity]*.

The reader is referred to the work by Hermann v. Hase, "Breitkopfsche Textdrucke zu Leipziger Musikaufführungen zu Bachs Zeiten," *BJ*, 1913, pp. 69–127, for further details. Here too the cantata texts are referred to as "Carmina" and the printing costs, on average, match those in Köthen.

25.   In the entry that relates to Bach's salary in the household accounts, we find after the sums paid to the composer the following:

his wife should receive 16 Thalers, 16 Groschen each month and has received:

for the month of May . . . . 16 Thalers, 16 Groschen
for the month of June . . . . 16 Thalers, 16 Groschen

From then on Anna Magdalena's salary appears regularly after that of her husband, e.g., for the fiscal year 1722/23 we find:

J. S. Bach July 1722 to April 1723: 333 Thalers, 8 Groschen.
A. M. Bach July 1722 to April 1723: 166 Thalers, 16 Groschen.

26. Credit is due to Arno Werner for having pointed this out (cf. *BJ*, 1907, pp. 178f., where the document relating to the baptism in question is discussed).

27. The first mention of the Monjou daughters in the household accounts runs as follows:

1720.	Sept. 16.	To the Master of the Pages Jean Francois Monjou, Madame Monjou, and their daughters who occasionally gave vocal performances: 20 Thalers.
	Oct. 8.	To the same for his and his family's maintenance: 25 Thalers per month.
	Nov. 27.	for the months of October and November: 50 Thalers. for the months of December 1720 and January 1721: 50 Thalers.
1721.	Feb. 1.	for the months of February and March: 50 Thalers. for the months of April and May: 50 Thalers.
	March 1.	for the month of June: 25 Thalers.

In the following year of the household accounts (1721/22) the Master of the Pages was likewise paid 25 Thalers monthly "for himself and his two girls who sing."

28. According to the household accounts, honoraria were paid to visiting instrumentalists:

1718.	Dec. 16.	To Konzertmeister Lienigke from Merseburg To Konzertmeister Volger from Leipzig.
1719.	April 8.	To Konzertmeister Lienigke from Merseburg. To Konzertmeister Volger from Leipzig.
	July 31.	To a visiting musico who played the "Bandoloisches Instrument."
	Aug. 17.	A lutanist from Düsseldorf.
	Oct. 21.	A "musico."
1721.	Sept. 6.	Two French horn players.
	Sept. 19.	Two Berlin musicians.
1722.	June 6.	Two French horn players.

29. The household accounts show the following visiting singers to have received payment:

1718.	Oct. 20.	A *Diskantist* from Rudolstadt.
	Dec. 16.	A *Diskantist* Preese (Bröse) from Halle.
1719.	March 21.	The Castrato Ginacini.
	April 8.	A vocalist from Wittenberg. The bass singer Riemenschneider. The *Diskantist* Preese (Bröse) from Halle.
	July 24.	A singer from Weissenfels.
	Aug. 24.	A *Diskantist*.

30. According to the household accounts, the following fees were paid to visiting musicians during the years 1723 (after Bach had left Köthen) to 1728. Bach's own visits are not included here:

1723. Aug. 8. To Joh. Friedrich Bohnando, who sang, in settlement: 5 Thalers.

1724. March 4. To the Royal Saxon Cammermusicus who had performed here: 50 Thalers

May 10. To the two French horn players Hans Leopold and Wentzel Franz Seydler from Barby, who had performed here, in settlement: 24 Thalers.

July 1. To a visiting musician, who had performed here and had lodged with Spiess, in settlement: 24 Thalers.

July 10. Two traveling Italian noblemen musicians, by the gracious order of trumpeter Krahl: 20 Thalers.

July 18. (At the same time as Jo. Seb. and A. M. Bach).
To the organist Schneider, in settlement: 20 Thalers.
To the tenor Vetter, in settlement: 20 Thalers.

Aug. 31. To the Landgrave of Cassel's French horn player who performed here for a while: 24 Thalers.
To the oboist Rose junior, who applied for permission to audition, in settlement: 4 Thalers.

Sept. 18. To the Berenburg oboist in settlement, in the presence of the pheasant hunter Bartel, by gracious command: 9 Thalers.

Oct. 9. To the oboist Gottlieb Siegmund Jacobi, who performed here for a time with the court orchestra, in settlement: 50 Thalers.

Oct. 11. To the same, in addition to the previous 50 Thalers: 32 Thalers.

Oct. 10. To a visiting musician who had performed: 12 Thalers.

Oct. 18. To the musician Rose junior, who performed again: 12 Thalers.

1725.   *Feb. 10.* To a visiting musician Vogler for delivering scores and performing: 50 Thalers.

March 15. To the vocalist Cetombi from Hamburg, who performed: 20 Thalers.

May 9. To Kapellmeister Fasch from Zerbst, who performed here: 50 Thalers.

May 31. To the musician Riedel, who gave a cello performance: 30 Thalers.

Aug. 18. To the French hornist Beda, who performed simultaneously on two horns, in settlement: 6 Thalers.
To the two French horn players from Barby, in settlement: 10 Thalers.

Aug. 25. To a musician who played on glasses, as on a glockenspiel, in settlement: 6 Thalers.

Sept. 17. To the town musician Würdiger for providing musical accompaniment to Brockes's comedies in the theater, with four companions, on seven occasions: 7 Thalers.

Oct. 20. To the court councillor von Wülkenitz, in recompense for paying a vocalist who had performed: 6 Thalers

Dec. 11. To a bass singer from Gotha who had performed (at the same time as J. S. and A. M. Bach): 10 Thalers.

1726.   *Feb. 6.* To two musicians from Gotha, a German castrato, and the violinist Weissmann, who performed here: 20 Thalers.

March 2. To the vocalist from Gotha, Hoborth, who performed here: 12 Thalers.

March 9. To a traveling bassoon player Zwanziger, in settlement: 2 Thalers, 16 Groschen.

March 21. To the lutanist Jacobi, who once again performed here, at the gracious command of the footman Schirrmann, in settlement: 20 Thalers.

March 25. To Grunwaldt for providing lodgings for the lutanist Jacobi for 8 weeks: 2 Thalers.

April 1. To the cook Weidlinger, for providing for Jacobi: 1 Thaler, 1 Groschen.

April 6. To the carter Gramm, for transporting Jacobi: 6 Thalers.

1728.   *May 1.* To a musician Bönigk from Halberstadt, in settlement: 2 Thalers.

31. Hans Löffler ("J. S. Bach's Orgelprüfungen," *BJ*, 1925, pp. 95f.) assumes that Bach visited in Köthen to inspect the newly restored organ at the Lutheran St. Agnes Church. He bases this view on a statement by Wilhelm Rust (BG 25, 2, pp. viii f.), who says on the subject of the rebuilding of the organ: "We may safely assume that Bach took part in these modifications, particularly since the fact that he enjoyed the personal friendship and favor of the prince would enable him to carry out the work exactly as he wished." But as early as C. F. Harmann's *Geschichte der evangelischen St. Agnuskirche* (Köthen, 1803), pp. 19f., we have it that the repairs to the organ did not begin until six months after Leopold's death. No evidence has materialized of visits by Bach after 1729.

   Vetter (see note 5) has a special chapter that he heads "Köthenscher Kapellmeister von Haus aus" (pp. 254–56 in his book). However, he ignores Bach's visits to Köthen, two of which Terry had already mentioned.

32. The household accounts record:

   1725.   *Dec. 22.* To Gänseler for accommodating the Kantor Bach and his wife, paid: 24 Thalers.

33. Bernh. Paumgartner (*Bach*, p. 344 n. 36) takes this opportunity to correct the author of the standard biography of Bach, calling him somewhat patronizingly but benevolently the "redoubtable Spitta." He writes: "The description of the cantata as a celebratory piece on the occasion of the princess's first (!) birthday is a minor lapse of concentration on the biographer's part." The title of the poem as it appears in Picander's collected poems (2d edition, part I, 1732, p. 14), however, is as follows: "On the occasion of the celebration of the first birthday of Her Serene Highness, the Princess of Anhalt-Köthen, 1726" (cf. BG 34, p. xviii).

34. Cf. note 30 above, listing entries in the household accounts relating to the period from July 18, 1724, to Dec. 11, 1725.

35. Entry in the household accounts:

   1728.   *Jan. 12.*   Paid to the Conrector for the New Year singing by the Lutheran school: 4 Thalers.
   To the Lutheran pupils of same: 2 Thalers.

36. Rudolf Bunge first published the list of the salaries of the entire orchestra in the *Bach-Jahrbuch* for 1905, pp. 22ff.

37. The father of the well-known musician Karl Friedrich Abel (1725–87).

38. Würdig was at the same time a town musician. In addition to his duties in the court orchestra, he was called on to play dance music, e.g., on Friederike Henrietta's birthday (Jan. 24, 1722). The household accounts record:

   1722.   *Feb. 7.*   To the musician Würdig for performing at the Royal Birthday and playing dance music, on 12 occasions: 30 Thalers, 12 Groschen.

39. Cf. *Bach-Urkunden*, ed. Max Schneider, Veröffentlichungen der Neuen Bach-Gesellschaft, vol. 17, no. 3 (Leipzig, 1917).

40. For further details relating to visiting French horn players see note 28 above, the entries of Sept. 6, 1721, and June 6, 1722, and note 30, the entries of May 10, 1724 and Aug. 18, 1725.

41. In the eminently readable text that accompanies the magnificent facsimile edition of the Brandenburg Concertos (Leipzig: C. F. Peters, 1950, p. 6) Peter Wackernagel also states that this refers to a copy in his own hand. Here Bach brought together six of the numerous, now for the most part lost, concertos he had composed for Prince Leopold's orchestra. Vetter (see note 5) writes on page 215 of his book that the "multicolored

instrumentation" of these works one could describe "in an ideal sense as Bach's Köthen orchestra." I believe I have been able to show that this was indeed very much the case. Nevertheless, it is clear that Bach had an entirely artistic intention in mind when he chose these pieces to go together. This is evident from Vetter's excellent observations on the internal coherence of the six concertos. Bernh. Paumgartner (*Bach*, p. 321) adheres to the idea that the works were composed for the margrave of Brandenburg but adds that Bach would have played through the pieces with the Köthen chamber musicians "before the painstakingly written fair copy by the master himself set off on its journey into the archival dust of the library of Christian Ludwig of Brandenburg."

42. Cf. note 30 for details relating to the appearances of visiting oboists.

43. Philipp Spitta (German edition, I:821) also places Cantata No. 47, *Wer sich selbst erhöhet*, in the Köthen period in the year 1720. [*Ed.: This chronological attribution is no longer credited.*]

44. [*Ed.: The texts of these libretti by Hunold may be found in Werner Neumann, ed., Sämtliche von J. S. Bach vertonte Texte (Leipzig, 1974). They were first printed in facsimile in Smend's original volume.*]

45. The forthcoming event is unmistakably hinted at in the penultimate number of the "Pastoral Dialog," where we hear that the shepherd, i.e., Prince Leopold, has chosen for himself "the most beautiful shepherdess."

46. If what is so near to Vetter's heart (see note 5) is indeed the case, i.e., that we must speak of denominational broadmindedness, then this must be primarily with an eye to the Köthen royal household and the Anhalt clergy. Leipzig adhered to the tradition banning the use of women's voices in art song that formed part of the divine service. Elsewhere, however, even in Lutheran churches, this rule was being relaxed. (Cf. Arno Werner, *Städtische und fürstliche Musikpflege in Weissenfels bis zum Ende des 18. Jahrhunderts* [Leipzig, 1911], p. 67).

47. Vol. 44 of the complete edition of the Bach-Gesellschaft (BG), *Manuscripts of J. S. Bach* (1895), reproduces on sheet 8 the first side of the score of *Durchlauchtster Leopold*. Here Bach had written the parody text below the original wording.

48. Philipp Spitta discovered this fragmentary score and immediately realized that it was to all appearances a composition for the turn of the year and must in fact have been written for the end of 1721 (*Bach*, German edition, 2:480, 822ff.). When Terry ascribes the work to the time of Princess Gisela Agnes's birth (Sept. 21, 1722), he disregards Spitta's clear statements. (Cf. *Bach*, 1st German edition [1929], p. 161; reprint [Leipzig and Berlin, 1950], p. 124). Terry's grounds for his assertion, namely that "the princess" appears in the text of the cantata, are without foundation; Spitta showed that only the dowager princess Gisela Agnes, Leopold's mother, could have been intended here. Equally unfounded is Bernh. Paumgartner's hypothesis (*Bach*, p. 324) that the cantata was written for Leopold's wedding (Dec. 11, 1721).

49. [*Ed.: Smend here listed for comparison various facsimile publications that were available as specimens of J.S. Bach's handwriting; since this subject has been considerably expanded on since 1950 and the number of discussions of Bach's handwriting, as well as of examples of it available through photography, is vast, we have omitted this list and recommend the curious reader to consult literature listed in the Bach bibliography in* The New Grove Dictionary of Music and Musicians *under the heading "Source Material" for a proper introduction to this subject.*]

50. Bernh. Paumgartner transfers the serenade *Durchlauchtster Leopold* to the royal birthday in the year 1718 without, however, any source reference or other form of justification (*Bach*, p. 322).

51. Concerning this movement, Arnold Schering writes (*BJ*, 1930, p. 78 n. 4): "The choral element is admittedly scantily defined. The movement gives the clear impression that four solo voices are intended. If ripieno voices had been available, they could only have entered after bar 40, in conformity with the instruments. They are not assigned any particularly rewarding task." With these remarks Schering is defining decisive characteristics of Bach's cantata choruses.

52. Cf. *BJ*, 1938, p. 79.

53. Spitta, *Bach*, German edition, 2:273.
54. Cf. *BJ*, 1938, p. 79.
55. [*Ed.*: *Smend here appended a list of works supposedly arranged by Bach for subsequent use and reuse from earlier vocal compositions; however, there is evidence that some of these had been conceived in two forms from an early stage in the compositional process.*]
56. *Bach*, 2:216.
57. [*Ed.*: *In this note, Smend discussed the cantata* Das ist je gewisslich wahr, *and declared that, if it were by Bach* (it was considered doubtful that this might be the case), *it could only have been composed at Köthen. The cantata, cataloged by Schmieder as BWV 141, has since been proved to be a composition of G. P. Telemann that Bach is unlikely to have known; it was composed for 1717 and is listed in Menke's catalog of Telemann's vocal works (Frankfurt am Main, 1982) as TVWV 1:181. Smend extends his hypothesis to speculate whether, in fact, that cantata was itself thematically associated with a (Bach) birthday homage cantata for Prince Leopold's birthday.*]
58. Cf. *Archiv f. Musikforschung* 7 (1942): 3ff.
59. Bach himself followed this method of notation particularly when he was writing out fair copies. This may be seen, e.g., from the autograph score of the *St. Matthew Passion*. Only in this way can we explain the oversight in the copying down of the words "Und Joseph nahm den Leib und wickelte ihn in ein rein Leinwand und legte ihn in sein" (And when Joseph had taken the body, he wrapped it in a clean linen cloth, and laid it in his own—Matt. 27:59–60). By mistake, these words, which fill a complete line of the manuscript, are placed not between the vocal part and the basso continuo but below it. This escaped Max Schneider's notice; he imagined that Bach had used in the recitatives the highly impractical method of notation whereby he first wrote down the musical notes and only then the text (cf. BG 4, New Edition, p. xviii, to p. 211, bar 6).
60. The same phenomenon occurs fairly often in Bach's parodies, e.g., in the duet (in the final version, the chorus) of the *Easter Oratorio*. Originally, the text here ran "Kommt, gehet und eilet." Only later did Bach convert this to "Kommt, eilet und laufet."
61. Spitta, *Bach*, German edition, 2:464.
62. *BJ*, 1934, p. 76.
63. Spitta, *Bach*, German edition, 1:724. The movement, which was previously accessible only in the collected edition (BG 9, pp. 252–257) is appended in this volume. [*Ed.*: *It is now readily available, besides being included in the New Bach Edition (NBA); therefore the example has been omitted from this edition.*]
64. Cf. note 45.
65. For the text, see Appendix A, pp. 211–13.
66. The household accounts record:

> 1721.   *March 1.* To the same (Monjou) for the Carmina most humbly presented on the royal birthday in the presence of the councillors: 4 Thalers.

Thus, the payment of the fee took place somewhat late, though it could only have dealt with Leopold's birthday. Among similar family celebrations only the birthday of Princess Christiane Charlotte, the prince's unmarried sister (Jan. 12) fell between Dec. 10 and March 1. But in none of the years is there any evidence of a musical performance on that day.
67. Cf. note 27.
68. My view of Bach's knowledge of French differs from that of Gustav Fock (cf. his excellent book *Der junge Bach in Lüneburg* [Hamburg: Merseburger, 1950], pp. 43f.).
69. Cf. the work by Wäschke in the *Zerbster Jahrbuch* 3 (1907): 38.
70. The household accounts record:

> 1722.   *Nov. 28.* To the same (J. S. Bach), in connection with the cantata for the royal birthday: 2 Thalers.

> 1723.   *April 3.* To the same (J. S. Bach) for having had the "poetry" [text]

for New Year prepared and bound: 2 Thalers.

71. The full title runs as follows:

> When, by the grace of Almighty God, His Serene Prince and Highness, LORD LEOPOLD, Prince of Anhalt, Duke of Saxony, Engern, and Westphalia, Count of Ascania, Lord of Berenburg and Zerbst, etc., etc., and his most beloved wife and consort, Her Highness FRIDERICA HENRIETTA, by birth and marriage the Princess of Anhalt, Duchess of Saxony, Engern, and Westphalia, Countess of Ascania, Lady of Berenburg and Zerbst, etc., etc., and Her Serene Highness, the young Princess, in the year MDCCXXIII after the birth of the Lord our Savior, in special good health and sovereign well-being, had taken their places, the Kapellmeister, together with all the chamber musicians, was to perform most respectfully his humble bounden duty with a musical DRAMA. Köthen. Printed by the Löffler press.

> [Ed.: For the German text, see Smend's original, p. 161 n. 71, or the facsimile of the only exemplar in Werner Neumann, Sämtliche von Johann Sebastian Bach vertonte Texte (Leipzig, 1974), pp. 386f.]

72. Vetter declares (see note 5; Der Kapellmeister Bach, p. 6), that Bach's petition for release from his duties at Mühlhausen of June 25, 1708, and his letter to Georg Erdmann of Oct. 28, 1730, are "quite simply the most illuminating documents we have in relation to Bach's life." Even though we must concede that the letter (Vetter refers to it again and again unflatteringly as the "Erdmann letter") is "not an outburst of anger" (p. 7), it still should not be accorded the importance that Vetter gives it. (On page 355 he even speaks of its "immeasurable significance.")

73. The household accounts record:

> 1726.   October 21. For covering the chamber music Carmina and producing 10 copies bound in gilt paper for the churching of Her Serene Highness our Most Gracious Princess held yesterday: 1 Thaler, 3 Groschen.

74. Bach's poem addressed to the heir to the throne is reproduced in J. S. Bach: Briefe, complete edition, ed. Hedwig and E. H. Müller von Asow, 2d augmented edition (Regensburg: G. Bosse, 1950), pp. 87f. [Ed.: It is also to be found in Bach-Dokumente (Leipzig, 1963), item 155, pp. 223f.]

75. Cf. BG 20, 2, pp. x–xii, where, however, the text from Picander's verses is reproduced only in a very incomplete form. In the first place, the division of the work into four parts has been ignored. Then the recitatives have been omitted, as well as the comment at the end of the second part, "Repetatur Dictum," i.e., the instruction to repeat the movement (Ps. 68:21) with which this part opens. Regrettably, the inappropriate image of the work that results from these omissions has been carried over into Wolfgang Schmieder, Thematisch-systematisches Verzeichnis der musikalischen Werke von Joh. Seb. Bach (Leipzig: Breitkopf and Härtel, 1950), p. 345, no. 244a. See also Spitta, Bach, German edition, 2:449f. [Ed.: The complete text of the work may be found in Werner Neumann, ed., Sämtliche von J. S. Bach vertonte Texte (Leipzig, 1974), pp. 398ff.; see also pp. 182, 344f. Smend included the complete text in the first edition of Bach in Köthen.]

76. [Ed.: Smend here discussed the presumed musical relationships between the Köthen funeral music and Bach's musically unpreserved St. Mark Passion (the Markuspassion, BWV 247). These supposed relationships stem from metrical and emotional similarities between the two preserved texts. Attempts to reconstruct the Markuspassion, incorporating materials derived from Bach's own music, have been made since 1951.]

77. Cf. my postscript to the first edition of Bach's pastoral cantata, Entfliehet, verschwindet, entweichet, ihr Sorgen (Kassel: Bärenreiter-Verlag, 1943).

78. Cf. BG 20, 2, p. xviii. [Ed.: Also KB to NBA I/36 and I/37.]

79. Bernh. Paumgartner (Bach, p. 345) makes the correct assumption here but cites the Biblical reference incorrectly (Ps. 48:20).

196

80. The volume of documents contains in the first instance the following:

Sheet 1r–8r	Report of the death and burial of Leopold.
8v–14v	"Regulations for the conduct of the funeral of the mortal remains of the erstwhile Most Serene Prince and Lord, Lord Leopold, Prince of Anhalt, Duke of Saxony, Engern, and Westphalia, Count of Ascania, Lord of Berenburg and Zerbst, on March 23, 1729."
15r–38v	There now follow individual instructions to all groups of persons taking part in the ceremonies (quartermasters, equerries, leaders of the noble young torch-bearers, leaders of the bodyguard, chief marshals, marshals with various other functions, representatives of the guilds, sundry artisans, and the palace guard).
39r–40v	"Regulation for the Conduct of the Mortal Remains of His Royal Highness the Prince, March 23, 1729."
40v–41r	A brief description of the funeral ceremony during the night of March 23–24, together with the divine service held on the morning of March 24, 1729.
41r–48r	"Account of the burial of the mortal remains of the erstwhile Most Serene Prince and Lord, Lord Leopold, Prince of Anhalt, March 23, 1729, and of the funeral oration on the following day."
49r–61r	Report of the doctor on the death and causes of death of the Prince.
62r–74r	Drafts, etc., of the final versions of the preceding documents.
75r–88r	Leopold's career.
89r–89v	Another description of the funeral ceremonies.
90r–91v	Two pages of the handwritten text of the funeral music of March 24, 1729 (there having been an error in the enumeration of the documents in this volume!).
91r–94v	The printed text of the same piece of music.
95r–95v	A page of the handwritten text, continuation of sheet 91v.
96r–107r	Instructions concerning guests to be invited and provision for their accommodation.
108r–111r	Allocation of places for the guests at the individual tables at the royal banquet.
112r–123r	Succession of the bill of fare of the dinner at the individual tables.
124r–128r	List of the special allowances to servants for funeral clothing, etc.

81. Sheets 91–94 in the volume of documents referred to in note 80. The title page is reproduced in the appendix on page 204 of this book [*Ed.: i.e., Smend's original edition; it has not been included in this translation*].

82. [*Ed.: All the detailed variants are presented in the original edition of Smend's Bach in Köthen on pp. 209–19; see also the full and shortened printed versions reproduced in facsimile from Löffler's separate print (Köthen, 1729) and Picander's third volume of Collected Poems (Leipzig, 1732) in Neumann's Collected Texts; cf. note 75 above.*]

83. Sheets 90 and 95 of the volume of documents listed above under note 80.

84. Here again curiosities in the text are closely linked to the parody process itself, as we found in the case of the cantatas *Ihr Häuser des Himmels* and *Ihr Tore zu Zion*, as well as in the *Easter Oratorio*.

85. This is not included in the documentary record of the expenditures incurred at Leopold's funeral (see end of note 80). Neither do the musicians figure among the guests noted at the banqueting tables. [*Ed.: Maybe they helped to serve, or played* Tafelmusik.]

86. Sheet 89ʳ of the volume of documents described in note 80. The other accounts in that volume are worded as follows:

> Sheet 40ᵛ   At the burial of His Serene Highness on Wednesday evening, March 23, 1729, music will be performed as the mortal remains of His Serene Highness enter the church. A prayer will be read and the hymn "Nun laßt uns den Leib begraben" sung. After the blessing, the hymn "Herzlich lieb hab ich dich, o Herr."

> 41ʳff.   The "account of the burial . . . and the funeral oration on the following day" begins with a description of the removal of the coffin from the royal chapel and its transference to the Jakobikirche, giving the order of the procession in the most minute detail. Then follows:

> 44ʳ–46ʳ: "When the cortege passed the palace guard in the above order, the latter stood at arms and presented arms without beating the drums. Outside the church all the torches remained behind including, the 12 taper columns borne by the young noblemen. Inside the church all the galleries and the choir seats were draped in black, likewise were the burial vaults in the form of two portals draped in black and illuminated with lamps and lights. The central aisle of the church between the seats of the women was similarly decked in black drapes, with lights everywhere overhead. As soon as the procession, including the prince's mortal remains, in the aforesaid order, reached the high gallery of the church, the horses were unharnessed, the admitted attendants dismounted, remaining by the third chief marshals, while the other marshals led the guests in their charge to their appointed places. Meanwhile the music began, whereupon Consistorial Councillor Friedel said a prayer before the Communion table, and when they began to sing the hymn "Nun laßt uns den Leib begraben," the funeral carriage was drawn most gently by the guildsmen into the royal vault, the third chief marshals, attendants, and guard preceding. As soon as these had all left the vault again, the Blessing was said and a funeral hymn was sung. After this each and every one returned home in his own time."

87. Sheet 89ᵛ of the volume of documents described in note 80. The remaining accounts are worded as follows: [*Ed.: Here Smend quoted two further accounts of the funeral that in most important respects corroborate that quoted in full in the main text. See, however, also note 88.*]

88. There is no mention in any of the manuscript reports of the funeral music of March 24, 1729. The two descriptions that form note 87, where court ceremonial is clearly considerably more important to the authors than the arrangements for the divine service, are inconsistent. Sheet 40ᵛ mentions only two occasions when music was performed, whereas sheets 46ff. speak of three musical performances; thus in this respect the accounts are incomplete. The compelling reason for the belief that all four parts of the ceremony were accompanied by music is the extant original printed libretto and the note on the manuscript of the text.

89. [*Ed.: Here Smend devoted considerable attention to conflicting opinions concerning the order of composition of the Köthen funeral music and parallel sections of the St. Matthew Passion, BWV 244. The redating of the first performance of the Passion to*

Good Friday, 1727, in an early form (BWV 244b), established by Joshua Rifkin in 1975, as well as an article by Paul Brainard, "Bach's Parody Procedure and the St. Matthew Passion," Journal of the American Musicological Society 22(1969): 241ff., render many of Smend's arguments invalid today.]

90. Joh. Nikol. Forkel, *Über Joh. Seb. Bachs Leben, Kunst und Kunstwerke* (Leipzig, 1802), p. 56. (Reprinted with the same pagination by Bärenreiter-Verlag, Kassel). Forkel dedicated his book to Baron van Swieten. Both Vetter (see note 5) and Gerhard Herz (J. S. *Bach im Zeitalter des Rationalismus und der Frühromantik* [Kassel: Bärenreiter-Verlag, 1935], p. 67) regard this dedication as "proof that the author wanted to win over the Viennese circle to the Bach cause" (Vetter, p. 41). In 1802, however, this was no longer necessary in Baron van Swieten's case (cf. Alfred Einstein, *Mozart* [Stockholm, 1947], pp. 212ff.).

91. Spitta's remark that Forkel's knowledge of the *St. Matthew Passion* was "probably in any case only superficial" (*Bach*, German edition, 2:450 n. 19) is of relevance here. At any rate, it is clear that this great worker in the field of Bach research recognized at this early stage the irreconcilability of Forkel's account with Rust's statements in connection with the Köthen funeral music. Bernh. Paumgartner correctly concludes that there could never have been a score of Bach's funeral music that exactly set Picander's published text. When he points out elsewhere (*Bach*, p. 345) that Forkel maintained in 1802 he had seen a copy of this score, we are obliged to draw our own conclusions regarding the Göttingen scholar's reliability.

Unfortunately, J. Müller-Blattau, in his postscript to the above-mentioned reprint of Forkel's Bach biography, does not deal with the crucial and decisive issue in connection with any assessment of this work, namely the extent of Forkel's knowledge of Bach. In trying to answer this question, we must first consult the *Verzeichniß der von dem verstorbenen Doctor und Musikdirector Forkel in Göttingen nachgelassenen Bücher und Musikalien, welche den 10ten May 1819 . . . meistbietend verkauft werden* (Göttingen: F. E. Huth, 1819). It is evident from this auction catalog that the only vocal works by Bach in Forkel's possession, apart from a problematical "Missa a 8 voci reali e 4 repiene coll'acc. di due orchestre" (No. 52 in the catalog) and the "Missa a 5 Voci 6 Stromenti e Continuo" (No. 67 in the catalog), were the two pieces of funeral music that he discussed. These were described there as follows:

95   (Bach, J. Sebast.) Funeral music on the death of the electress of Saxony, Christ. Eberhard. Original score of Oct. 18, 1727, stitched.

124ᶜ   (Bach, J. Sebast.) Funeral music. Score, Parts 1–3.

(According to a statement by Wilhelm Rust [BG 13, 3, p. vi], Forkel possessed the autograph score of the funeral ode of 1727. The addition of the word "stitched," which appears at the end of the description of catalog number 95, is either a mistake or could refer to a single printed copy of the text that certainly did exist originally but had been lost in the meantime and that had stood at the beginning of the score).

Forkel had none of the remaining vocal works by Bach, including the Passions, and was only indirectly aware of their existence. In other words, there was no way in which the identification of certain movements in the Köthen funeral music with passages from the *St. Matthew Passion* could have occurred to him. On the other hand, this fact could not have escaped his notice had the first section of the funeral music listed under catalog number 124ᶜ begun with the opening chorus of the funeral ode of 1727 and ended with its final chorus. This adds further support to the view that Bach composed two works for Köthen ceremonies, one of which, now entirely lost, was performed at the nocturnal burial and came into Forkel's possession later.

92. In his letter of resignation from his post at Mühlhausen (dated June 25, 1708) Bach spoke of his "ultimate objective, which was to perform regular church music in God's honor and according to your will." Historically speaking, one can apply this statement in the first instance only to Bach's activity in Mühlhausen. "In God's honor and according to your will" were the words Bach addressed to his previous municipal authorities in his effort to comply with their intentions. If one transfers these words, as is so frequently

the case in the church's view of Bach's work, to his entire output, they are taken out of context and their import is diminished. In his move to Weimar, Bach was anticipating that he would there too be able to pursue his "ultimate aim of improving church music." At Köthen, however, even though thanks to the prince's love of music and the denominational tolerance of the clergy figural music did feature in certain religious festivals, Bach's intentions were fulfilled only to a limited extent. It is unfortunate when we read over and over again in Vetter's book (see note 5) that the author, in the context of Bach's "ultimate intention" in respect of "church music," merely substitutes the term "music" and in doing so believes that the composer fulfilled his intentions as expressed in the 1708 letter in the *Wohltemperiertes Klavier* and the Brandenburg Concertos just as well as in the religious works, perhaps even more satisfactorily. And when Bach, some five and a half years later, moved from Köthen to Leipzig, he was entering a territory where the realization of what he described as his "ultimate intention" in 1708 was feasible in a way that was entirely different from what he had been able to achieve at the small court of the Reformed principality of Anhalt. In this respect Bach returned in 1723 to a path he had abandoned in 1717. The Köthen period, however, should not be seen as a detour but as an inwardly essential stage in Bach's own development, in that the fruits of his Köthen activities, particularly including the works that were not intended for the church and divine service, were of benefit to the Leipzig vocal compositions, especially those of his early years in that city. In fact, without a knowledge of Köthen, the early Leipzig cantatas are not fully comprehensible. On this higher plane, if one wishes to stress the statement of 1708 so forcibly, Bach did remain faithful to his "ultimate purpose." [*Ed.: The modern reader should bear in mind that Smend's assumptions regarding the chronology of Bach's Leipzig church music were mainly based on outdated theories that Alfred Dürr's "Zur Chronologie der Leipziger Vokalwerke J. S. Bachs" (BJ, 1957, pp. 5–162) was to alter completely. Indeed, one of the criteria used to place each early Leipzig years previously was its inclusion of apparent Köthen (mainly Brandenburg or other concerto) influence.*]

93. This work, *Entfernet euch, ihr heitern Sterne*, of which only the text composed by Christian Friedrich Haupt has survived, was performed on the evening of May 12, 1727 (cf. BG 34, pp. xliii–xlv; Spitta, *Bach*, German version, 2:450, 459). Terry (*Bach*, 1st German edition [1929], p. 222. Reprint [Leipzig and Berlin, 1950], p. 166) says on this point: "On May 12 Elector August II came to Leipzig. His visit was in connection with the Jubilate Sunday Mass. In 1727 Jubilate Sunday fell on May 4." In actual fact, the sovereign's arrival in Leipzig, as Spitta had already told us, occurred on May 3, the Saturday before Jubilate Sunday. The incorrect statement in Terry is due to an error by the translator.

94. BG 36, p. 316.

95. Dance forms also figure prominently in Bach's Köthen concertos. Note particularly the sequence of dances at the end of the first Brandenburg Concerto.

96. Spitta, *Bach*, German edition, p. 424.

97. Cf. Bernh. Friedrich Richter, "Über J. Seb. Bachs Kantaten mit obligater Orgel," *BJ*, 1908, pp. 49–63. [*Ed.: The cantatas having obbligato organ parts are today, however, considered to come mostly from the years 1726–27.*]

98. Among the best sections of Vetter's book, *Der Kapellmeister Bach* (see note 5), belong the parts that are dedicated to these transcriptions. His comments on the opening number of Cantata No. 174, *Ich liebe den Höchsten*, and its relationship to the third Brandenburg Concerto (Vetter, pp. 224ff.) may be cited as an example. [*Ed.: See also KB to NBA I/14, p. 65.*]

99. This phenomenon was not entirely new in the Köthen works either. In his essay "Die Meisterzeit Bachs in Weimar" (*Bach in Thüringen: Festgabe* [Weimar, 1950], pp. 106ff.) Heinrich Besseler draws attention to individual movements from those years, e.g., the final duet of Cantata No. 152, *Tritt auf die Glaubensbahn*, which is related to the slow dance known as the Loure. We find a similar connection between the soprano aria "Wirf, mein Herze" from Cantata No. 155, *Mein Gott, wie lang, ach lange*, and the gigue. [*Ed.: See also the much more detailed treatment—not all of it supporting Smend's*

assumptions—in Doris Finke-Hecklinger, Tanzcharaktere in Bachs Vokalmusik, *Tübinger Bach-Studien 6 (Trossingen, 1970).*]

100. Cf. in particular Bernh. Friedr. Richter, "Die Wahl J. S. Bachs zum Kantor der Thomasschule i. J. 1723," *BJ*, 1905, pp. 48ff.). [*Ed.: However, see editorial note 56 below.*]

101. "Die Johannes-Passion von Bach, auf ihre Form untersucht," *BJ*, 1926, pp. 105ff.

102. *BJ*, 1928, p. 43.

103. Earlier, in my study of the *St. Matthew Passion* published in the *Bach-Jahrbuch* (1928, p. 42), I compared the structure of this piece with that of the first Brandenburg Concerto.

104. I have already explained in note 92 that I attach qualified importance to the programmatic significance of Bach's remark about the "ultimate purpose" of his music (cf. the Mühlhausen petition for release, 1707) in terms of his life's work as a whole.

105. Wilhelm Rust in the preface to BG 12, 2, pp. v f.; Bernh. Friedr. Richter, "Über die Schicksale der der Thomasschule zu Leipzig angehörenden Kantaten J. S. Bach," *BJ*, 1906, pp. 43ff.; Rud. Wustmann, *J. S. Bachs Kantatentexte* (Leipzig, 1913), introduction, p. ix.

106. Reprinted version, arranged by Bernh. Friedr. Richter, *BJ*, 1920, pp. 13ff.

107. *List of the items of music in the estate of the late Kapellmeister Carl Philipp Emanuel Bach* (Hamburg, 1790). Reprint arranged by Heinrich Miesner, *BJ*, 1938, pp. 106ff.; ibid., 1939, pp. 81ff.; ibid., 1940/48, pp. 161ff. The list of J. S. Bach compositions in their original printed form may be found reproduced on pp. 66–81 (reprint in *BJ*, 1939, pp. 87–93). [*Ed.: Also in* Bach Dokumente, *vol. 3 (Leipzig, 1972); translation:* The Catalog of C. P. E. Bach's Estate . . . *(New York and London, 1981).*]

108. Cf. my study "Neue Bach-Funde," *Archiv f. Musikforschung* 7 (1942): 1ff.

109. Cf. the comments on the *B Minor Mass* [BWV 232]: in *BJ*, 1937, pp. 10–44, in particular those on "Osanna" and "Dona nobis pacem." The *Easter Oratorio* [BWV 249] should also be mentioned in this context.

110. See, for example, the recent discussion in Walter Blankenburg, "J. S. Bach und die Aufklärung," *Bach: Gedenkschrift* (Internationale Bach-Gesellschaft, 1950), pp. 25ff.). [*Ed.: See also* Bach-Studien 7, Johann Sebastian Bach und die Aufklärung *(Leipzig, 1982).*]

111. The very verses by Hunold that Bach set to music bear eloquent witness to this point. The reader's attention is drawn to the alterations undertaken to Picander's original text for Bach's funeral music on the occasion of the death of Leopold of Köthen [BWV 244a]. Picander himself was inclined to glorify world rulers in the sense of the heroes of antiquity. On Feb. 27, 1723, he sent a poem to Augustus the Strong on the occasion of his recovery after a grave illness. There he wrote:

> Die Schrifften mögen viel von jenem August sagen
> Und des Trajanus Lob bis an die Sterne tragen!
> Es schließe beyder Ruhm sich in ein Wesen ein,
> So werden beyde doch kein Sachsens August seyn.

> (The Ancients may say much of their Augustus
> And they may praise Trajan to the skies!
> If you put the fame of both together in one man,
> The pair of them would still not equal Saxony's Augustus.)

The inclusion of the name of Augustus alongside that of Trajan as a praiseworthy emperor matches Tacitus's view. Added to the poem is a quotation from the works of Horace (c. I. 2, vv. 45f.), from the ode for the end of the year 28, in which the *princeps* is celebrated as "Novus Mercurius" immediately before the name Augustus is conferred. Further echoes of Horace may be found in Bach's cantata *Ihr Häuser des Himmels* [BWV 193a], composed to a text by Picander. Here the ruler Augustus the Strong, on "the advice of the gods" is set among the stars, in the same way as in Horace (c. III. 25, 6), Augustus, in accordance with the "consilium Jovis," is consigned to the heavenly realm. Just as Horace (c. IV. 5, 25ff.) lauds the stable rule of Augustus under whom

Rome has nothing to fear from the Parthians in the east or the wild tribes of Spain in the west, so Picander cleverly transposes the situation:

Soll ich von Englands Pein,
Von Moscaus Plagen
Noch ferner sagen?
Nein! Nein!

(Need I say more
Of what troubles England
Or plagues Moscow?
No! No!)

Similarly, Horace's words "Praesenti tibi largimur honores" (ep. II. 1, v. 15), which come at the end of the cantata text, are directed at the *princeps*. I am indebted to my esteemed friend Hildebrecht Hommel for this information. (See his book *Horaz, der Mensch und das Werk* [Heidelberg, 1950], in particular p. 119.)

112. Cf. in this context, apart from the statements made by Wilhelm Rust (BG 12, 1st Preface) and Phil. Spitta (*Bach*, German edition, 2:349ff.), the latter's study "Die Arie 'Ach, mein Sinn' " in *Musikgeschichtliche Aufsätze* (Berlin, 1894), pp. 101ff. Also, Rud. Wustmann, "Zu Bachs Texten der Johannes- und der Matthäus-Passion" *Monatschrift f. Gottesdienst u. kirchl. Kunst* 15 (1910): 126ff., 161ff.

113. Menantes (i.e., Christian Friedrich Hunold), *Theatralische, galante und geistliche Gedichte* (Hamburg: Liebernickel, 1706), containing "Der blutige und sterbende Jesus, wie selbiger in einem Oratorio musicalisch gesetzt und in der stillen Woche aufgeführt worden durch Reinhard Keisern, hochfürstl. Mecklenburg. Capell-Meistern." Cf. Spitta, *Bach*, German edition, 2:321f. The Hamburg performance took place in 1704.

114. G. F. Händel, *Werke*, ed. Friedrich Chrysander for the Deutsche Händel-Gesellschaft, vol. 9.

115. This movement, including the preceding recitative may be found below, p. 215.

116. The opinion of Heinrich Besseler in the final paragraph of his study, "Die Meisterzeit Bachs in Weimar," in *Bach in Thüringen: Festgabe* (Weimar, 1950), p. 119.

117. The first to relate Gerber's verdict to Bach's *St. Matthew Passion* was C. H. Bitter, *Bach*, 2d edition (1881), 2:58. Terry (*Bach*, 1st German edition [1929], p. 231. Reprint [Leipzig and Berlin, 1950], p. 173) quotes the passage incompletely and therefore misleadingly. At the same time he confuses the clergyman Christian Gerber with Bach's pupil Heinrich Nikolaus Gerber. Similarly, in the first-rate collection of source extracts relating to Bach's life that H. T. David and A. Mendel published in English under the title *The Bach Reader* (New York: W. W. Norton and Co., 1945), Gerber's statement is taken to refer to the *St. Matthew Passion*. Here too the key opening sentences are omitted.

118. Spitta, *Bach*, German edition, 1:474.

119. F. Blankmeister, *Der Pfarrer von Lockwitz Christian Gerber* (1893).

120. Cf. F. Bosse, *Realencyklopädie für protestantische Theologie und Kirche*, 3d edition (1898), 4:460–64.

121. Credit is due to Rudolf Wustmann for having pointed this out in *J. S. Bachs Kantatentexte* (Leipzig, 1913); cf. p. xxxiv.

122. See the notice in the Leipzig Council Records, "Die Schule zu St. Thomae betr.," of March 17, 1739, which Spitta reproduces (*Bach*, German edition, 2:868). I have shown elsewhere that this refers directly to the *St. Matthew Passion* (*BJ*, 1928, pp. 78f.).

123. Cf. note 110.

Editor's Notes

E1. Since the 1950s, during the preparation of the NBA, a number of the listed works—the ensemble suites partly or wholly, the sonatas for viola da gamba in their preserved form, other concertos and sonatas (but not the Brandenburg Concertos), as well as parts of the harpsichord suites (BWV 806–17)—have been ascribed to Bach's Leipzig years. There is also at least some possibility that some of the remaining chamber music, keyboard music, and possibly certain early parts of the Brandenburg and other concertos had existed in earlier forms during Bach's Weimar period (1708–17). For full discussion of this instrumental part of Bach's music, the reader is advised to consult the relevant commentary (*KB*) volumes to the NBA, together with other recent studies by authorities such as Hans Grüss (preface to miniature scores of the ensemble suites, BWV 1066–69, Bärenreiter/Deutscher Verlag), Hans Eppstein (studies of Bach's sonatas in various scholarly and editorial contexts), Christoph Wolff (commentaries on J. S. Bach's chamber music accompanying phonograph recordings issued by Teldec and Phonogram [DG 'Archiv']), besides subsequent volumes of the *Bach-Jahrbuch* and the usual international journals of music scholarship.

E2. The Brandenburg Concertos are obviously outstanding as examples of music of their genre, but they are perhaps not as unique in instrumentation or style as some scholars have suggested; rather they are superlative examples of the multiconsort ensemble concerto, a kind of music current in Germany for nearly a century (or more than a century) when they were copied out in 1721 and of which there are interesting preserved examples by Telemann, Heinichen, Vivaldi, and others of J. S. Bach's contemporaries.

E3. Unfortunately, this has by no means been continued since the time of Smend's postwar researches. The Oranienbaum Anhalt-Archives do not seem to respond to inquiries (either from this editor or from others), even when these are nominally supported by national bodies or international authorities from within and outside the German Democratic Republic; as with so much original research that reaches publication, the material outlined only leads to a multiplicity of further lines for inquiry; many questions arise regarding the life of the Köthen court (e.g., regarding the prince's periods of absence from the town: Did he never visit Dresden, Weissenfels, Weimar, Halle, or Bernburg [from which town he married a princess] during the years of Bach's service? Did he visit Berlin or Potsdam? Was Karlsbad the only fashionable spa visited by the prince?). There must be archival records resulting from the arrangements for these visits (surely there were some). As Smend himself admitted, he only considered that he had begun to investigate the implications of these archives, which have since become—most tantalizingly—inaccessible.

E4. Frederick William I of Prussia laid the foundations for the rising military and economic strength of Prussia between 1713 and the Napoleonic Wars, which was eventually to lead to the unification of Germany in both political and cultural respects. However, unlike his more celebrated heir Frederick II ("the Great"), he was uninterested in the arts.

E5. Further discoveries concerning the management and even the constitution of the Köthen Hofkapelle were revealed by the local historian Ernst König in his article "Die Hofkapelle des Fürsten Leopold zu Anhalt-Köthen," *BJ*, 1959, pp. 160ff.; these are included in the material supplied in chapter 18.

E6. Further evidence regarding Brandenburg Concerto No. 5 indicates that it was composed some time before 1721 (cf. Alfred Dürr, "Zur Entstehungsgeschichte des 5. Brandenburgischen Konzerte," *BJ*, 1975, pp. 63ff.); since the discovery by Ernst König (cf. *BJ*, 1959) of a number of additional string players available in Köthen around 1720, the argument that Bach omitted a second ripieno violin part from this concerto *out of necessity* is certainly weakened, and in any event, the omission of the third violin line was surely deliberately chosen by Bach for good, *purely musical* reasons, since the increased prominence of the viola in the ensemble would offset the transverse flute to special advantage, and this was *one of Bach's first compositions for transverse flute, if not his very first.*

E7. Although it is possible that the trumpet was involved in Cantata 66a (it is inessential to the later Leipzig parody, BWV 66), there is absolutely no certain evidence of the trumpet's involvement in any Köthen cantata; Smend was here relying on the by no means watertight suppositions that all parodies involve common instrumentation and that all of the supposed relationships between Hunold's texts and Bach's preserved music provided clearcut evidence that these were originally associated. Posterity has tended to dispute the latter; the former is by no means supported by Bach's more fully documented parody processes, which were often far less direct.

E8. Although it was quite usual until well into the 18th century for flutists and oboists to exchange instruments with one another and to play the recorders, to assume that these players in particular played recorders in this specific work is somewhat speculative.

E9. It is equally possible that Bach led the ensemble with his violin, surely; in his references to other works also, Smend tends to miss possibilities and probabilities—more likely in the light of Ernst König's revelations (*BJ*, 1959)—that the total ensemble available to Bach at Köthen was quite flexible and rather larger than Smend, Terry, and others had supposed.

E10. The Overture in C (BWV 1066) may not have been composed in Köthen at all; the earliest preserved performing materials were written out at Leipzig in 1724–25. The oboist Rose's son was also earning money at the Schloss before Bach left, in any case; he too became a professional oboist.

E11. The wedding cantata BWV 202 was composed to a text that displays the strong influence of the Weimar poet Salomo Franck; its earliest preserved source is a copy made by Johannes Rinck (?b. 1717) and dated "anno 1730." These two factors cannot be said to support an ascription to Bach's Köthen period, despite certain aspects of its style and form. It is a pity that this work, of which Smend himself admits that "precise dating . . . is not possible," forms so central a part in many of his arguments concerning the vocal music of the Köthen years.

E12. This date is accepted by modern scholars, and the work has been printed in its complete form in the NBA (ed. Alfred Dürr, I/35, p. 51).

E13. A good short biography of C. F. Hunold is in the introduction to Alfred Dürr, *Die Kantaten von Johann Sebastian Bach*, 1st edition (Kassel, 1971), pp. 34f. This excellent work is currently being prepared in an English translation (of the 1984–85 revised edition) for publication ca. 1986 (Chicago and London).

E14. This table is only partly acceptable by the standards of the NBA; cf. *KB*, I/35, pp. 8ff., where Alfred Dürr presents a more accurate summary of the situation regarding the Köthen secular cantatas. The association of the text *Lobet den Herren, alle seine Heerschaaren* (BWV Anh. 5) is slightly tenuous, but a work of that title was performed on the date shown by Smend.

E15. The ascription of BWV Anh. 7 to this date (by which time the librettist would have been dead several months) is considered improbable; cf. *KB*, I/35, pp. 118f. (Alfred Dürr). It seems that Smend was unaware of Spitta's discussion of the work (in P. Spitta, "Über die Beziehungen Sebastian Bachs zu Christian Friedrich Hunold und Mariane von Ziegler: Historische und Philologische Aufsätze," *Festgabe an Ernst von Curtius zum 2. September 1884*).

E16. It is improbable that Anna Magdalena Bach—or the Monjou sisters—performed in church music, although that might have been allowed in the palace chapel; her fee does indicate her professional involvement in the funeral music, however, and this is itself interesting in that it signifies her continuing activity as a singer.

E17. Cf. supporting evidence in *KB*, I/35, pp. 62–86 (by Alfred Dürr).

E18. It is possible to identify dance forms in arias and ensembles throughout Bach's career as a composer of cantatas; they are by no means solely a Köthen phenomenon. Cf. Doris Finke-Hecklinger, "Tanzcharaktere in Bachs Vokalmusik," *Tübinger Bach-Studien* 6 (Trossingen, 1970).

E19. There is little doubt that BWV 184a was in many respects the model for Cantata BWV 184 (itself first heard on May 30, 1724); however, the exact extent of the similarity is uncertain; see *KB*, I/35, pp. 138ff. Most of the instrumental parts for BWV 184 involve Köthen copies of several movements, written on paper that Bach is known to have used at Köthen.

E20. It has long been agreed that the first two movements of Cantata BWV 145 are not by Bach and were probably added to the rest (presumably part of an earlier Bach church cantata) after his death. The second movement, the chorus "So du mit deinem Munde," has been shown to be by Telemann. The duet "Ich lebe, mein Herze" for soprano and tenor and the bass aria "Merke, mein Herze" are probably derived from music composed at Köthen; cf. *KB*, I/10, pp. 128ff. Incidentally, a copy of the score and parts of the Telemann Easter cantata *So du mit deinem Munde* was owned by C. G. Meissner of Gotha, Bach's former *Hauptkopist B*; cf. *KB*, I/10, p. 133.

E21. Bach is not thought to have used the oboe d'amore in Köthen. However, see Hans-Joachim Schulze, "Johann Sebastian Bachs Konzerte: Fragen der Überlieferung und Chronologie," in *Bach-Studien 6* (Leipzig, 1981), pp. 9–26; this paper was originally delivered as a series of lectures in English at universities in the United States.

E22. The copyist was Johann Andreas Kuhnau (known as Alfred Dürr's *Hauptkopist A*); cf. *KB*, I/4, pp. 14, 16. Kuhnau wrote his contribution in the last days of 1723.

E23. Cf. note E21 above; besides, oboes d'amore included in Leipzig music do not necessarily indicate their requirement in earlier versions of which they are parodies.

E24. There can be no certainty that there was a Köthen early version of Cantata BWV 190, although it is possible that some movements might derive from Köthen stylistically. See Werner Neumann's comments in *KB*, I/4, p. 22.

E25. Cf. note E24.

E26. Perhaps not so much a *passepied* as a country dance?

E27. The impression is, indeed, beautiful; but so are the oboe solos of several Weimar and many Leipzig arias, and there is little indication, indeed, that BWV 202, *Weichet nur*, was composed at Köthen.

E28. This is still considered to be possible, but the suggestion has not been reinforced through support from the evidence of those examining the sources; indeed, the similarities to *Weichet nur* (BWV 202) cannot be said to support the theory.

E29. This does not necessarily follow, and some of the later portions of Smend's text go to considerable lengths to stress the avoidance of any distinction between the sacred and the secular sides of musical expression in Bach's musical language.

E30. The final $\frac{6}{8}$ movement of the sonata for violin and obbligato harpsichord was, however, not a part of that composition until the 1730s; it is also possible that sonatas BWV 1015–19 and 1019a partly originated before, partly after, or possibly even entirely after the Köthen period.

E31. This sonata movement in E minor for harpsichord alone is organically related to the bass theme of the ensuing Adagio in B minor; this seems to indicate that whereas at the earliest stage of composition of the sonata, Bach was aiming to produce symmetrical structures built on contrasting moods, by the late 1730s he was more intent on the creation of progressively developing structures that reached forward motivically from one movement to the next.

E32. The Augsburg Confession Bicentennial was celebrated throughout the Lutheran world on June 25–27, 1730; the first of these days was also a Sunday, Trinity 3. For the full translated text of the Augsburg Confession, see Tappert, et al., *The Book of Concord: The Confessions of the Evangelical Lutheran Church* (Philadelphia, 1959), pp. 23–96. Its nine original signatories included the Elector John, Duke of Saxony, and Prince

Wolfgang of Anhalt.

E33. Since 1951, the idea that Bach's chamber music—and even his concertos—all originated in Köthen has had to be modified somewhat; it is improbable that either Cantata BWV 35 or Cantata BWV 120 is a parody of a Köthen cantata, and although BWV 35 is clearly derived from the concerto whose fragmentary opening is cataloged as BWV 1059, the fact that both of these were notated in D minor probably indicates that each originated in Leipzig. See, however, note E37.

E34. See note E20. The duet "Ich lebe, mein Herze" and the bass aria "Merke, mein Herze," both to texts by Picander, might have been partly derived from Köthen music.

E35. *Ihr Häuser des Himmels* (BWV 193a) is a Leipzig homage cantata celebrating the name day of Augustus the Strong for 1727 with a text by Picander but without preserved music. The music possibly derives wholly or partly from Köthen music; there is also a sacred cantata from the Leipzig years that survives complete, and the music of which fits the aria numbers of *Ihr Häuser des Himmels;* this is Cantata BWV 193, *Ihr Tore zu Zion.*

E36. There is now considered to be too little evidence for Smend's ascription of Cantata BWV 32 to the Köthen period.

E37. The date given by Smend for BWV Anh. 7 is reasonable and has not been either proved or disproved by subsequent research.

E38. Binenschneider should be Riemenschneider/Riemschneider. Johann Gottfried Riemschneider was born in Halle on or around Bach's own birthday (i.e., ca. March 21) in 1791. His subsequent career took him to Hamburg and London, where he participated in Handel's *Lotario* and *Partenope.* He was the son of Kantor Gebhardt Riemschneider of Halle and will have known Handel from his school days. Riemschneider is the only performer known to have performed as a soloist under both Bach and Handel in their own music.

E39. However, French was the normal language of the German courts of the time, and the dedication of the Brandenburg Concertos presentation autograph is written by a scribe with a sure and a fluent hand—probably a professional secretary or clerk.

E40. However, no choral movement of Cantata BWV 145 apart from the final chorale is now thought to be by Bach at all.

E41. This argument is weakened considerably by the fact that there is far less certainty to be attached to Smend's ascription of the later Köthen cantatas to their supposed dates (in association with Bach's preserved music) than there is with regard to the earlier ones.

E42. It is now considered highly probable that the *St. Matthew Passion* was already performed in recognizable form on Good Friday 1727 (or maybe 1728)—long before Leopold's death could have been anticipated. Cf. Joshua Rifkin, "The Chronology of Bach's *St. Matthew Passion,*" *The Musical Quarterly* 61 (1975): 360–387.

E43. See note E42.

E44. Friedrich Smend was one of a number of Bach specialists who have placed high significance on the supposed use of number symbolism by Bach and his contemporaries. In one of the various languages of number symbolism, the letters of the alphabet are accorded numbers consecutively ($A = 1$, $B = 2$, $C = 3$, $H = 8$). The total of the letters of Bach's surname is therefore, in this schematic system, $2 + 1 + 3 + 8 = 14$.

E45. This is true to a limited extent, but our impressions of Bach's Köthen compositions have been somewhat modified since 1951. See note E33 and Appendix C.

E46. This is by no means certain. The Weissenfels homage cantata, *Was mir behagt, ist mir die muntre Jagd!* (BWV 208, the "Hunting Cantata") was supposed by Friedrich Smend (and others around 1950) to date from 1716; today, it is generally agreed that it is likely to have been composed for the birthday of Duke Christian of Weissenfels in 1713 (on Feb. 23). There is no preserved evidence that Bach was in Weissenfels at all in 1716.

E47. See notes E20 and E34.

E48. This ingenious argument is invalidated by the critical studies carried out since 1951 during the preparation of the NBA. The two preserved early sources for the Suite in A Minor (BWV 818a) in the collections (Leipzig Mempell-Preller MS. 8; Berlin P804) are not in Kellner's handwriting, although both are written by the same anonymous scribe, who worked for Johann Nikolaus Mempell (1713–47). Although Mempell and Kellner seem to have had quite close relationships and did exchange copies, these anonymous ones of BWV 818a (a revised version of BWV 818) are from the 1740s—well into Bach's Leipzig period.

E49. Since the establishment of the new chronology (see editor's preface), our notion of what constitutes an early Leipzig cantata has changed; although BWV 249a was first performed on Feb. 23, 1725, it was about the 90th of Bach's vocal works thought today to have been performed under Bach by that date in Leipzig. Of the preserved vocal works, all but a few had been performed by 1731, whereas in 1950, when Schmieder first published his thematic catalog of Bach's music—in full cooperation with Friedrich Smend—no fewer than 95 vocal works were considered to have been composed after 1731.

E50. Here Smend originally wrote: "during the Trinity season of 1731"; since nearly all of the cantatas that he supposed to come from the late summer and autumn of 1731 have been reattributed to 1726 or 1727, a direct adjustment seemed most appropriate. To clarify, the dates of the cantatas are shown in brackets in the following discussion.

E51. It is not strictly identical, but is thought to have been reworked from an earlier version of the suite [Ouvertüre] for strings, woodwinds, and continuo without trumpets and drums. Whether this early version of the suite BWV 1069 comes from the Köthen years or the early Leipzig ones (before Christmas 1725) is, however, completely unknown. Smend and his contemporaries generally supposed that all four of Bach's ensemble-Ouvertüren (orchestral suites) had been composed at Köthen; there is only insubstantial evidence that any of them may have been composed before Bach's removal to the city of Leipzig—"kleiner Paris."

E52. This date has been confirmed by subsequent researches.

E53. The part for obbligato organ was added for a later performance than that given on Christmas Day, 1723, indicating that the line was originally written for the oboe; however, the Christmas cantata Christen, ätzet diesen Tag (BWV 63) comes from the Weimar period and has no obvious Köthen associations; preserved parts for the soprano, bass, and oboe for the duet in question, written by Bach himself in Weimar, are preserved today in West Berlin (Bach St 9); their existence invalidates Smend's theory.

E54. See note E51, third sentence.

E55. This certainly applied to the two cantatas, although at that stage BWV 23 did not include its final movement (the chorale, "Christe, du Lamm Gottes," which was later incorporated from the St. John Passion). However, the St. John Passion (BWV 245) was almost certainly not composed in Köthen; at one time it was supposed that Bach wrote the work to reinforce his application to Leipzig and for performance on Good Friday, 1723 (i.e., before his provisional appointment), a hypothesis first presented by B. F. Richter in BJ, 1911. Richter's theory, which Smend adopted, can hardly be totally disproved, but there is little evidence to support it. Cf. Arthur Mendel's summary of the arguments against it in KB, II/4, p. 67 n 1. Mendel prudently stated in conclusion that, while the first performance of the St. John Passion in a form that we might easily recognize was almost certainly first heard in Leipzig on Good Friday (April 7), 1724, it may well have been the case that parts of the work had been in preparation in earlier years, either incomplete or in distinct, but today unrecognized or unpreserved, musical contexts. To state baldly that BWV 245 was composed in advance with the Leipzig Kantorat in mind is, nevertheless, untenable in 1985.

E56. In fact it now appears that Bach probably performed both Cantata BWV 22 and Cantata BWV 23 (without the final chorale) as one cantata in two sections as his trial composition. It seems most likely that the complete work consisted of the following—or as the original one work from which the later two cantatas were developed:

PART 1 (before the sermon)

1. Arioso, aria, and chorus "Jesus nahm zu sich die Zwölfe"
2. Aria "Mein Jesu, ziehe mich nach dir"
3. Rec. "Mein Jesu, ziehe mich, so werd ich laufen"
4. Aria "Mein alles in allem"
5. Chorale "Ertöt uns durch dein Güte" (5th stanza of "Herr Christ, der einig Gottes Sohn")

PART 2 (after the sermon)

6. Duet "Du wahrer Gott und Davids Sohn"
7. Rec. incorporating chorale "Ach, gehe nicht vorüber"
8. Chorus "Aller Augen warten, Herr"
9. Chorale music as 5. above, but combined with a text from another stanza of "Herr Christ, der einig Gottes Sohn"

This scheme, in which the movements of the later Cantata BWV 22 form Part 1 and the concluding movement of Part 2, which is otherwise the original for movements 1–3 of Cantata BWV 23, is based on Martin Geck, "Bachs Probestück," in *Quellenstudien zur Musik: Festschrift Wolfgang Schmieder zum 70er Geburtstag* (Frankfurt/London/New York, 1972). The notion of the returning chorale setting to conclude each part (cf. Cantatas BWV 75, 76) is the present editor's.

E57. See note E55. In any case, the combined cantatas as outlined above in note E56 would have created a very fine impression.

E58. The usual ensemble for which Bach wrote in Leipzig consisted of strings, continuo, and two oboes, to which other instruments were added appropriately from time to time. There are numerous movements for strings and one oboe throughout Bach's vocal output, and indeed, an ensemble of strings with two oboes was the most "usual" German orchestral resource of the day. Little may therefore be deduced from this instrumentation in itself.

E59. Although Smend's thesis regarding the relationship between the "sacred" and the "secular" music of Bach is extremely attractive and is to be extensively developed in the next chapter, we cannot be sure that he is correct in ascribing so heavy a proportion of even Bach's Köthen vocal music to religious purposes in the sense indicated; there is too little certainty here. He might have been better advised to have introduced here the argument that Bach, as a relatively receptive man of his own time, probably accepted without question the doctrine of the "divine right" of hereditary rulers; therefore, every homage cantata he ever wrote—including those prepared at and for the Köthen princely household—was actually for him a glorification of his God.

E60. That idea is reinforced by the amazingly productive rate of composition of the subsequent early Leipzig years, which since 1951 have been discovered to have witnessed the genesis of the larger part of Bach's total preserved output. However, some of the music that Smend and Schmieder considered to have its origins in the Köthen period is today thought to have been composed later—and some of it (though less) is thought to have originated earlier or to have had earlier, pre-Köthen versions that are today lost.

E61. The new chronology—and particularly Georg von Dadelsen's brilliant studies of the *Mass in B Minor* (BWV 232)—has changed and to some extent has reversed this argument, although it was quite reasonable when so many of the chorale cantatas (which contain little elaborate parody) were mostly thought to come from between 1730 and 1750.

E62. It should perhaps be mentioned that it has been suggested that at least some of the oratorio parodies may have been conceived as paired works from an early stage of their creative process; both the librettist Picander and Bach could have been involved in this process, which can occasionally explain why the "later," "parodied" version of a movement sometimes seems more unified between text and music than the "earlier" one.

E63. The "late" Cantata BWV 38 was, however, very probably first performed on 29 October 1724.

E64. See note E55.

E65. This Passion setting was not by Handel, it is now generally agreed; however, Postel's text did furnish Bach with some material for his own *St. John Passion*, and it is also possible that, if Bach knew the setting, he may have believed that it was Handel's work.

E66. See note E65.

E67. However, it is usually agreed that BWV 245c was composed by Bach in Weimar.

E68. This is true, but it was also a characteristic of his Weimar cantatas; indeed, it is a continuing feature of his music until the early Leipzig period. This does nothing to diminish Friedrich Smend's present argument, however (but see note E65).

E69. This *Alla breve* indicates the proportionate tempo of the central section of the area (in $\frac{3}{4}$ time, rather than common time); it is present in the autograph score (Source A of the NBA edition).

E70. Probably five years earlier. See note E42.

E71. The dates in brackets have here been adjusted from Smend's original "1723 and 1727," both of which do not accord with the new chronology.

E72. This was not so; see note E55.

E73. The *St. John Passion* may have been conceived in whole or in part at Köthen, but it was not performed in a form we should recognize before April 7, 1724; see note E55.

E74. The idea that Bach *never* reused music composed for a liturgical or religious purpose for a subsequent secular one was an imaginative interpretation of evidence available in the first half of the 20th century by the musicologist Arnold Schering (1877–1941). This has since been shown not to be invariably true; see Paul Brainard, "Bach's Parody Procedure and the *St. Matthew Passion*," *Journal of the American Musicological Society* 21 (1969): 241ff.

E75. J. Anderson, *Royal Genealogies* . . . 2d ed. (London, 1736), p. 558.

E76. Ibid., p. 559.

E77. Cf. Herbert Zimpel, "Der Streit zwischen Reformierten und Lutheranern in Köthen während Bachs Amtszeit," *BJ*, 1979, pp. 97–106.

E78. Cf. Hermann Wäschke, "Die Hofkapelle in Köthen unter Johann Sebastian Bach," *Zerbster Jahrbuch* 3 (1907), p. 35.

E79. Cf. Günther Hoppe, "Bachs Abendmahlgebrauch in seiner Köthener Zeit," *BJ*, 1981, pp. 31–42, referring to a preserved *Catalogue des Livres appartenans en propre à Son Altesse Serenissime Monseigneur le Prince August Louis . . . d'Anhalt*.

E80. Wäschke, "Die Hofkapelle." This troupe of theatrical comedy actors might well have been that which had visited the court of Duke Christian of Weissenfels during the winter of 1717 and that included the later famous actress Karoline Friederike Neuber (1697–1760). See Ingo Bach, et al., *Stadtchronik Weissenfels* (Weissenfels/Saale, 1981), p. 29.

E81. The acquisition and adaptation of the Neue Schloss around 1710 may not have been the only external building program on a lesser scale, of course. More concerning the architecture of Anhalt and the various residences within the principality may yet materialize.

E82. Most important here is the research of the late Köthen archivist Ernst König, whose most important articles were published in *BJ*, 1957, pp. 163–67; ibid., 1959, pp. 160–67; and ibid., 1963/64, pp. 53–60. The 1959 article reveals much concerning the constitution of the Kapelle, and the last article contains a helpful calendar of Bach dates, which, used in combination with the J. S. Bach *Kalendarium* (2d, revised edition; Leipzig: Bach-Archiv, 1979), should be the basis of future historical investigations of Bach with regard to Köthen.

E83. There has been a little bibliographical confusion concerning this excellent short study of Bach's life. It was first issued in Munich in 1960, but a revised edition followed on the heels of the first one in 1961. However, publications of English and Danish translations of the revised edition appeared in advance of the second German one, and were dated 1960. The basis of our quotation is the second English edition of Neumann's revised work, entitled *Bach and His World* and translated by Stefan de Haan (London, 1964). We have taken the liberty of slightly adapting the translation.

E84. Most regrettably, Neumann names no source for Mattheson's interesting job description.

E85. *Bach and His World* (London, 1964), p. 52.

E86. Prince Victor Amadeus of Anhalt-Bernburg, born Oct. 6, 1634, died Feb. 14, 1718, aged 84; he was succeeded by his son Karl Friedrich (then aged 49), born July 13, 1668. He in turn died April 22, 1721, and was succeeded by his son Victor Friedrich, born Sept. 20, 1700, who ruled until his own death in 1765. Prince Karl Wilhelm I of Anhalt-Zerbst, born Oct. 16, 1652, ruled from 1667 until his death at 66 on Nov. 3, 1718; he was succeeded by his direct heir Johann August (born July 29, 1677), who ruled from the age of 41 (in 1718) until he died at 65 on Nov. 7, 1742.

E87. For further details see Stephen Daw, "Bach Celebrates an Anniversary," *Early Music*, 1986 (in preparation); also *Dok* II, p. 167.

E88. Cf. *Dok* II, pp. 164–67.

E89. See note E78.

E90. Cf. E. Haetge and M.-L. Harksen, eds., *Die Kunstdenkmäler des Landes Anhalt: Landkreis Dessau-Köthen*, part 1, "Die Stadt Köthen und der Landkreis ausser Wörlitz" (Burg bei Magdeburg, 1943), p. 135.

E91. This list is available very largely as the result of generous help from Dr. Klaus Hofmann and, even more particularly, Dr. Yoshitake Kobayashi of the Göttingen Johann-Sebastian-Bach-Institut, without whose authoritative assistance the editor might not have dared to risk supplying such a list.

E92. See Wolfgang Schmieder, *Thematisch-systematisches Verzeichnis der Werke Johann Sebastian Bachs* (Leipzig, 1950), pp. 651–53. The long title is often abbreviated—with the compiler's and publisher's approval—to *Bach-Werke-Verzeichnis* or BWV as a prefix to the catalog numbers.

E93. Much of Schmieder's list and several of Friedrich Smend's arguments in the preceding text are based on the (surely questionable) assumption that Bach wrote in a recognizably consistent style during the Köthen years. Even if such a style is identifiable, it is very hard to see how it might be clearly defined without becoming so subjective as to be meaningless or so generalized as to be practically inapplicable.

E94. As Smend has himself pointed out, the 1768 catalog of music held in the Schloss library (printed by Rudolf Bunge in *BJ*, 1905) can have but little representative bearing on the Hofkapelle's activities 50 years earlier—especially since the ingredients had mainly been published since 1723 and the Kapelle had been dissolved in 1754.

Appendix A

Als der Durchlauchtigste Fürst und Herr, Herr Leopold, Fürst zu Anhalt Cöthen, bey Dero Hohen Geburts-Feste, den 10. Decemb. 1719. in Dero XXVI. Glorwürdiges Alter traten, wolten ihre Devotion bezeigen der Capell-Meister und sämtlichen Cammer-Musici.

MENANTES.

So bringt, Durchlauchtigster, Glorwürdger LEOPOLD,
Der Tag des Landes Heil, der Zeiten bestes Gold.
Es trägt diß Hohe Fest in Deinem theuren Leben
Des Himmels Gnad und Huld den Unterthanen zu.
Der Seegen krönet uns, hier wohnt die süsse Ruh.
Das Glücke lacht uns an, das Dich der Welt gegeben.
Wir ehren diesen Glantz, der durch die Wolcken bricht,
Denn von dem Himmel nur kommt dieses Fürsten-Licht.

Zwar Anhalt jauchzete, da Dich die Welt empfing.
Doch als Dein zarter Fuß der Tugend Wege gieng,
Und man in Deinem Geist der Ahnen Preiß erblickte,
Brach bey dem Hoffnungs-Strahl die Freude mehr hervor,
Und ward vollkommen groß, als auf Aurorens Thor,
Auf Deine Morgen-Röth' auch Gott die Sonne schickte,
Die Sonne, die durch Dich an Anhalts Himmel steht,
Und mit den Jahren nur in größre Klarheit geht.

Denn als die Reisen nun mit Höchstem Ruhm geschehn,
Sah' Anhalt den vergnügt, der vor die Welt gesehn;
Und seufzete darauf, Dein Scepter anzubeten.
Die Klugheit führte dich durch manches schöne Reich;
DU sahst der Fürsten Kunst; wer aber war Dir gleich,
Als DU, o Edler Fürst, der Väter Thron betreten?
Du brachtest Weisheit mit: Allein daß Anhalt blüht,
Bringt Dein Erlauchter Geist, Dein Fürstliches Gemüth.

Es ziert Dein hohes Haus ein graues Alterthum,
Noch mehr, Ascaniens geprießner Helden Ruhm.
Dein Götter Stamm ist reich von tausend Lorbeer-Zweigen;
Doch herrlicher durch Dich, o Baum, der Schatten giebt,
O schöner Fürsten Baum, von jedermann geliebt,
Auf dessen Aesten sich nur güldne Früchte zeigen,
Und unter Dessen Schutz kein Blitz das Land erschreckt,
Weil es der Lorbeer-Crantz von Deiner Tugend deckt.

Groß bist Du von Geburth, noch größer selbst durch Dich:
Es zieret die Natur Dein Ansehn Königlich.
Allein was Dich erhebt bis zu der Sternen Kertzen,
Macht Deiner Klugheit Strahl, die Tugend, so Dich küßt.
Weil Du viel größer noch in Deiner Seelen bist,
Ein Saul zwar von Gestalt, doch David in dem Hertzen,
Ein Salomon am Geist, und ohne Purpurs-Pracht
Zum Fürsten von Natur und vom Verdienst gemacht.

Du machst Dein Land berühmt, doch aber auch beglückt,
HERR, den der Lebens-Fürst mit Huld und Weisheit schmückt.
Wer seufzet unter Dir? nur Fremde hört man klagen,
Gepreßt von mancher Noth, gequält von vieler Pein.
Nur von den Gräntzen dringt manch Jammer-Lied herein:
Da wir von GOttes Preiß und Deinem Lobe sagen.
Da wir durch Deine Gnad' in lauter Wohlergehn
Und gleichsam, HErr, durch Dich im Paradiese stehn.

Wir jauchzen unter Dir in unserm Canaan;
Da, wie zu Babylon, manch fremder Unterthan
Die Geigen höchst-betrübt an seine Weiden hanget.
Hier klingt ein Jubel-Thon vom Hofe durch das Land:
Denn, wenn der Fürst vergnügt, wenn Seiner Musen-Hand
Die frohen Saiten rührt, wenn der in Freuden pranget,
Der aller Menschen Wonn'. und Seines Landes Lust,
So rührt Sein Saiten-Spiel der Unterthanen Brust.

Ein Herr, der reich an Huld und Hoher Gütigkeit,
Ist zur Music geneigt, und liebet allezeit
Der Fürsten beste Lust, der Edelsten Ergetzen.
Der aller Menschen Feind, verträgt kein Saiten-Spiel.
Hingegen liebt es GOtt. Was diesem wohlgefiel,
Mag Götter dieser Welt auch wohl in Freude setzen.
Und zwar, wie Dein Gemüth, HErr so schön und ungemein,
Muß Dein Music Geschmack auch nur der Schönste seyn.

Fürst, der uns im Triumph durch Seine Güte führt,
So lieblich aller Brust, wie man die Saiten rührt,
Heut ist ein Hohes Fest, des Himmels Huld zu loben.
Es klinge GOtt zum Ruhm, was nur die Kunst erdacht,
Und durch die Harmonie, so Treu und Tugend macht,
Der Hertzen GOttesfurcht, sey dieses Heil erhoben,
Daß Anhalt, dessen Glück auf Deine Lieb' erbaut,
In dir sein höchstes Gut, den besten Fürsten schaut.

Dein Leben friste GOtt; Er stärcke Deine Krafft;
Er segne Dein Gemüth, so unsre Wohlfahrt schafft;
Dein göttlicher Verstand regier in späte Zeiten.
Huldreich-Gerechter Fürst, leb' in vollkommnen Wohl.

GOtt sende Deinen Flor von jenem Sternen-Pol,
Daß wir in Deiner Lieb', in Deinen Seltenheiten,
   Die Helle Gnaden Sonn' im Auf und Niedergehn,
   Und was dem Himmel gleicht, in Deinen Augen sehn.

Appendix B

Evangelist
Continuo
Da stand ein Ge - fäß voll Es - sig, sie a - ber fül - le - ten ei - nen Schwamm mit
Es - sig und leg - ten ihn um ei - nen Y - so - pen und hiel - ten's ihm
dar zum Mun - de. Da nun Je - sus den Es - sig ge - nom - men hat - te, sprach er:
Violino I
Violino II
Viola
Jesus
Es ist voll- bracht! es ist voll-bracht! es ist voll - bracht!
Bass
Grave
Basso
Bassi
O gro - ßes Werk, o gro - ßes Werk, im
Pa - ra - dies schon an - ge - fan - gen: o Rie - sen - stärk', o
Rie - sen - stärk', die Chri - stus läßt den Sieg er - lan -

Appendix C

List of music attributable to Bach's Köthen period (December 1717 to May 1723) on positive documentary and/or historical grounds.

Note: The editor wishes here to acknowledge especially the help most generously afforded by Dr. Yoshitake Kobayashi of the Johann-Sebastian-Bach-Institut, Göttingen; without Dr. Kobayashi's invaluable assistance, it is highly doubtful that such a list could have been presented in this book, and it is the more valuable in that the extremely interesting supporting information is known to come from a source that is internationally respected for its consistent authority.

Abbreviations used in the table below:

DSB   prefix to abbreviated shelfmarks of the East Berlin Deutsche Staatsbibliothek, Musik-Abteilung, Unter den Linden 8, DDR 1080 Berlin, East Germany

SPK   prefix to abbreviated shelfmarks of the West Berlin Stadtsbibliothek Preussischer Kulturbesitz, Musik-Abteilung, Potsdamer Strasse 1407, D1 Berlin 30 (Tiergarten), West Germany

Weiss   watermark identification numbers according to Wisso Weiss, "Katalog der Wasserzeichen in Bachs Originalhandschriften," in preparation, NBA, IX/1 (Kassel/New York and Leipzig)

AMB   in the handwriting of Anna Magdalena Bach

JSB   in the handwriting of Johann Sebastian Bach

WFB   in the handwriting of Wilhelm Friedemann Bach

NBA   in this table, NBA refers to the commentary volume (*KB*) first of all, although clearly these volumes are of little value without the text they are designed to illuminate

BWV

21   *Ich hatte viel Bekümmernis* (second version)
Source: DSB St 354, parts 1 (Soprano)
                       11 (violin 1)
                       13 (violin 2)
                       14 (viola)
                       22 (bassoon)
                       24 (cello) (numbering as per NBA, I/16)
Watermark: Weiss 9 (Fisch im Kreis + EN)

Scribes: part 1: JSB?
parts 11, 13, 14, 22, and 24: probably Emanuel Leberecht Gottschalck, also identified with "Anonymous 6" by Paul Kast (see
Tübinger Bach-Studien 2/3 [Trossingen, 1958]: 138); re Gottschalck, see H.-J. Schulze's reported address in *Bach-Studien* 6
(Leipzig, 1981).

Paul Brainard has reported that this cantata was probably arranged in such
a way that all of its arias were sung by two singers (the one a "high" voice—
soprano or tenor—the other a "low" one—alto or bass); one possible occasion for the work's requirement may have been Bach's application for
the post of organist of the Jakobikirche, Hamburg, in November 1720.
See NBA, I/16.

22 *Jesus nahm zu sich die Zwölfe*
Source: DSB P119, score, (also P46, pp. 1–10)
Watermark: Weiss 104 (Wappenschild mit gekreuzten Schlägel und Ei-
sen, darunter Buchstaben), also 97 (IMK, kleiner Halbmond)
Scribe: JSB, also Johann Andreas Kuhnau.
Kuhnau's copy is on Leipzig paper, but may represent Bach's first con-
ception, whereas the autograph, written on paper that is unique in Bach
manuscripts, might stem from Köthen. See Weiss (NBA, IX/1).

23 *Du wahrer Gott und Davids Sohn* (**C minor version**)
Source: SPK P69, score; also DSB St 16, parts copied in Leipzig
Watermark: Weiss 1 (Wilder Mann), also 97 (IMK, Kleiner Halbmond)
Scribe: JSB, also Johann Andreas Kuhnau, Christian Gottlob Meissner
The score is written on Köthen paper, which may indicate that it was
composed there; this version has unusual transposing oboe parts for
Leipzig and no fourth movement (see note E56).

66a **Text:** *Der Himmel dacht auf Anhalts Ruhm und Glück*
No performing materials preserved, but probably in some movements an
early version of BWV 66, performed on April 10, 1724, and at least twice
subsequently. The printed text refers directly to Leopold I's birthday on
Dec. 10, 1718.

134a *Die Zeit, die Tag und Jahre macht*
Sources: o/b Bibliotheque du Conservatoire de Paris, shelfmark *Ms.* 2;
score

DSB St 18, parts 6 (oboe 1)
7 (oboe 2)
8 (violin 1)
10 (violin 2)
12 (viola)
13 (continuo)
14 (continuo copy of 13) (numbering as per
NBA, I/10 and NBA, I/35)

Watermarks: Weiss 2 (Wilder Mann, andere Form), 76 (Gekrönter Li-
lienschild, darunter CV)
Scribes: Paris *Ms.* 2: JSB
SPK St 18: most of parts 6, 7, 8, 10, 12, and 13 copied by an

BWV

unknown scribe, here *Köthen Anonymous 1*; the same parts finished by a second unidentified scribe, here *Köthen Anonymous 2*; part 14, the second continuo copy is in the hand of yet a third unidentified copyist, here *Köthen Anonymous 3.*

The vocal parts are not preserved separately but may be reconstructed from the score and the earlier continuo part, which includes the vocal line of the recitatives without text. The score is written in appropriate handwriting and on appropriate paper to signify a Köthen origin. Contrary to the implications of Alfred Dürr and sources quoted by him in editing NBA, I/10 and I/35, "Köthen Anonymous 1" is probably neither Johann Bernhard Bach nor a contributor to the *Mollerscher Handschrift* or the *Andreas Bach Buch.*

172   *Erschallet, ihr Lieder, erklinget, ihr Saiten!* (C major version)
Source: o/b Stadtarchiv Leipzig, shelfmark Mus. ms. 9, formally part of set of parts DSB St 23, nos. 14(15): bassoon; 15(14): cello (as per NBA, I/13); the remainder of the parts of the C major version were copied for performance in Weimar.
Watermark: Weiss 9 (Fisch im Kreis + EN)
Scribe: unknown scribe, here *Köthen Anonymous 4* (This link with Köthen is not mentioned in NBA, I/13, nor in Alfred Dürr, *Studien über die frühen Kantaten Johann Sebastian Bachs*, 2d revised and extended edition [Wiesbaden, 1977], presumably because of confusion concerning watermarks; credit for inclusion here rests with Dr. Yoshitake Kobayashi.)

173a   *Durchlauchtster Leopold*
Source: DSB P42, 1; score
Watermarks: Weiss 1 (Wilder Mann) and 129 (S neben Viererhaken)
Scribe: JSB

184a   (Text not preserved)
Source: SPK St 24, parts 5: flute 1
                 6: flute 2
                 7: violin 1
                 8: violin 2
                 9: cello (numbering as per NBA, I/14)
Watermark: Weiss 13 (Springendes Einhorn; Monogram)
Scribes: all parts started by "Anonymous 6" (probably Emanuel Leberecht Gottschalck; see under BWV 21 above) and completed in Köthen handwriting by JSB; also some autograph corrections

194a   (Text not preserved)
Source: SPK St 346, parts 1: oboe 1
                   2: oboe 2
                   3: oboe 3
                  (4: violin 1
                   5: violin 2
                   6: viola) (numbering as in NBA, I/35)
Watermarks: Weiss 108 (EN; Gekreuzte Schlägel und Eisen über Wellenlinie im Schild) and 109 (EN; Gekreuzte Schlägel und Eisen

über Zierstück, in Zierschild). There is no watermark on the paper of the string parts, but it is of the same type.
Scribe: An unknown copyist, here *Köthen Anonymous 5*

199 ***Mein Herze schwimmt im Blut*** **(second traceable performance)**
Sources: SPK 459, parts 3a: violin 1
10a: viola
15: basso continuo in d
16: basso continuo in d (numbering as in NBA, I/20)
o/b Archiv, Gesellschaft der Musikfreude, Vienna, part: viola da gamba
Watermark: in both sources, Weiss 13 (Springendes Einhorn; Monogram)
Scribes: JSB and one unknown copyist, here *Köthen Anonymous 6*

572 **Fantasia in G (composed at Weimar?)**
Source: SPK P1092
Watermark: Helms (see NBA, V/7, p. 185) describes it as "Buchstaben IGB (in bekröntem Zierstück)"; it is not mentioned by Weiss
Scribe: "Anonymous V" in Paul Kast's list (see *Tübinger Bach-Studien* 2/3 (Trossingen, 1958, p. 138); *An 5a* and *An 5b* are treated as the same copyist by Helms in NBA, V/7.
The watermark is visible on a single sheet contained within a bifolio; the latter displays no watermark. The manuscript is dated "late 1722" by Helms (NBA, V/7, Anh. 1); it was later the property of Johann Christoph Oley (1738–89).

573, 728, 812–15, 816 (opening), 841, and 991
Excerpts from Anna Magdalena Bach's first Album (fragment of the original started early in 1722)
Source: DSB P224
Watermark: Weiss 1 (Wilder Mann)
Scribes: as indicated below in right-hand column

	Scribe(s)
573 **Fantasia in C (fragment, compositional draft)**	JSB
728 ***Jesus, meine Zuversicht*** **(keyboard setting)**	JSB
812–15 **Suites 1—4 of** *Six Suites* **(first version)**	JSB
816 **(opening few bars) Suite 5** in G of *Six Suites,* Allemande (to be completed in Leipzig) The remaining section of 816/1 and further movements were added by Bach later, to form the earliest version of the Suite. See NBA, V/4, p. 14n, and NBA, V/8.	JSB
841 **Menuet in G**	AMB(?)
991 **Air in C minor**	JSB

BWV

691, 753, 772–87, 789–801, 836, 837, 841–43, 846a, 847/1, 848/1, 849/1, 850/1, 851/
1, 853/1, 854/1, 855a, 856/1, 857/1, 924a, 926, 927, 928, 929, 930, and 994

Excerpts from Wilhelm Friedemann Bach's Album (started in 1720)
Source: Yale University Library (no shelfmark)
Watermark: Weiss 2 (Wilder Mann, andere Form)
Scribe(s): see below, in right-hand column

		Scribes
691	"Wer nur den lieben Gott läßt walten" (keyboard setting)	JSB
753	"Jesu meine Freude" (keyboard setting)	JSB
772–87, 789–801		JSB & WFB
	The **Praeambulae** complete, followed by the **Fantasien** (i.e., the Inventionen, followed by the Sinfoniae except BWV 788 in C minor); there is no preserved Fantasie in C minor	
836	Allemande in G minor*	JSB & WFB
837	Allemande (fragment) in G minor*	JSB, WFB, and an unknown copyist, here *Köthen Anonymous 7*
841	Menuet 1 in G major	JSB & WFB
842	Menuet 2 in G minor	JSB & WFB
843	Menuet 3 in G major	JSB & WFB
846a	Praeludium 1 in C	JSB & WFB
847/1	Praeludium 2 in C minor	JSB & WFB
848/1	Praeludium in C-sharp	JSB & WFB
849/1	Praeludium in C-sharp minor	JSB & WFB
850/1	Praeludium 4 (fragment) in D	JSB & WFB
851/1	Praeludium 3 in D minor	JSB & WFB
853/1	Praeludium in E-flat minor (fragment)	JSB & WFB
854/1	Praeludium 6 in E	JSB & WFB
855a	Praeludium 5 in E minor	JSB & WFB
856/1	Praeludium 7 in F	JSB & WFB
857/1	Praeludium 7 in F minor (fragment)	JSB & WFB
924a	Praeludium in C	JSB (revised Leipzig WFB)
926	Praeludium 2 in D minor	JSB (revised Leipzig WFB)

---

*These Allemandes, besides other works from the list below, may have been exercises partially written by Wilhelm Friedemann Bach rather than compositions by his father.

BWV

927 Praeambulum in F	JSB (revised Leipzig WFB)
928 Praeludium in F	JSB (revised Leipzig WFB)
929 "Trio von J.S.B." in G minor	JSB (revised Leipzig WFB)
930 Praeambulum in G minor	JSB (revised Leipzig WFB)
994 Applicatio	JSB

772–801   Inventions and Sinfonias (complete)
Source: DSB P610
Watermark: Weiss 78 (Kleines Posthorn an Schnur)
Scribe: JSB
This autograph is dated 1723.

806, 1–5 Suite avec Prélude ("English Suite") in A,
*Prélude, Allemande, Courante I, Courante
II avec Doubles, Sarabande*
Source: SPK P1072
Watermarks: Weiss 2 (Wilder Mann, andere Form)
and 9 (Fisch im Kreis + EN)
Scribe: "Anonymous 5" (see under BWV 572 above)
The first three movements were copied in 1720 or
earlier, the *Courante II avec Doubles* and the *Sar-
abande* towards the end of 1722 (see NBA, V/7, Anh.
1).

812, 1–4; 813, 1–4; 814, 1—4*
Suites 1—3 of *Six Suites* (the French Suites) **and**
818 Suite in A minor
Source: DSB P418
Watermark: not listed in Weiss (Krone über Buch-
stabengruppe J ? K, darunter Traube
zwischen Stegen). See Helms (NBA, V/7,
Anh. 1, p. 184).
Scribe: "Anonymous 5" (see under BWV 572 above)
This manuscript contains also other works appar-
ently copied from the Bach family albums of Köthen
or their sources.

846–69   *Das wohltemperirte Clavier*, **Part I**
Sources: DSB P415 (autograph fair copy)
SPK P401
Watermarks: DSB: Weiss 28 (Gekreuzte Schwerter

---

* These are copies of the above-listed first versions of the *Six Suites* (see NBA, V/4 and
V/8).

BWV

zwischen Zweigen: bei Dürr *BJ*, 1957, mit
Schwerter I)
SPK: Weiss 1 (Wilder Mann) and 9 (Fisch
im Kreis + EN)
Scribes: DSB: JSB
SPK: "Anonymous 5" (see BWV 572 above)
The autograph is dated 1722; the copy by "Anonymous 5" is ascribed
to "1722/23" by Helms (see NBA, V/7, Anh. 1).

1001–06   *Sei Solo* [sic] (the sonatas and partitas for unaccompanied violin)
Sources: SPK P967 (autograph fair copy)
SPK P968
Watermarks: P967: Weiss 50 (Wappenschild, geteilt, oben drei Turmspitzen mit Fähnchen, unten bekreuzte Schlägel und Eisen, darunter JBA) and 107 (Gekreuzte Schlägel und Eisen zwischen Palmzweigen, darunter JBA)
P968: not listed by Weiss; "Gekreuzte Schlüssel" (Kobayashi)
Scribes: P967: JSB
P968: "Anonymous 6," i.e., probably Emanuel Leberecht Gottschalck (see BWV 21 above)
Autograph dated 1720

1013   **Partita in A minor for unaccompanied flute**
Source: SPK P968
Watermark: not listed by Weiss; "Gekreuzte Schlüssel" (Kobayashi)
Scribes: 2 unidentified scribes, here *Köthen Anonymous 8* and *Köthen Anonymous* 9

1046–51   **Six Concertos (the six Brandenburg Concertos)**
Source: DSB Am. B. 78 (autograph fair copy—but see Scribes below)
Watermark: Weiss 28 (Gekreuzte Schwerter zwischen Zweigen: bei Dürr *BJ*, 1957, mit Schwerter I)
Scribes: JSB and one unidentified scribe, here *Köthen Anonymous 10*

1050   **Concerto in D (Brandenburg Concerto No. 5, first version)**
Source: DBS St 130
Watermarks: Weiss 13 (Springendes Einhorn; Monogram) and Weiss 93 (Posthornwappen; HI), the latter forming the titled wrapper of the portfolio only
Scribe: JSB

Included last, because it is least certainly an indication of use or copying at Köthen:

BWV

1014–18 and 1019a
6 Sonatas for violin and cembalo obbligato
Source: DSB St 162 (autograph cembalo part)
Watermark: Weiss 9 (Fisch im Kreis + EN)
Scribe: JSB
N.B. Together with the cembalo part under this shelfmark is included a part for violin, copied out by Johann Heinrich Bach (1707–83) on Leipzig paper. We cannot be sure whether or not Bach simply used Köthen paper to make copies in Leipzig on this occasion.

The list above is complete. But textual evidence (from the printed poetry of Hunold/Menantes) indicates that besides BWV 66a listed above, the following texts were set to music by Bach during this period:

BWV Anhang 5 *Lobet den Herrn, alle seine Heerscharen*
date: Dec. 10, 1718

BWV Anhang 6 *Dich loben die lieblichen Strahlen der Sonne*
date: Jan. 1, 1720

BWV Anhang 7 *Heut ist gewiß ein guter Tag*
date: Dec. 10, 1720(?)

In addition, **BWV Anhang 8** was performed at Köthen on Jan. 1, 1723, but its text is not known (Hunold had died in 1721), and Friedrich Smend's theory that it formed an early antecedent to BWV 190 (see above) is perhaps somewhat fanciful.
There will have been further Köthen works, some of which have no doubt been preserved in rearrangements (especially the concertos for cembalo/cembali, BWV 1053–65, many of which are transposed rearrangements, may have had Köthen origins; the violin concertos [BWV 1041–43] have late sources, and are usually considered to have been composed at Köthen, especially owing to the surviving Leipzig autograph harpsichord transcriptions of BWV 1041 and 1042 in notation one tone lower as BWV 1058 and 1054 respectively). However, as research continues, it becomes increasingly clear that what was once thought to be Bach's "Köthen style" is as broadly general chronologically as it has to become analytically.

Works by Other Composers
Associated with Bach in the Köthen Period

Composer	Work
Francesco Conti	**Cantata *Languet anima mea***
	Sources: DSB Mus. ms. 30098 (Bach's score)
	SPK Mus. ms. 4081 parts (a complete set including basso continuo transposed for Köthen)
	Watermark: SPK ms. 4081: Weiss 13(Springendes Einhorn; Monogram)
	Scribes: JSB, *Köthen Anonymous 6*, and two further unknown copyists, here *Köthen Anonymous 11* and *Köthen Anonymous 12*
Stölzel	**Partita in G minor for keyboard**
	Source: Yale University Library (Friedemann Bach Album; see BWV 691, etc., above)
	Watermark: Weiss 2 (Wilder Mann, andere Form)
	Scribe: WFB
Telemann	**Suite in A (discontinued copy)** (= BWV 824)
	Source, watermark and copyist as Stölzel above

N.B. In selecting items from the albums of Wilhelm Friedemann Bach and Anna Magdalena Bach, an effort has been made to restrict references to those for which a Köthen association seems particularly probable.

Index
of Compositions

References to the works of Bach are given by BWV number and title and are grouped by type of composition. Works of Bach's contemporaries are given alphabetically at the end.

Index of Persons and Places

Note: In an attempt to clarify entries, undated descriptions refer to persons active after 1800 with regard to the present subject of study.

229